JAMES E. WHITE

A
Life Span and Reminiscences

OF

Railway Mail Service

BY

JAMES E. WHITE

Ex-General Superintendent of Railway Mail Service

BLACK LETTER PRESS
1201 Butler, S.E.
Grand Rapids, Mich. 49507

Reprinted 1973 by BLACKLETTER PRESS

SBN 0-912-382-11-2

This edition consists of five hundred copies of which this is

Number **211**

PREFACE

In the late Summer of 1908 I wrote a reminiscent article on "The Railway Mail Service," which was published in the September issue of "The Railway Post Office." This article was prepared in response to the request of a large and important association of the splendid men who had served with me, and under my supervision, during part or all of my long career in that most remarkable branch of the civil service of our government.

The reminiscences began with my entry into the service—March 5, 1866—nineteen months after the inauguration of the first railway post office, and when the whole corps of its employees, railway postal clerks, route agents, mail route messengers, and local agents, numbered only 703; and more than a year and a half before the first full railway post office car was placed in service.

As I wrote, my memory awoke and presented in the order of time, clear recollections of events with which I was connected in the earliest years of the improved service and they were chronicled so that those who joined the devoted corps later might become familiar with the details of its inception, inauguration and development; the hardships and disadvantages under which the work was performed; the desperate struggle preceding its firm establishment, and the gradual breaking of the clouds between the rifts of which could be seen the coming of the magnificent service of to-day.

As the story progressed, the educational methods employed to strengthen the minds and memories of the clerks, to increase the efficiency of their work while its scope was enlarging, and its character becoming more complexed, the system of discipline instituted to insure obedience of orders, instructions, regulations and laws, and thus gain the confidence and support of the public, were introduced and discussed.

The strength and favorable consideration thus obtained, fostered and advanced the work the service was created to perform; improved facilities for distribution, storage, and dispatch of the mails were furnished more readily by the railway companies, and the frequency of train service and consequently of dispatch of mail was increased.

The salaries of the clerks serving in the two highest classes in full railway post offices had been raised and lowered again; the fight for their restoration, and for traveling expenses for chief clerks, was on and growing more vigorous but without visible effect for many years, nevertheless it was wearing away the opposition and apathy that was predominant in the law making power.

As I wrote, the panorama moving before my mind became intensely interesting, and something of the same feeling must have touched some of the friends who read the reminiscent articles and urged me to publish them in book form when completed. This I concluded to do after revising what I had written, and taking up and describing to the best of my ability the salient features of the administrations of the nine gentlemen who had occupied the office of General Superintendent and the one who is at the head of the service at present.

This has been done. Reference to the list of contents will show that many subjects and incidents, covering the period from 1863 to 1909, have been passed upon and that much of the work is historical. I believe it will prove interesting and valuable not only to my late associates and co-workers in the railway mail service, but to railroad officials, and all others who may be directly or indirectly interested in the past and present of that great system, which has become a blessing to the American people, individually and collectively.

It is not possible to present in this book portraits of all who are employed in the service, therefore, there will be exhibited those of some who have grown from the ranks and had much experience in the service, and are in full sympathy with the working force and anxious to secure for it all it should receive.

CONTENTS.

ILLUSTRATIONS.

HON. GEORGE B. ARMSTRONG
Founder of the Railway Post Office

HISTORY

OF

THE INAUGURATION OF THE RAILWAY POST OFFICE

The railway post office, as distinguished from that portion of the railway mail service equipped with route agents, mail route messengers, and local agents prior to August 1, 1882, first became a factor in the operations of the Post Office Department August 28, 1864, about nine months before the close of the Civil War. Up to that date it was an outline or skeleton of a system, having a home in the mind of Mr. Geo. B. Armstrong, its founder, and expression in his letters of May 10 and 14, and June 10, 1864, which constituted the introductory prospectus he forwarded to the Postmaster General through Mr. Zevely, his Third Assistant.

This prospectus represented ten years' experience as the supervisory officer of one of the most important distributing post offices on this continent, during which he discovered the weak spot in our postal establishment, and thought out a system capable of eliminating it when applied and developed by trained officers and employees. In the years that have passed since those historic days that system has been applied and developed, the skeleton has become robust and vigorous, mentally and physically, and because of the great service it has rendered the commercial, professional and social worlds, is clothed with the benedictions of all classes and conditions of men.

Many of the fundamental principles laid down by the author of that prospectus are as essentially true now as they were then, which shows that he had pondered the subject until he became satisfied that the scheme had in it all the elements of success; nevertheless, there is in his letter of May 10, 1864, a feeling of doubt as to the possibility of introducing the new service in its entirety, in view of the opposition it would likely encounter from those wedded to the old system;

because of its emoluments and political power; therefore, he counseled gradual change in this language:

"Although it would doubtless be difficult to a certain degree to introduce a system under the present precarious tenure of office, which would at once violently revolutionize the order of things, yet such changes may be made as would gradually, yet effectually, accomplish the purpose, retaining so much of the present system as would not bring improvements into too sudden conflict with long habit and practice. * * * *

"Certainty and celerity in the transmission of letters are primary considerations. No postal system may be regarded as perfect that does not give to the whole public the largest possible facilities in extent and frequency of communication between all important places, and rapid, frequent local delivery. * * * * The working out of this reformation in the service is second in universal interest to no other measure touching the welfare of the public at large. This final result may be attained by wise planning and patient, persistent effort; beginning the reform with the simplest changes, for the reason hereinbefore named, and gradually introducing the more radical improvements till the end is accomplished."

The founder seems to have had a premonition that the new service, if launched, would pass through a stormy period before its enemies would be overthrown, and the people and Congress become convinced that it, and it alone, of the proposed so-called advanced methods of handling the mail, was the only one capable of keeping pace with the growth and progress of the country; that without it prosperity would be retarded, because intercommunication would be sluggish, less frequent, uncertain and incorrect; in short he seems to have seen the gathering of a storm, such as broke over the service in 1873 and 1874, and from which it emerged adjudged by the court of public opinion and the highest legislative tribunal in the land the most expeditious, efficient, and economical system of distribution, dispatch and supply. It is probable that his familiarity with the methods in vogue in distributing post offices then caused this anxiety or apprehension. That it was not baseless is shown in the proceedings of the commission of special agents of the Post Office Department, which met in Cleveland, Ohio, on June 24 and 25, 1863, by order of the Postmaster General, to consider the conditions of this class of offices, especially with reference to the distribution of letter mail, which had become a menace to the successful transaction of public and private business, to that social tranquillity essential to peaceful homes, and cheerful communities, on account of the intolerable delays resulting from the accumulation of this class of matter therein, and lack of enterprise and system in handling it. A paper was read before this commission, of which the following is an extract:

"The emoluments derived by postmasters at distributing offices consist of a commission on the letters distributed. Originally the commission was 5 per cent. on letter postage paid and unpaid. This was afterwards increased by law to 7 per cent., and then to $12\frac{1}{2}$ per cent., at which it now stands. It is obviously to the interest of those having charge of such offices to increase business of this kind to the utmost, and though expressly forbidden by the Department to invite distribution from its legitimate channel, it has often been done, and it is believed that the post office revenue has in this manner been largely defrauded. Letters have been subjected to so many distributions as entirely to absorb the postage charged upon them; and in some cases the distribution commission of a postmaster has largely exceeded the whole proceeds of his office and required a balance to be paid him quarterly from other sources. Even when no abuse is practiced and letters are subjected to only the necessary and proper distribution, a large portion of the correspondence of the country pays an unnecessary tax of 25 per cent., besides the regular commission of 40, 50, or 60 per cent., to which the mailing office is entitled. For instance, a hundred letters on which the postage is $3.00, originating in small offices in Ohio and west of Pittsburg, and destined for New England, are sent to Pittsburg for distribution and there subjected to a commission of $12\frac{1}{2}$ per cent.; from Pittsburg they are sent to New York or Boston and there charged with a second commission of $12\frac{1}{2}$ per cent., and then forwarded to destination. Assuming the average commission taken at the mailing to be 50 per cent., this three dollars' worth of letters pays a tax of 75 per cent. in the shape of commissions while passing through the mail, or $2.25 out of $3.00."

Some of the discoveries of the commission, which did not reflect credit upon the methods and practices of the distributing post offices, but the contrary, were made public either through the Department or otherwise, and as most of those who clung to the old system were not as obtuse as they were obstinate, they read the signs and prepared to oppose the introduction of any change likely to lessen their emoluments and influence socially and politically. Therefore, it is not strange that the founder of the system should have felt some trepidation when drawing up his prospectus for the consideration of the Postmaster General and his advisers. Search may be made through all of his subsequent writings and official acts with full confidence that no misgivings, as to the soundness of the plan or of its success when put to the test, will be found—of that he had no doubt.

On May 14, 1864, he forwarded the second letter of the series, composing the prospectus, to the Postmaster General through Mr. Zevely; from it the following extract is given, because it opens his scheme more fully—shows what he expects to accomplish and how:

"The classification of offices above given is for the twofold purpose of arranging a system of mailing, combining more comprehensiveness and simplicity than the present one and thereby to attain greater accuracy in the dispatch of letters, and in the case of distributing offices the design in the classification is so to relieve them of the vast amount of letters now necessarily thrown upon them under the present system as to enable them, together with the assorting offices in the classification given, to make more extended and frequent interchange of mail with other offices of the same classification, both for local delivery and distribution. But the main feature of the plan, which after its introduction and final adaptation to the service would undoubtedly lead to the most important results, is the system of railway distribution. To carry out the true theory of postal service there should be no interruption in the transit of letters in the mail and therefore, as little complication in the internal machinery of a postal system as possible, to the end that letters deposited in a post office at the last moment of the departure of the mails from the office for near or distant places should travel with the same uninterrupted speed and certainty as passengers to their places of destination as often as contracts with the Department for the transportation of the mails permit. It is well known to the public that passengers traveling over railroad routes generally reach a given point in advance of letters, when to that given point letters must pass, under the present system, through a distributing office; and when letters are subjected to a distributing process in more than one distributing office, as is largely the case now, the tardiness of a letter's progress toward its place of destination is proportionately increased. But a general system of railway distribution obviates this difficulty. The work being done while the cars are in motion, and transfers of mails made from route to route and for local deliveries on the way as they are reached, letters attain the same celerity in transit as persons making direct connections. This is obvious; but to reach this perfection would necessarily be a work of time. The plan I now submit looks to that end in time; and if it be proved by trial to be adapted to the service in a new form, the time may not be distant.   *   *   *   *

"In passing, however, to this final improvement I remark that the classification of offices above given would be so far changed as to abolish the distinction between distributing and assorting offices, reducing the former to the character with the simple functions of the latter. The other question of frequent local deliveries in cities and towns by carriers I will not touch upon only so far as to say that the two questions are correlative; and that the success of one depends upon the perfection and thoroughness of the other. To carry out the design, therefore, each railroad corporation under contract with the Post Office Department, or otherwise, employed in transporting the mails shall furnish for the exclusive use and occupancy of the railway clerks a sufficient number of cars suitable in dimensions and conveniences as may be deemed necessary for the proper discharge of distributing and other duties; these cars, or railway post offices, to be under the direction and control of the Department while the corporation is engaged in carrying the mail."

The letters of May 10 and 14, 1864, announced the primary principles which served as the groundwork of the system; they were not proclaimed publicly by any one before the dates named, and they have not been modified since; upon them the whole superstructure has been built; the methods employed, the details of the work of development were beyond his ken, undoubtedly, for they have unfolded gradually, each step in advance suggesting the succeeding one, and the wonderful growth made must be counted the product of many minds. The letter of June 10, 1864, and parts of the others not quoted, enter more largely into the details incident to the classification of post offices, and the method of making up and post-billing mails.

This last had been in existence many years, was cumbersome, expensive, and was discontinued in 1873, in favor of a simpler, more efficacious, and economical method, known as the "Postage Due Stamp."

See section 513, P. L. & R., which reads:

"No mail matter shall be delivered until the postage due thereon has been paid (R. S. No. 3900). That all mail matter of the first class upon which one full rate of postage has been prepaid shall be forwarded to its destination, charged with the unpaid rate, to be collected on delivery; but postmasters before delivering the same, or any article of mail matter upon which prepayment in full has not been made, shall affix or cause to be affixed and canceled, as ordinary stamps are canceled, one or more stamps equivalent in value to the amount of postage due on such article of mail matter, which stamp shall be of such special design and denomination as the Postmaster General may prescribe, and which shall in no case be sold by any postmaster nor be received by him in prepayment of postage."

One who reads these letters will understand, if he never did before, that when a man of a studious and thoughtful nature, with a well trained and resourceful mind, is engaged in a special line of business and reaches a point in the transaction of the same where the methods previously employed with reasonable success fail to meet demands, he will instinctively commence making an analytical examination of the whole machinery to discover the defects, and the remedy.

The distributing post office system reached that point during the Civil War; it had been anaemic for years, but did fairly well when there were but 22,616 miles of railway, and about one third of our present population to supply; no rapid development of our resources—the extent of which was not comprehended, because it had not been explored—and no great national emergency to provide for; but when all these conditions were changed, and mail began to pile up in most of these offices, and to lie there for weeks, awaiting distribution, it was unbearable and caused protests to pour in upon the President, his cabinet and the press, from all quarters. It would have been singular, under these circumstances, if an officer of one of the post offices most affected by these changes, having the experience, capacity, and energy for which Mr. Armstrong was noted, had not anticipated what happened long before it reached its greatest magnitude, and prepared a scheme to meet the emergency. This is just what he felt and did. We are told that he sounded the keynote to the situation and the solution of the whole problem when he remarked to Mr. Francis A. Eastman of *The Chicago Times* in 1861:

"I tell you, we do not yet know what to do with our post offices. We have but a village here, compared to the city we shall have. This vast western country is still almost empty of settlers, and even so, the mails that are hourly dumped into the post office fill up the entire space and paralyze the men. Unless something is done towards relief, the post office system will break down of its own weight."

And in 1862, when he said to the same gentleman:

"I am going to put the post office on wheels."

He made substantially the same remark to Colonel Carr of Galesburg, Ill.; to Mr. George S. Bangs of Aurora, Ill.; Mr. Fernando Jones of Chicago, Ill.; Hon. E. W. Keyes of Madison, Wis.; Charles R. Harrison of the same state; and to many other gentlemen of national reputation, all of whom became earnest supporters and advocates of his plan. Strong indorsements were forwarded to Washington, which with the clear statement in the prospectus evidently appealed to the Postmaster General, for on July 1, 1864, he addressed a letter to Mr. Armstrong, of which the following is a copy:

Post Office Department, July 1, 1864.

Sir: You are authorized to test by actual experience, upon such railroad route or routes as you may select at Chicago, the plans proposed by you for simplifying the mail service.

You will arrange with railway companies to furnish suitable cars for traveling post offices; designate "head offices," with their dependent offices; prepare forms of blanks and instructions for all such offices, and those on the railroad not "head offices;" also for clerks of traveling post offices.

To aid you in this work, you may select some suitable route agent, whose place can be supplied by a substitute, at the expense of this Department.

When your arrangements are complete, you will report them in full.

(Signed)   M. Blair,

George B. Armstrong, Chicago, Ill.   Postmaster General.

Upon receipt of this authority Mr. Armstrong and the management of the Chicago and Northwestern railroad arranged to test his plan upon the Galena division of that line. The company remodeled some old cars, after drawings furnished by him, and as soon as these came from the shops Percy A. Leonard and James Converse of the "east room," of the Chicago post office, because of their familiarity with the Eastern distribution, were detailed to take charge of them, and to run between Chicago, Ill., and Clinton, Iowa; the route agents who were on this route became their assistants. Everything being ready, on the 28th of August, 1864, Mr. Leonard and Mr. Bradley started from Chicago on the initial trip of this remarkable service; the originator of the system, with a few commercial and newspaper acquaintances, and some personal friends, accompanied these gentlemen on that occasion; not all of these guests returned from the trip favorably impressed with the scheme; many who long afterward were visitors in railway post offices better equipped, more skilled and effective than this one was, did not enthuse over its work, or possibilities; it was beyond their comprehension, that was all, just as it was beyond that of many who entered the service but did not survive the tests of adaptability and fitness. The trips made over this route regularly thereafter soon demonstrated, to those upon whose good opinion the introduction and fair trial of the system depended, that it embraced all the elements of success, but that like all innovations of the higher order put in operation by the Government to ameliorate the condition of its people, education of a special character, financial and the strongest executive support, perseverance, faith and time were necessary to its development. A month and more after this initial trip, the New York and Washington railway post office was introduced and ran on the rails of the P., W. & B. R. R., the B. & O. R. R. and the Camden & Amboy R. R. companies—now known as the Pennsylvania Railroad Company—time, twelve hours, now reduced one-half. Then followed the Chicago, Ill., & Davenport, Iowa, on the C. R. I. & P. R. R.; the Chicago & Quincy, Ill., on the C. B. & Q. R. R.; the Chicago, Ill., & St. Louis, Mo., on the Chicago & Alton R. R.; the Chicago & Centralia, Ill., on the Illinois Central R. R.; the Clinton & Boone, Iowa, Chicago & Northwestern R. R.; Quincy, Ill., & Hannibal, Mo., Hannibal & St. Joseph R. R., in the west; the last two were introduced in the fall of 1866. Following the New York & Washington R. P. O. came early in 1865, the New York & Dunkirk, New York & Erie R. R. and the Philadelphia & Pittsburg—Pennsylvania Railroad Company, in the east. No more were introduced there until 1867. In fact the new service east seemed to move with halting and uncertain steps for a considerable time, after these lines were opened to it, due to the opposition it met with from without and within; the difficulty experienced in securing exceedingly moderate accommodation for it on the desirable railway lines, and the active hostility of the heads of the great distributing offices who, instead of welcoming it with open hands, encouraging words, and a "God speed," antagonized it, sought to array public and legislative sentiment against it, to destroy it in its swaddling clothes. Not so in the west. There a different spirit prevailed; the railway managers were responsive to reason, and furnished such facilities as were needed for the new service as rapidly as requested; nothing extravagant or excessive was asked for, as is shown in the fact that for more than three years after its introduction it was housed in apartments of cars wholly. The fact that it was regarded as an experiment was not lost sight of for a moment, consequently all were on their mettle. The distributing offices were friendly also—no jealousies existed—the two branches of the postal service worked in harmony; besides, the service there was under the immediate direction and supervision of the author of the system, and the clerks assigned in charge of these first railway post offices were experts detailed from the Chicago post office, of which he was the assistant postmaster, all known to him personally.

Thus the conditions were more favorable than in the east, and naturally the service moved from the outset with less friction, with more freedom and confidence, which insured it greater vigor and progress. However, the service in the east passed through this crucial period and in 1867 many additional railway post offices were inaugurated in that section, New England, the south and west; but the greatest extension in mileage, for those days, occurred during the period from 1868 to 1870 inclusive.

Until 1868 nothing official or systematic was done toward building schemes of distribution to guide railway post offices in the work they were gradually assuming. That feature of the service, which long since became almost a science, studied as diligently and intelligently as the astronomer studies the heavens to locate the planets and the stars, was not organized then or subject to supervision; each clerk provided himself with such lists of distribution as he used and these were the essence of information obtained from other clerks, from postmasters, contractors, stage drivers and county and state maps—an amalgam not always reliable because too large a per cent. of it was tradition—nevertheless, in an age when post route maps, star route lettings and other reliable official helps were not available, it was the best that could be done. These lists were devoted quite largely to offices supplied by lines connecting at junctions and head and terminal offices, as distinguished from those purely local to the line, and contributed to a more extended knowledge of distribution; but the greater portion of the mail, not more or less local in character, continued to be massed on distributing offices, though fair headway was being made in the distribution of more remote states when not too complicated; as, for instance, we made such a distribution of Massachusetts and the other New England states as avoided delay in Chicago for that purpose, because it was simple. The scheme of Massachusetts was:

Massachusetts to Boston. D. P. O.

Except Berkshire, Franklin, Hampden, Hampshire and Worcester counties to the Boston & Albany railway post office.

New Hampshire was Boston. D. P. O.

Except Cheshire, Grafton and Sullivan counties to the Boston & Albany railway post office.

Danbury and South Danbury, of Merrimack county, same.

The offices in these counties were listed for reference until memorized.

The distribution of the other New England states was as simple. The first official scheme used in railway post offices was printed this year and issued to lines with headquarters in Chicago; it was small, simple and just suited to the times and conditions. "Express Mails" also became an important feature of the service during this year, for by means of these offices located not more than twelve hours from Chicago, north, south, east or west from the meeting point of railway post office trains, on lines provided with double train service but single railway post office service, were given twice daily supply, and the most important offices, and their dependent offices, between Chicago and the meeting points were also given a double supply, by means of "night pouches" made up in the Chicago office and, as with "express mails," dispatched by night trains in care of baggage men, who delivered them as per the address on the pouch labels. The railway post offices centering at Chicago made up packages for these pouches, threw them into the Chicago office, which pouched them, as per their address, with similar packages made up in that office. The "express mail" was carried past the meeting point to the terminal, usually, where it was transferred to the inward bound railway post office, by which it was distributed and delivered from one to six and, in rare cases, twelve hours earlier than if held for the next regular outbound railway post office. This was not understood at first, and, as was quite natural, complaints were made that this mail was carried past destination and delayed in delivery.

In the book of schemes, which I have before me now and which I printed with pen and ink in 1868 and 1869, I find many of these "express mail" lists and "night offices," also general and standpoint schemes—some by offices, and some county and exception. I assure you they bring to my mind very vividly those early days, and the disadvantages under which we performed our duties, as compared with the excellence of the fittings, the accuracy of the guides, and the order and system which surround and help the clerks of to-day in their work, and which prevail throughout our whole postal establishment, a condition due largely, unquestionably, to the new life, progressive ideas, and energy brought into it by the railway post office, which through a cumulative process of infection and transfusion leavened the whole. Notwithstanding these advantages, I believe I was never happier in my life, for I soon came to love the occupation, the research and study, the exhilarating movement of the train, the rhythmical sound of the wheels as they revolved quickly and smoothly over the rails under my feet, the quietude and absorption of the employment after the excitement, anxiety, storm and crash, and woe and mortality of more than four years of war.

The year 1868 also witnessed the first official effort to ascertain the quality of the distribution made by the clerks centering at Chicago. To this end the originator of the service caused mails made up in railway post offices, awaiting dispatch from Chicago, to be taken to his office and examined critically by his able secretary, Mr. William P. Campbell, and others of the service, whose efficiency had been established. The fact that this was being done was not trumpeted abroad; otherwise, as a means of ascertaining who were conscientious workers, it would have been abortive. As it was, the indolent and incompetent were caught "red handed" and those believed to be beyond reformation were separated from the service. This good work was continued with beneficial results into 1869, when the facing slip, which proved one of the most helpful factors in advancing the service in efficiency, was introduced.

This slip performs its mission by bearing upon its back, to the officers in charge of the distributers, a statement of the quality of the work done on each trip, if the employees who distribute the mail covered by it check thereon the errors they discover, as directed by the Postal Laws and Regulations, and thus points out those who must be urged forward in their studies, and cautioned to greater care in their work, or be removed in order that the patrons of the Post Office Department may not suffer great inconvenience or loss through their incompetency, and the record of the division or line, especially interested, be lowered. The facing slip is not an educator, but is an indicator of the degree of special knowledge, need in the work, that each clerk possesses, and in this capacity does much to advance the service. These slips were not furnished the clerks for some time after they came into use, but large sheets of wrapping paper were supplied—such as was used to wrap packages of letters in theretofore—these they cut into slips of prescribed dimensions and wrote, or caused to be printed upon each, the address of the package it was to cover, the name of the employee using it, the direction moving, and just before placing it upon the package they made a clear impression of the postmark of the route, with the date of the run, upon it. Upon the face of these early slips was written, or printed, substantially this: "The clerk who opens and distributes this package will please note upon the back of this slip all errors of distribution found therein, and send it to his superintendent." Later blank slips were furnished by the Department; still later printing plants and cutting machines were introduced in the offices of the division superintendent, through the appointment of qualified printers as clerks, under an agreement that they would furnish this equipment and do the printing if detailed to that duty. Long after this the slips were cut and printed in these offices and turned over to a clerk detailed in charge of a slip room fitted up with long cases of pigeon holes, into which he assorted them, and from which he filled the requisitions received from the clerks; some of the clerks, however, have always preferred to have their slips printed outside, because they could deviate from a prescribed formula—have their names, train numbers, and other details printed upon them, and have them made up in runs, which would be impractical in preparing a general supply for the postal service. Finally the exigencies of the service became so great and pressing that these offices could not meet them economically, and outside printing establishments were called upon to help out. Now the Feist Printing Company of White Haven, Penna., furnishes the Post Office Department nearly all the slips used. The clerks make requisition through their chief clerks upon their division superintendents and they forward them to the Department, which gives an order covering them to the company with such shipping directions as will minimize the handling and cost of transportation. Any clerk can have his slips printed by the same company as he likes, at the same price, but must pay the transportation charges.

It did not require a long trial to convince such officers as Messrs. Armstrong and Bangs that the facing slip would be a valuable aid in the development of the service; from 1869, the year it was introduced, to 1872, the year a systematic record of errors in distribution was first made, was ample, and it has been a potent factor in determining the relative efficiency of the service, one year with another ever since.

On April 4th, 1869, Mr. Armstrong's assignment was changed from Chicago, Ill., to Washington, D. C., and under the designation of General Superintendent of railway mail service the supervision and responsibilities of the whole service centralized in his office, and the possibilities of a conflict of ideas, and procrastination, in applying tested methods universally and uniformly, ceased; after this whatever was found conducive to the public welfare in one section was promptly utilized in the other. As soon as he entered upon his new assignment he selected as his successor at Chicago, Mr. George S. Bangs, a very able man, and his personal friend, and this selection was confirmed by the Postmaster General. One of the first things that engaged Mr. Armstrong's attention, and perhaps the most important of all, in the favorable development of the service, was such an organization of it as would insure immediate and personal supervision and inspection of the whole; more intimate knowledge of its needs, condition, resources, helpfulness, and prospective development. To this end he recom-

HON. GEORGE S. BANGS
Inaugurator of the First Fast Mail—New York to Chicago.

mended to the Postmaster General that the territory of the United States be segregated into six divisions, with headquarters in each at a central transportation point. The plan was approved and five special agents, designated assistant superintendents railway mail service, were assigned one to each of the first five divisions named in the list. The sixth, which embraced a very large and sparsely settled country west of the Rocky Mountains, within which was a very limited railroad trackage and service, but a vast number and mileage of star routes, remained as before, practically in the hands of such special agents as were assigned to the territory on the general business of the Department, except that the chief head clerks railway mail service at Omaha, Nebraska, and San Francisco, California, handled nearly, if not quite, all of the railroad service west of the Missouri river until 1871, when the division lines were readjusted so as to condense the six divisions into five, the fourth of the original organization being merged into the third and fifth, the latter becoming, numerically, the fourth and the sixth the fifth, which then comprised Arizona, California, Idaho, Montana, Nevada, Oregon, Utah, Washington and Wyoming, except the Union Pacific R. R., Alfred Barstow, assistant superintendent, San Francisco, Cal.

This organization was the initiative of that systematic and sympathetic conduct of the service, which by degrees brought order out of confusion, interest out of indifference, subordination in place of disobedience, and efficiency, where poor and unsatisfactory service existed.

Mr. Armstrong resigned May 3, 1871, and died on the 5th.

GEORGE S. BANGS,

who had been in charge of the service reporting to the Chicago headquarters, from April 4, 1869, and who had developed great executive ability and grasp of postal affairs, and, as well, a firm belief in retaining in the service all employees during good behavior and efficiency, was fortunately selected for the vacant office, which he filled to the satisfaction of the public, the Department, and the employees of the service for almost five years.

During his administration the service was extended very materially. The "miles of railroad upon which mail was carried" increased from 49,834 to 72,348, or 22,514 miles; and the corps of employees from 1,382 to 2,415, an increase of 1,033; the mail more than doubled; the supervisory force was increased as was the number of divisions; scheme making became active in division headquarters, and they were approved, printed, and supplied more freely by the general superintendent; some of the most capable and intelligent subordinate officers were appointed superintendents of mails and assigned in charge of mailing divisions of the most important post offices—this to harmonize and perfect the distribution more readily; and to impress this upon those most interested it was provided that all distribution, in such offices should be made according to schemes prepared in the office of the superintendent of mails and approved by the proper division superintendent of railway mail service; that the dispatch and exchange of mails, the record pertaining to these and the distribution, and all else relating to this work, in these offices, be subject to orders and instructions emanating from the railway mail service. This action was of inestimable importance in elevating the old system and establishing the new. During this period the "Fast Mail," between New York and Chicago, via the New York Central & Hudson River and the Lake Shore & Michigan Southern railroads was inaugurated, as was full fast railway post office service—known as "The Limited Mail"—between New York, Philadelphia and Pittsburg, via the Pennsylvania Railroad Company, at which latter city the mails dispatched by and distributed in it were pouched out and forwarded by connecting trains —not railway post office—in charge of baggage men, to Chicago, Cincinnati, important intermediate offices and routes, and St. Louis, making morning connections with outward bound railway post offices at the two first, and some of the way junctions, and afternoon and night at the latter.

So, too, the civil service reform movement bore its first fruit in these years. Under the Act of March 4, 1871, Section 1753, Revised Statutes, which authorized the President to appoint a civil service commission, to draw up rules for his consideration, he appointed Messrs. George William Curtis, Dorman B. Eaton, and Joseph Medill —three men of excellent repute, strong convictions, clear understanding, and each in his field of labor devoted to the public interest, and not only willing but anxious to accept and weigh information respecting the work upon which they were entering from conservative men experienced in public service. They commenced their work early, and on December 18, 1871, presented the rules they had drafted to the President, who approved them the following day to take effect January 1, 1872; but they were not applied to the railway mail service until the commission completed grouping them, and made recommendations for carrying them into effect.

When this was finished President Grant issued a supplementary executive order announcing it and his approval, and stating that the provisions adopted would be enforced as rapidly as the proper arrange-

HON. THEODORE N. VAIL
Third General Superintendent R. M. S.

ments could be made. This order was issued April 16, 1872, and provided for a tenure of office based upon good behavior and efficiency. The methods of ascertaining and promoting these were practical, being such, in the main, as had been applied to the service successfully by its own officers, and as were then coming into general use. Among these may be mentioned, in the order of their introduction, the facing slip, case examination, schedule of connections, and the probationary period; this last kept fresh in the minds of new appointees the fact that while entry into the service was usually secured through political influence, it might not be sufficient to retain them therein unless they demonstrated fitness for it; this was an incentive to the highest usefulness. Nevertheless many failed—it is claimed as high as 30 per cent. previous to 1885—and were dropped at the end of either the first or second probation, the latter being frequently granted. These civil service rules were reasonably satisfactory as long as the political complexion of successive administrations of the Government remained unchanged, which was until March 4, 1885; after that date they were of no effect, but on May 1, 1889, a civil service that was, and is, effective, was established by law. Mr. Bangs also faced the fight made upon the service in 1873 and 1874, and had the satisfaction of seeing it overcome. Resigned February 3, 1876.

THEODORE N. VAIL

succeeded to the general superintendency February 4, 1876. He had been a route agent on the Union Pacific railroad, west of Omaha, Nebraska, and a head clerk in the Omaha & Ogden railway post office, on the same road, for several years. Early in the seventies he was detailed to the office of General Superintendent Bangs, and in 1873, I think, was promoted to assistant superintendent, and assigned as before. He was active, industrious, efficient, with a mathematical turn of mind, when in my jurisdiction, and lost none of these desirable qualities afterwards. He assumed charge of the service at a period in its history when the tide of progress, which had been full, was beginning to ebb, and he worked energetically to stay it, but it was a stupendous and discouraging task, for Congress had ordered a reduction of ten per cent. in the compensation of railroads for transporting the mails, July 12, 1876, and a further reduction of five per cent. June 17, 1878. This antagonized the companies, in the East especially, for the principal lines in that section had held that the old rates were non-remunerative, and expected an increase. Being disappointed in this, those that had provided exceptional service withdrew it on July 22, 1876, and the facilities for the quick transit of the mail and for the distribution thereof, in some sections of the country, became less satisfactory than before the exceptional service was inaugurated; but during the less than three years of this administration the miles of railroad upon which mail was transported increased about 5,372, the annual mileage about 15,500,000, the number of railway mail service employees 193, cost of the employees about $90,000, and the cost of transportation about $50,000. This small increase in cost was due to the reduction in rates, just alluded to, and not for any other reason, for the mail continued to grow as phenomenally as before.

In this emergency Mr. Vail adopted a wise policy with respect to the railway post office service on long railroad lines in the west, southwest, and south. When such lines were covered by two single railway post offices, both day lines, he took up the one farthest from headquarters, established a route agency in lieu of it, and ordered an additional railway post office on the other end of the route. To illustrate, there were two such offices between Chicago, Ill., and Council Bluffs, Iowa, on the Chicago, Burlington & Quincy R. R., one designated Chicago & Burlington and the other Burlington & Council Bluffs R. P. O.; the latter was discontinued and a night line established on the former—such clerks of the discontinued railway post office as desired transfer to this night line were accommodated, and route agent service was resumed west of Burlington. This left the service west of Chicago unimpaired, because the lines so arranged covered all the through trains in both directions, caught all connections, kept all but the local mails out of the head offices, and provided an improved supply to the double line, and as good service to the territory of the Burlington & Council Bluffs as it had before.

It was during the early part of this administration that our service had its first experience with strikes on railroad lines, and these were more extensive and troublesome in the east than in the west; in fact, I believe they only extended to the Lake Shore & Michigan Southern, the Michigan Central, and the Chicago, Burlington & Quincy roads west of Buffalo, New York.

I remember that the division superintendents were called in convention at Lake Mahopac, New York, by General Superintendent Vail in 1876, and that when we adjourned Superintendent Cheney of the First Division escorted us through the Northern portion of New England, stopping on the way down to Boston at Hampton Beach, a beautiful spot with a fine hotel, on the Atlantic coast in New Hampshire, on a Saturday afternoon; two of us at least intended to remain there a week or two for recreation and rest, but on Monday I received a telegram from Chicago telling me that the railway employees were very restless, that trouble was anticipated, and that I had better come home; so Superintendent Hunt and I started westward that day. On our arrival at Buffalo, New York, we found travel over the Lake Shore & Michigan Southern railroad interrupted by labor troubles, and changed our course via Suspension Bridge, London and Windsor, Canada, to Detroit, Michigan, and thence over the Michigan Central railroad to Chicago. The train that carried us through to Chicago was about the last that got through on this line for some days; they were held up and the mails discharged from them at the station where the blockade existed until a great pile accumulated, then decisive action was taken to release it. Up to this time all the reasoning powers I possessed were exerted to have the embargo raised; the laws respecting the transportation of mail, and the obstruction of it in transit, were cited but without avail, so I telegraphed Thomas H. Bringhurst, a special agent of the Post Office Department residing at Logansport, Indiana, a request that he proceed to the point of blockade and address the recalcitrant parties respecting their violation of law, and advise them in the "round up" of his talk that unless they ceased to interfere with the mails, and the trains carrying them, they would be arrested by the United States marshals and prosecuted.

Mr. Bringhurst complied and was successful; the mail that had been held was released, and thereafter mail carrying trains passed over the route unmolested. But I was reprimanded; not, however, by the General Superintendent. The following year these troubles covered a wider territory and became more aggressive east; but one line in the west was involved, I believe, and that was the Chicago, Burlington & Quincy; this was soon relieved, but while it lasted it impaired the service materially and seemed to require action on the part of the railway mail service. Therefore, a notice of which the following is a copy was sent out:

Chicago, Illinois, July 27, 1877.

To Strikers, Rioters and Other Parties Whomsoever:

You are hereby notified that the Post Office Department contracts with the railroad companies to carry mails over their lines as often as said companies may run passenger trains thereon.

Therefore, All passenger trains carrying mails are mail trains, and if such trains are delayed by violence the United States mails are necessarily delayed, and the United States postal laws violated.

You are further notified that all trains carrying United States mail must not be delayed on any pretense whatever, and parties delaying the same will be vigorously prosecuted under the United States laws. All officers are instructed to find out the names of parties who are or may be found obstructing the mails and report same to this office.

By authority.   JAMES E. WHITE,
                         Supt. Railway Mail Service, Chicago, Ill.

Additional blanks were issued, and fuller instructions as to the use of facing slips and the conduct of case examinations were promulgated this year also.

Considering the little encouragement General Superintendent Vail had received in this field of labor, and the excellent opportunity for advancement urged upon him in another, which he realized when others did not, it would have been strange indeed if he had not severed his connection with the one and affiliated with the other immediately. This he did on November 25, 1878, and became the manager of the now famous Bell Telephone Company.

During Mr. Vail's administration the record of efficiency in the service was about as follows:

No. of employees in 1876, when he assumed charge,
    about   2,415
No. of employees in 1878, when he retired   2,608
Miles of R. R. carrying mail 1876, when he assumed
    charge   72,400
Miles of R. R. carrying mail 1878, when he retired,
    about   78,000
Annual miles, 1876, when he assumed charge   77,000,000
Annual miles, 1878, when he retired, about   92,537,060
Pieces of mail matter distributed, 1876 ....   No record
Errors in distribution, 1876 ....   No record
Pieces correct to each error, 1876 ....   No record
Pieces of mail matter distributed, 1877, about........   864,723,927
Errors in distribution, 1877, about   264,917
Pieces correct to each error, 1877, about .... $3,226\tfrac{1}{2}$
Pieces of mail matter distributed, 1878 2,215,080,650
Errors in distribution, 1878   625,662
Pieces correct to each error, 1878   3,540
Number of case examinations, 1878   3,979
Number of cards handled, 1878   3,996,782
Correctly handled, 1878   2,811,899
Per cent. correct, 1878 ....   70.35

The year 1877 the first facing slip record appeared in the annual report of the General Superintendent, and the report for 1878 contained the first case examination record of the entire service, though

Hon. William B. Thompson
Fourth General Superintendent R. M. S.
Restored the Fast Mail—New York and Chicago

the former was introduced in 1869 and the latter in 1870. The scattering reports of divisions prior to 1878 showed that the average per cent. correct made in the beginning of its general use was about 50; from 1878 to 1884 it rose but once above 78.10—that was in 1883, when it reached 87.46 per cent.

As has been indicated, the reduction of 10 per centum, in 1876, and 5 per centum, in 1878, in the rates of compensation, fixed by the law of 1873, for the transportation of the mails by railroad companies, created widespread dissatisfaction among the managers of all companies, and deep indignation on the part of those who, in expectation of increased compensation therefor, were providing unusual facilities, such as fast and limited mail trains, which they withdrew upon receipt of the information that the Act of July 12, 1876, had become operative, and that beginning with the first of that month, those rates would be reduced 10 per centum. The reduction of 5 per centum which followed in 1878 emphasized the opinion, held by the companies, that Congress was not willing to grant them fair remuneration for the services they rendered the government, so they emphasized their justifiable action in withdrawing the special trains, by the questionable one of curtailing ordinary accommodations.

The result of the first step in this unfortunate controversy was much to the disadvantage of public and private interests, for it was responsible for the defensive or retaliatory measures of the companies, that brought about the impairment of the service, and the aggressive demand which ensued for the restoration of the lost facilities, or for compensating service, culminating in the series of annual appropriations for special facilities, which began with the one of March 3, 1877, for $150,000, to be used during the fiscal year 1878, in the discretion of the Postmaster General, to improve the service on trunk lines. This did not restore the lost service, but it did provide some compensating service.

The withdrawal of the exceptional service, and the initiation of the movement to minimize its effect, occurred during Mr. Vail's incumbency of the office of General Superintendent, and undoubtedly prepared him to enter another field of labor without regret.

WILLIAM B. THOMPSON,

superintendent of the Ninth Division, succeeded Mr. Vail December 1, 1878. Mr. Thompson entered the service December 8, 1868, as a route agent on the Lake Shore and Michigan Southern railway—between Toledo, Ohio, and Chicago, Ill., at $900 per annum; promoted to second clerk, $1,200 per annum, in the Toledo & Chicago railway post office, September 17, 1869; to head clerk, $1,400 per annum, same office, February 21, 1870; assigned as chief head clerk (chief clerk, without change of pay) at Toledo, Ohio, September, 1871; commissioned special agent, Post Office Department, at $1,600 per annum, May 1, 1875, and later assigned as assistant superintendent railway mail service in charge of the New York & Chicago fast mail—which was inaugurated September 16 of the same year—promoted to superintendent of division, with headquarters at Cleveland, Ohio, July 18, 1878; to General Superintendent December 1st, of the same year, and appointed Second Assistant Postmaster General January 1, 1885. A record of advancement in class brilliant enough to satisfy the most ambitious. The fact that he served as a soldier during the Civil War attests his patriotism, as does his membership in the Loyal Legion.

In assuming the office of General Superintendent he took up its duties and responsibilities, agreeable and burdensome, where they were laid down by his predecessor. Chief among these was the rehabilitation of the service, and its advancement in extent, efficiency, and usefulness to the level it should have reached had it not slipped a cog in 1876; and though he set about this task earnestly, and persistently, the most that was accomplished in the expedition of the service prior to March, 1884, was secured through the use of special facility funds, and the greater portion of this fund during all the years it was appropriated was expended in expediting the service south of New York City, Philadelphia, Baltimore, Alexandria, and Washington, D. C., to Richmond, Lynchburg, and Danville, Va., Wilmington and Charlotte, N. C., Charleston, Columbia, and Florence, S. C., Atlanta and Savannah, Ga., New Orleans, La., Jacksonville, Sanford and Tampa, Fla., and intermediate points; though, during the earlier years, part of each appropriation was expended in expediting the service on the Pennsylvania railroad between New York City and Columbus, Ohio; on the New York Central system between New York City and Cleveland and Toledo, Ohio, and the 4:35 a. m. train between New York City, Poughkeepsie and Albany, N. Y.; also on the 5:00 a. m. train of the New York, New Haven & Hartford railroad between New York City and Springfield, Mass.

For the fiscal year 1882 the appropriation was $425,000, and the facilities provided covered a greater mileage. Of this sum $142,985.-71 was expended on the special service between New York and Springfield, Mass., between New York and Albany, N. Y., via the 4:35 a. m. train, and between New York and Cleveland, Ohio, with extension to Toledo, Ohio, and Chicago, Ill.; also from New York to Columbus,

Ohio, with extensions to Cincinnati, Ohio, St. Louis, Mo., and Chicago, Ill. None of these, however, were fast mail trains. Of the remaining appropriation $231,544.93 was used in maintaining the expedited service south of New York City, Philadelphia, Baltimore, Alexandria, and Washington, D. C. The residue ($50,469.36) was unexpended.

The largest special facility appropriation ever made was for the fiscal year 1883, which amounted to $600,000, but only $185,121.32 was expended. Of this $42,647.06 was used to continue the 5:00 a. m. service between New York and Springfield, Mass., and the 4:35 a. m. between New York and Albany, N. Y.; the remainder—$142,474.26— was used on a line from Philadelphia, via Baltimore and Washington, D. C., to Richmond and Wilmington, and Florence to Charleston Junction, S. C., and from Florence to Columbia, S. C.

The appropriation for 1884 was $185,000; it was expended to maintain the 1883 arrangement. For the fiscal year 1885, $250,000 was appropriated, of which $249,999.82 was expended as for 1883 and 1884, except that the line south was extended from Charleston Junction to Jacksonville, Fla., and special service was provided between Baltimore and Hagerstown, Md.

From 1885 down to and including 1891, with one exception, the annual appropriation for this special service amounted to a little more than $295,000, while the territory covered by it remained practically unchanged. But in 1892 the appropriation dropped to $196,614.16, and in 1894 a further reduction to $171,238.75, occurred, on account of the discontinuance of all the expedited service, save the line to the south, which was changed from the Pennsylvania and Atlantic Coast Line railways, to the Pennsylvania and Southern railroads, and extended from New York City via Philadelphia, Baltimore, Washington, D. C., Danville, Greensboro, Charlotte, Atlanta, Montgomery, and Mobile to New Orleans, with connections at Charlotte for Florida points. In 1898 it rose to $195,000 on account of the establishment of an expedited line from Kansas City, Mo., to Newton, Kas.—the only one ever established west, north, or south of Chicago or St. Louis— it was continued at this rate until 1903, when the Pennsylvania allotment of the fund was discontinued and the appropriation was reduced to $167,175. Of this, $142,005 was apportioned to the line from Washington, D. C., to New Orleans, La., and $25,000 to the one from Kansas City to Newton. The allowance, Washington to New Orleans, was discontinued January 5, 1907, and the Kansas City and Newton with the close of that fiscal year.

No appropriation for special facilities was made thereafter; none was needed, but they subserved private and public interests quite largely during the years immediately following the discontinuance of the first fast and limited mail trains; more so than during any other period. This was natural and as anticipated; it was not intended at any time that they should become perpetual; their mission was to assist in providing a service that would more nearly meet business demands, encourage increase and expansion of industries; secure concessions in the hours of arrival and departure of mail trains at terminal and junction points, thus fostering the growth of the mail and providing for the more efficient handling of it and, as a sequence, gradually and naturally increase the revenue derived from its transportation upon the basis provided by the law, until it became sufficiently remunerative to justify the withdrawal of special facility pay, and the continuance of the improved service without that stimulant. That is what happened; the mail increased in weight, not so much in pay, about 23 times between the dates of the first and last special facility appropriation—1878 and 1907.

The growth was much more rapid on the New York Central, Pennsylvania, and New York, New Haven & Hartford railroad systems than on the other special facility routes, as was known would be the case when they were established; consequently they were in condition to provide the service without aid earlier; therefore, it was discontinued on them first, i. e., mainly with the close of the fiscal year 1883, and wholly with 1893, except so much as was allotted the Pennsylvania for maintaining that portion of the southern route—New York City and New Orleans—between the former city and Washington, D. C., which was also discontinued in 1903. In 1907 special facility payments ceased entirely—having fulfilled their mission by building up, in connection with concentration of eligible mail upon them, certain great mail arteries, leading into different sections of the country, by which subsidiary routes and dependent offices were supplied.

The arrangement and rearrangement, from time to time, equipment, and harmonious working of these, and their tributary routes, was a constant care to General Superintendent Thompson, and added greatly to his official responsibilities, but they were borne with cheerful equanimity, and discharged as graciously, "by my troth," as if he had been a cavalier of the old school. However, righteous indignation was appeased by a little blood letting occasionally. During all this time he labored assiduously for the establishment of an improved fast mail between New York City and Chicago, and for the same class of service west and northwest of the latter city, via connecting routes and trains. This was finally accomplished on March 9, 11 and 13, 1884, by the extension of the train leaving New York City via the New York Central system at 8:50 p. m. and arriving at Toledo, Ohio, at 4:57 p. m.; to Chicago over the L. S. & M. S. R. R.—arriving at the latter city seven hours and thirty-eight minutes later (12:35 a. m.). Two days afterward (March 11th), the Chicago and Union Pacific Transfer, Iowa, fast mail, made its first run over the Chicago, Burlington & Quincy railway, departing from Chicago at 3:00 a. m. and arriving at the western terminus at 7:00 p. m., where it connected with the regular passenger and mail train for the Pacific coast, via the Union Pacific railroad. Two days later (March 13), a fast mail made its initial trip over the Chicago, Milwaukee & St. Paul railway, between Chicago and St. Paul, Minn., leaving Chicago at 3:00 a. m. and arriving at St. Paul at 3:30 p. m., making connection there with the west bound night trains.

These and all other fast mails west, north, and south of Chicago have been established without the use of special facility funds. In fact, they were secured, and have been wonderfully successful in expediting the mails, with a saving in the cost of transportation charges; a condition due to the law of March 3, 1873, which based these charges on the average weight of mail carried the whole length of routes for a certain number of days, not less than thirty, and taken not less frequently than once every four years; fixing a descending rate of compensation for an ascending weight. Reductions of 10 and 5 per cent. have been made from those rates in pursuance of the Acts of July 12, 1876, and June 17, 1878, but the feature of the law which made for economical transportation remains unimpaired, viz.: A decrease in the rates of pay as the weights increase. This encouraged the concentration of the mails on trunk lines as far as could be without delaying it, and moved such lines to accept them and to provide most excellent accommodations for their proper and prompt handling. This action by those interested recognized the well established business principle that the ratio of expense to the earnings in operating a healthy business decreases with its growth, leaving a larger margin of profit to invest in expansion, in improved service, or to be disposed of in any other way the owner of the business deems best; sometimes experience leads him to reduce the price of the traffic he offers; in that case he has learned the lesson that a small profit on each transaction of a large business aggregates a greater net income than is realized from a larger profit on each transaction of a smaller business.

The law of March 3, 1873, is provided with another economical feature, but one that does not seem to be predicated upon any known equitable business principle, and would—if applied to merchandising —bankrupt those engaged in it who are transacting a progressive business; only those whose business is on the decline could benefit by it, and then only at the expense of others who, because of superior advantages, have acquired part of their trade, or stopped the natural increase from flowing in its accustomed channel; reference is made to that clause which reads: "That the pay per mile per annum shall not exceed the following rates, namely: * * * the average weight to be ascertained, in every case, by the actual weighing of the mails for such number of successive working days, not less than thirty, at such times after June 30, 1873, and not less frequently than once in every four years."

The mail increases rapidly day by day, year by year; the farther away the closing day of the last weighing is from the opening day of the next, the more pronounced the extent of the increase becomes. This is most noticeable on the great trunk lines, which receive the lowest rates of pay and perform the highest class and most frequent service; the increase on these often amounts to twenty or more per cent. of the weight taken on them during the quadrennial weighing, and it matters not what it may average over the whole route, for the intervening four years it is hauled without increase of compensation until the next readjustment becomes effective. This, and the descending rates of pay provided for in the law of 1873, would seem to have brought the cost of transportation down to a point beyond which it cannot be reduced and leave a margin of reasonable profit, especially if just consideration is given the many details—more or less expensive —associated with it.

The pay per ton per mile on the largest routes, including paid car space, is about seven cents, excluding paid car space about six, and, ascending cent by cent as the tonnage decreases, it reaches in some instances enormous figures, often $16.00 or more and many times $12.00, but the lower and higher costs mentioned must be counted among the extremes.

During Mr. Thompson's administration, and chiefly through his untiring efforts, which secured for it the support of the Postmaster General and his Second Assistant, the Act—approved July 31, 1882— to designate, classify, and fix the salaries of persons in the railway mail service, became a law and was promulgated in the Postmaster General's Order No. 354, issued August 1st of the same year. This act discontinued the designations route agents, local agents, and mail route messengers, and thereafter all employees of the service, except the commissioned officers, were known as railway postal clerks. The order of the Postmaster General interpreting the law, and prescribing the regulations to carry it into effect, was very comprehensive and they worked satisfactorily.

The *Daily Postal Bulletin,* that most useful publication of the Post Office Department for the transmission of information indispensable to a prompt and orderly conduct of its business by its officers, and to a satisfactory understanding and utilization of the facilities, accommodations, and methods it provides for the benefit of its patrons, was introduced during this administration.

The Presidential election of 1884 resulted in the first change in the political complexion of the Government since 1861; most—if not all—who held Federal offices up to a short time subsequent to the inauguration of the incoming President—March 4, 1885—believed their doom was at hand, and those who could, secured positions elsewhere, but as a rule those railway mail employees who knew they measured up to the requirements of President Grant's tenure of office order of 1872—"efficiency and good behavior"—and who had not made themselves politically offensive to good citizens, though apprehensive, felt or hoped that they might rest secure on the implied, if not direct, assurances of that order as they had for more than twelve years. The officers of the service, I believe, did not expect to remain long, and I have always believed that Mr. Thompson, feeling that the office would be subject to unpleasant situations under the incoming administration and, therefore, undesirable, concluded, as he was perfectly independent of it financially, to accept the office of Second Assistant Postmaster General for the remaining months of the outgoing administration, and retire from public service with his political friends, knowing that his public career had been meritorious.

Under his administration the service improved steadily as the following records show:

No. of employees in 1878, when he assumed charge...	2,608
No. of employees in 1884, when he retired	4,175
Increase during the six years	1,567
Average annual increase	261
Miles of railroad carrying mail 1878, when he assumed charge	78,000
Miles of railroad carrying mail 1884, when he retired..	119,120
Increase during the six years	41,120
Average annual increase	6,853⅓
Annual miles carrying mail 1878, when he assumed charge	92,537,060
Annual miles carrying mail 1884, when he retired....	147,226,766

Increase during the six years 54,689,706
Average annual increase 9,114,951
Pieces of mail matter distributed 1878, when he as-
    sumed charge 2,215,080,650
Errors in distribution 625,662
Pieces correct to each error 3,540
Pieces of mail matter distributed 1884, when he retired 4,519,661,900
Errors in distribution, Dec. 31, 1884, 18 mos. 1,167,223
Pieces correct to each error 3,872
Increase in pieces distributed during the six years..... 2,304,581,250
Average annual increase 384,096,875
Average annual increase of errors 194,537
Average annual increase of pieces correct to each error 55
No. of case examinations 1878, when he assumed
    charge 3,979
No. of cards handled 3,996,782
Correctly handled 2,811,899
Per cent. correct 70.35
No. of case examinations 1884, when he retired 4,903
No. of cards handled 5,028,492
Correctly handled 3,927,290
Per cent. correct 78 3-5
Increased per cent. correct in 6 years 8 1-4
Annual increase correct 1 3-8
Pieces of mail separated for immediate city delivery, by
    carriers, in railway post offices from July 1, 1883,
    to January 1, 1885 89,694,475
        Being 48,824,750 for the fiscal year 1884, and
        40,869,725 for the first half of the fiscal year
        1885.
Average annual separation for city delivery 59,596,312

JOHN JAMESON

was appointed to the Washington & Petersburg, Va., railway post office May 4, 1867, at $1,400 per annum; resigned April 14, 1876; appointed special agent, to act as assistant superintendent railway mail service, April 15, 1876, at $1,200 per annum; pay increased July 1, 1878, to $1,600 per annum; promoted October 1, 1881, to $2,500 per annum as one of the ten inspectors, at that salary, authorized under the Act of Congress June 17, 1878; was promoted to be general superintendent January 1, 1885, at $3,500 per annum, and resigned February 4, 1887.

HON. JOHN JAMESON
Fifth General Superintendent R. M. S.

The incoming administration assumed the government of the nation little more than two months after Mr. Jameson entered upon the responsibilities of his office. The days that followed were not replete with joy—the mysteries of the morrow were a menace to the service, therefore an unfailing source of anxiety to him who had charge of it; many of his waking hours were devoted quite largely to the consideration of a probable and possible perilous situation that either threatened the integrity of the service by making indiscriminate breaches in the corps of trained and experienced distributers or unintentionally impairing it in other ways. In time these disquieting thoughts, with others relating to the regular business of his office, could not be shaken off when the doors of the great Department building closed behind him, they became his constant companions; accompanied him to and from his home; were with him day and night, and always making demands upon his time and strength; when he sought repose and sleep, to recuperate his jaded mind and weary body, the headsman with his axe stood at his elbow waiting for the examination and review of papers he brought from the office in his pockets for that purpose; therefore, he must forego rest, slumber and forgetfulness until "a more convenient season."

Undoubtedly the suave manner, phlegmatic disposition, and undertow of gentle resistance to indiscriminate removals from the service, characteristic of Mr. Jameson and his administration, qualified him for the emergency—enabled him to influence the Postmaster General to a conservative course in considering the demands for changes in office which poured in upon him continually. To Mr. Jameson, those who aided him, and above all to the business sense and grasp of mind of Colonel Vilas was due this

"SPECIAL NOTICE.

Post Office Department.

Office Postmaster General,

Washington, D. C., March 31, 1885.

Tenure of Office,—Railway postal clerks who have become efficient and valuable men, against whom no just complaint of neglect, inattention, or want of fidelity, honesty, or efficiency can be brought, and who have not turned their attention to political labors during their service, need have no fear of being disturbed so long as they continue to render meritorious and faithful service.

(Signed)   Wm. F. Vilas,
Postmaster General."

This notice exerted a quieting influence upon the men, and it is not believed that many valuable clerks would have been removed during the administration of Postmaster General Vilas, but for the ill advised organization of the "Brotherhood of Postal Clerks," in fact clerks, who affiliated with this society, but were not active in proselyting, were not disturbed. Each case known was carefully considered by Mr. Jameson, and action on it taken in conformity with rules determined in conference with the head of the Department to be necessary to destroy an association believed to be inimical to private and public interests, because its purpose was intimidation and retaliation; before action was taken upon any case the proper Division Superintendent was requested to inform his chief of all mitigating circumstances, the character, disposition, and capacity of the clerk, and all these were weighed. It has been my understanding that this association originated in the Fifth Division where the removals were the most numerous in the first years of the administration, but the men must be credited with excellent recuperative judgment, which led them to abandon the society and to resume their loyalty to their very honorable calling and to the people whom they served after a brief lapse.

That General Superintendent Jameson was faithful to his trust, realized the gravity of the situation, and labored to prevent its culmination, is attested in the following extract from his first annual report (1885) respecting civil service:

* * * "If continued in the service his studentship is by no means ended; in fact, if assigned to any one of the larger lines of the country, it is but commenced, and the appointee must look forward to several years of constant application before he can hope to attain the highest grades. I think I can safely say that it requires fully as much mental, and more physical, labor to become a first class postal clerk than it does to become proficient in any other trade or profession.

"Years of patient and assiduous labor and study have served to train up in the service a corps of energetic and faithful employees whose places could not be satisfactorily filled without the expenditure of an equal amount of time and labor in the preparation of their successors. The retirement of these skilled clerks could not but be followed by disastrous results to many of the commercial and social interests of the country, which depend in a great measure upon the prompt delivery of the mails.

"In view of these facts, I cannot close this annual report without reminding you that, while in other and less important branches of the public service the tenure of office of employees is covered by the civil service law, the railway mail service remains outside of its protecting influence, and to earnestly recommend that some action be taken by the Department in the matter, to the end that Congress may be prevailed upon to extend the benefits of that law to this service, and thereby insure the retention in office of postal clerks so long as they continue to render meritorious service, comply strictly with all of the instructions of the Department, abstain from undue interference in political matters, and conduct themselves in a gentlemanly manner.

"With a view to bringing this important matter to the attention of Congress, I have the honor to submit the following draft of a bill which embodies my ideas as to what is required in the premises, and with the hope that it may receive favorable action."

Then follows the draft of the bill, which is only fair as compared with the civil service laws and regulations of to-day. But we have been advancing with great strides during the past twenty-four years; what was only fair then, would be very crude now.

Mr. Jameson, like his predecessors and his successors, until Congress authorized it in 1900, urged that the chief clerks of the service be recognized by law, and be paid a higher salary than that allowed clerks in charge. These officers were, always have been, and always will be, indispensable. They are selections from those counted the most capable clerks in charge; have supervision of from fifty to two hundred or more clerks; in many respects their duties are like those of the superintendents to whom they are accredited, only in a lesser degree, and they lack the authority of final action in important cases. In Mr. Jameson's time few of them were provided with stenographers or other help; they did all the work themselves, as best they could; examined their subordinates, inspected the routes under their charge, scheduled the runs, filled those left vacant for any reason, made minor investigations, reported irregularities of service, conduct, morals and traveled "from pillar to post," day and night, in the discharge of their duties, and paid their expenses from the salary they were receiving as clerks in charge, which was very inadequate, by living on hopes, sleeping on piles of mail, dreaming of "Delmonico's" and of reposing in the favored guest chamber of the "Waldorf Astoria."

Consider the character, responsibilities, and hardships of their assignment; the knowledge and capacity—mental and physical—they had and exercised; the unending hours of duty—for they had no tours or reliefs; the expenses that could not be avoided; their fidelity, integrity, and loyalty; cheerful obedience and self-forgetfulness in their devotion to the advancement of the service in usefulness, and you will agree with me that there never was, and never will be, another corps of employees so able, successful, and faithful, paid so inadequately as this one was until the fifty-sixth Congress in 1900 and 1901 passed a bill increasing their salaries to $1,600 per annum, and allowed actual traveling expenses, not exceeding $3.00 per diem. This was a splendid battle won, and all who participated in it on our side were happy.

Mr. Jameson's term was short, but he was active all the time, and was what might be termed preventive medicine. The following is the statistical record of his administration—January 1, 1885, to February 4, 1887:

No. of employees January 1, 1885	4,175
No. of employees February 4, 1887	4,735
Increase for the 25 months about	560
Average annual increase about	268
Miles of railroad carrying mail January 1, 1885	119,120
Miles of railroad carrying mail February 4, 1887	128,033
Increase for the 25 months about	8,913
Average annual increase about	4,278
Annual miles carrying mail Jan. 1, 1885, about	147,226,766
Annual miles carrying mail Feb. 4, 1887, about	167,694,627
Increase for the 25 months about	20,467,861
Average annual increase about	9,824,573
Pieces of mail distributed last half of fiscal year 1885	2,474,024,700
Errors in distribution for same period	443,852
Pieces correct to each error	5,574
Pieces of mail distributed during fiscal year 1886	5,329,521,475
Errors in distribution, same period	1,260,443
Pieces correct to each error	4,228
Pieces of mail distributed the first 7 months 1887	3,413,313,197
Errors in distribution, same period	1,011,864
Pieces correct to each error	3,373
Increase in pieces distributed during the 25 months	900,086,499
Average annual increase	432,041,508
Average annual increase of errors, same period	406,518
Average annual decrease of pieces correct to each error	1,056
No. of case examinations, permanent, last half 1885	2,744
No. of cards handled, same period	2,844,328
No. correctly distributed	2,338,945
Average per cent. correct	82.23
No. of case examinations, probationers, last half 1885	1,658
No. of cards handled, same period	1,226,314
No. handled correctly	835,540
Average per cent. correct	68.13

Hon. Thomas E. Nash
Sixth General Superintendent R. M. S.

No. of case examinations, permanent, first 7 months
    1887 3,836
No. of cards handled, same period 3,801,962
No. of cards handled correctly 3,326,852
Average per cent. correct 87.50
No. of case examinations, probationers, first 7 months
    1887 2,614
No. of cards handled, same period 2,117,997
No. correctly handled 1,717,473
Average per cent. correct 81.09
Increase per cent. correct, permanent, for the 25 months   .5
Average annual increase per cent. correct, about 2 1-3
Increase per cent. correct, probationers, for the 25 months   13
Average annual increase per cent. correct, about 6
Pieces of mail separated for immediate city delivery, by
    carrier, in railway post offices, January 1, 1885,
    to February 4, 1887 255,996,940
        Being 40,869,725 for last half fiscal year 1885;
        129,025,155 for the fiscal year 1886; and
        86,076,732 for the first 7 months 1887
Average annual pieces of mail separated for immediate
    city delivery 122,866,368
Average annual increase from the close of Mr. Thomp-
    son's administration to the close of Mr Jameson's.. 63,270,056
The number of packages, pouches, and other pieces of
    registered mail handled during the fiscal year 1885 16,614,177
        421,249 less than during 1884, and the fiscal
        year 1886 showed a further decrease of 289,608
        pieces; this decline was due to extensions of
        the through registered pouch and inner regis-
        tered sack systems, which made many of the
        packages theretofore handled separately avail-
        able to them, and as they had numbers or
        addresses of their own, the numbers of record
        in railway post offices fell off, though the pieces
        actually mailed increased largely.
Mr. Jameson was a soldier, from Wisconsin, during the Civil War.

THOMAS E. NASH

of Wisconsin was appointed to succeed Mr. Jameson and entered upon the duties of the office February 14, 1887; he was
an able business man of excellent sense and judgment; a man

of strong convictions and determination; he was not in the service for blood, and proved it by championing the cause of faithful and efficient employees, and by separating himself from the very honorable position he had occupied for a brief time only, and in which he had hoped to make a record that would be a credit to himself and friends, rather than scuttle the ship he commanded, by discharging crews that were, in the main, thoroughly disciplined, and efficient, and taking on those that in the main would be undisciplined, uneducated, and consequently incompetent. Undoubtedly he would have continued in the office if permitted to conduct it as he believed the best interests of public and private business demanded, but he was not willing to sacrifice those interests to advance the selfish aspirations of any set of men, and when his business judgment clashed with what some considered party fealty —a grievous misconception of the facts—he re-entered business pursuits, and I am sure that all who know of his courageous stand rejoice that he has been successful. He has my most profound respect, and best wishes for a long, happy and prosperous life.

During his general superintendency the great strike of the Brotherhood of Engineers and Firemen, of which Messrs. Arthur and Sargent were the respective chiefs, against the Chicago, Burlington & Quincy railroad was ordered, and met by that company, and a desperate conflict between the two forces was waged for some time. The strike commenced about March 1st, 1888, and before it closed had extended to some other lines—the Santa Fe for one—and became embarrassing because the C. B. & Q. was, as it is now, the route of the fast mail between Chicago and Union Pacific Transfer, Iowa. We felt the effect of the strike, first, a day or two after it moved out in the open, through the stoppage of the train carrying the Chicago, Forreston & Dubuque railway post office at a place a little north of west of Aurora, Ill. This was then the Chicago & Dubuque night line R. P. O. and important. The report of this interference with the mail was received next morning. After reading it I visited the Grand Pacific Hotel in Chicago, and sent my card up to Mr. Arthur's rooms and was invited up. The conference that ensued was pleasant but earnest. I stated our grievance; he disclaimed responsibility for it, but said he would see that it did not occur again, and he took measures at once to prevent it; but they were not effective, for the train was stopped the following night, and my visit to Chief Arthur was repeated. This time he sent men out to see that his forces understood they were not to interfere with the mail, and assured me that their men would not be withdrawn from the Chicago & Union Pacific Transfer fast mail. Being superintendent at Chicago, I kept General Superintendent Nash informed

of the exact situation every day, and after the Sante Fe became involved he came out and remained with us a few days, bringing a confidential decision framed to meet emergencies, affecting the mails, due
to possible hasty or ill-considered action on the part of either party to
the controversy.

After Mr. Nash returned to Washington, the daily telegraphic
reports of the situation were resumed and continued until the strike
ended.

The schedule between New York and St. Louis was improved
during this administration, and a fast mail, St. Louis to Kansas City,
Mo., on the track of the Missouri Pacific railway established; it departed from St. Louis at 3:00 a. m., fifteen minutes after the arrival
of the Pennsylvania fast mail from New York, and arrived at Kansas
City at 11:00 a. m., making connections with trains bound north,
west, and southwest. This was a valuable improvement.

This administration covered a period of one year, three months
and nineteen days; its statistical record is:

No. of employees, February 15, 1887, the opening day.. 4,744
No. June 30, end of the fiscal year 1887 4,851
No. of employees June 4, 1888, the closing day 5,077
No. June 30, end of the fiscal year 1888 5,094
Increase during administration 333
Miles of railroad carrying mail Feb. 4, 1887 128,038
Miles of railroad carrying mail June 30, 1888 143,713
Increase for the 17 months 15,675
Annual miles of mail carried by railroad Feb. 4, 1887.. 167,694,627
Annual miles of mail carried by railroad June 30, 1888.. 185,485,783
Increase for the 17 months 17,791,156
Pieces of mail matter distributed from Feb. 4 to June
 30, 1887 2,438,080,860
Errors in distribution for same period 722,753
Pieces correct to each error 3,373
Pieces distributed for the whole fiscal year 1887....... 5,851,394,057
Errors in distribution, same period 1,734,617
Pieces correct to each error 3,373
Pieces of mail matter distributed during fiscal year 1888 6,545,876,202
Errors in distribution, same period 1,765,821
Pieces correct to each error 3,707
Increase in distribution for the 17 months 911,929,055
Increase in errors, same period 228,779
Pieces correct to each error for the whole time 3,542
Increase of pieces correct to each error 169

No. of case examinations, permanents, Feb. 4 to June
    30, 1887 2,740
Cards handled 2,715,688
Correctly handled 2,376,328
Average per cent. correct 87.50
No. of case examinations, probationers, same period... 1,867
Cards handled 1,512,855
Correctly handled 1,226,765
Average per cent. correct 81.09
No. of case examinations, permanents, fiscal year 1888.. 7,809
Cards handled 7,917,904
Correctly handled 7,165,988
Average per cent. correct 90.50
No. of case examinations, probationers, same period... 5,633
Cards handled 4,092,350
Correctly handled 3,223,964
Average per cent. correct 78.78
Increase per cent. permanents, correct for 17 months... 3.00
Decrease per cent. probationers, correct for 17 months.. 2.31
Pieces of mail separated for immediate city delivery by
    carriers in railway post offices Feb. 4, 1887, to June
    30, 1888 204,594,705
        Being 61,483,380 for the last five months of the
        fiscal year 1887, and 204,594,705 for the fiscal
        year 1888.
The number of registered packages, through registered
    pouches and inner registered sacks handled by the
    railway mail service during the 17 months of the
    administration of Mr. Nash was 24,063,802

W. L. BANCROFT

succeeded to the office of General Superintendent June 5, 1888,
and was succeeded March 19, 1889. The only thing I can say
in commendation of his administration is, it was brief. I do
not wish to say anything harsh, but it was the first, after the railway
post office was inaugurated, that threw up its hands, and apparently
permitted efficient and well behaved clerks, who had spent years in
perfecting themselves to discharge all their duties acceptably to the
people and their superiors, to be removed without protest. The only
comfort there is in the recollection is the assurance that Providence has
the happiness and prosperity of people and nations in its keeping, and
that experience is an excellent schoolmaster.

Hon. W. L. Bancroft
Seventh General Superintendent R. M. S.

HON. J. LOWRIE BELL
Eighth General Superintendent R. M. S.

J. LOWRIE BELL

succeeded to the General Superintendency March 20, 1889. He was without experience in the railway mail service, which is as essential to a real understanding and consequently to the best management of that system of skilled labor, as it is to success in most if not all professions. It has been repeatedly demonstrated that no matter how marked one's natural ability to command and manage may be in any calling requiring cultivated brain and brawn, he cannot be as effective without as with education and actual experience.

The great generals of our wars would not have attained their highest rank had they entered upon their careers without military education and actual experience in camps and on battlefields in actual war; so with clergymen, lawyers, surgeons, physicians, architects and builders; each one who enters a profession may be led to the one he chooses by natural genius in that direction, but he will not be as successful in it without as with training, in which large experience is woven.

There has been no time in many years, when a vacancy in any office of the service, from the lowest to the highest, could not have been filled better by promoting the refined material within, than by the introduction of raw material from without; besides the latter procedure is unjust, detrimental and uncalled for in such a magnificent service, whose distinction rests upon the fact that it moves upward all the time through the honest and intelligent skilled labor of its corps of more than sixteen thousand of the best trained and brightest men engaged in any vocation.

The service passed under Mr. Bell's supervision much impaired in efficiency, and in a somewhat demoralized condition, but he was a man of indomitable energy and courage, of great capacity for mental labor, and was trained in the field of railroad transportation; had full confidence in himself, was ambitious, restive under restraint, and somewhat intolerant; was a good organizer and, withal, of a kindly nature.

He served as an officer in emergency regiments during the Antietam and Gettysburg campaigns of the Civil War, in both of which the State of Pennsylvania was imperiled, and served well and faithfully.

Of the nine division superintendents in office at the close of Mr. Thompson's administration, only two remained when Mr. Bell entered upon his duties; all of these had been in the service many years, and had risen grade by grade during that time from the lowest to the highest office, save one, on merit alone.

Of the 4,175 clerks employed when Mr. Thompson retired from the railway mail service proper, only 1,250 were continued until Mr.

Bell's administration began. A large majority of those employed up to March, 1885, were excellent clerks; most of them had been drilled and trained for years; a large per cent. of those who were lacking in capacity or were habitual drinkers of intoxicants, or not suited to the service in other ways, had been winnowed out, but some were in; if these had been taken and the useful left, no one could have found fault.

As soon as inducted into office Mr. Bell took into consideration the advisability of reinstating the superintendents, and did reinstate all but two. The resignations of the two superintendents, who succeeded these two, were accepted, and the vacancies filled by promotion of two employees, who had served in lower positions long and efficiently. The two who passed from Mr. Thompson's to Mr. Bell's administration were continued as superintndents—one until death called him home— the other succeeded Mr. Bell when he was appointed Second Assistant Postmaster General and retired from the General Superintendency, after serving seventeen years in that office, on account of continued ill health.

In November, 1888, two additional divisions were organized, with headquarters in St. Paul, Minn., and Fort Worth, Tex., respectively. Those who had been placed in charge of them retired in March, 1889, and were succeeded by two employees who had seen much service and were selected for promotion because of experience and believed adaptability for the office.

The enthusiasm and activity manifested by the preceding administration in retiring employees, who had become indispensable to business and social intercourse, simply to gratify partisan feeling, undoubtedly aroused a spirit of retaliation that could not be gratified with due cautionary regard for fitness and justice in the limited time intervening between the inauguration of President Harrison, March 4, 1889, and May 1, 1889, the date the railway mail service found shelter within the classified civil service order of President Cleveland, dated January 4, 1889, and intended to become effective March 15th of the same year, but which was postponed to the first of the following May, by President Harrison, on request of the Civil Service Commission, to enable that body to organize boards of examiners throughout the country to examine applicants for admission to the service, and to forward the papers to the Commission at Washington, D. C., for inspection by experts, preparatory to the creation of an eligible register from which certifications were to be made to establish and maintain a certified substitute list from which regular probationary appointments were to be made in accordance with prescribed rules, to fill vacancies in the regular force, to equip new routes as they were established and to make additional appointments to old routes as they might be needed.

The lack of due deliberation in making removals of clerks appointed subsequent to March 4, 1885, and in the reinstatement of those appointed previous thereto, but removed between March 5, 1885, and May 1, 1889, was not in the interest of the service nor just; but, I presume, was quite natural from a human standpoint, being in accord with the old Mosaic law, "eye for eye, tooth for tooth, hand for hand, foot for foot," which, thank God, has been an outcast from the railway mail service for many years. Much was done immediately afterwards to rectify this haste and injustice. There were many who believed that discrimination in making removals and reinstatements, based upon capacity, health, knowledge, and habits, should be exercised carefully in that emergency; to them two wrongs could not make one right, and they used their influence in favor of careful selection, but it did not control as well as it should.

In replying to a letter received from a gentleman close to President Harrison, before and after his inauguration, the writer said, under date of January, 1889:

"The most expeditious way to restore the service to its former efficiency is to reinstate such of the old clerks as were competent and of good habits. This cannot be accomplished unless the rules are suspended, because with them in force if they come back, they can come as probationers only, and those who are desirable would not wish to return under those conditions, nor do I think it would be just to expect them to. The greatest care should be exercised in determining who may come back. Some who were removed were incompetent, some had bad habits, and a few were insubordinate; the restoration of those who were retired under those conditions would be a detriment, rather than a benefit, to the service. The fact that a clerk was removed does not, taken alone, constitute a reason sufficient to justify his reinstatement.   Very respectfully,

(Signed)   James E. White."

In March of the same year the writer included the following paragraph in a letter addressed to Mr. J. Lowrie Bell:

"Permit me to invite your attention to the necessity of determining, by close inspection of records, who of the clerks that have been removed, may be returned to the service with reasonable expectation that such action will be beneficial."   *   *   *   *

Very respectfully,

(Signed)   James E. White,

Superintendent."

The failure to fully follow the advice of the many interested business people, was responsible for the removal of some excellent, and the reinstatement of some very poor material; afterwards some of the best of the former were reinstated and some of the latter removed on the recommendation of the division superintendents; later others of the former class passed the civil service examination and their names were entered in the eligible register, which, as I have said, is the base of supply for the certified substitute list, and which in turn is the source from which vacancies in the corps of regular employees are filled and additional appointments drawn in the manner prescribed in the civil service rules.

I am justified, I believe, in saying that when these changes were made, and the service was within the full influence of the civil service methods ordained, the employees were about equally divided in political faith between the two great political parties. Since then all appointments have been made in pursuance of these methods, which constitute it an offense for any person in the executive civil service to discriminate against or in favor of an applicant, eligible, or employee in the classified service, because of his political or religious opinion or affiliation, or color; so that it is now impossible to know how the service is divided politically.

With these changes; with experienced captains in charge of the ships of the line once more; with the application of a sound civil service system in which protection stands for real protection; with the warm interest manifested in the success of the service by Postmaster General Wanamaker and the business public, the old inspiration revived and was intensified.

To inspire rivalry in the acquisition of knowledge of distribution, and in work and records, the fifth division, by the advice of Superintendent Burt, hung up medals for best records during the calendar year 1889, which were presented at a splendid reception held the evening of January 15, 1890, in the headquarters of the Superintendent. There was a large attendance of the employees of the division; their wives, mothers, daughters and sweethearts, and a number of official guests, among whom I remember Mr. J. Lowrie Bell, General Superintendent, Mr. R. C. Jackson, Mr. L. M. Terrell, and myself (then Superintendent of the sixth division). I presume other superintendents were present; if so, I cannot recall them, a fact that I sincerely regret. The occasion was very enjoyable and impressed me so thoroughly as being one of the most commendable acts taken to increase interest in the service then, that I applied the medal feature of it to my own division in 1890.

Following the reception at Cincinnati, Ohio, Postmaster General Wanamaker offered twelve beautiful gold medals as rewards for best records, "one to the clerk in each division who made, during the calendar year 1890, the best general record on the largest number of cards, representing post offices distributed by routes or by counties, modified by the class of the clerk, the number of separations, the cards per minute cased correctly, the error slip record, and the car work of the clerk."

The twelfth medal was to be awarded "to the clerk of any class in any division who, during the year, correctly distributed in the shortest time and largest number of separations, cards representing the greatest number of post offices, special consideration to be given the rapidity with which the distribution was accomplished."

These contests aroused the widest interest in the service and were the cause, in part at least, of very sharp emulation in all the divisions, which resulted in many phenomenal records at the case. As a natural result this was reflected in the general work as soon as the knowledge thus obtained had time to ripen in the crucible of application and experience.

During this administration the fast mails between Omaha and San Francisco via the Union and Central Pacific railroads and Green River, Wyo., and Portland, Ore., via the Union Pacific, the Oregon Short Line and the Oregon Railway and Navigation Company routes, and between Chicago, Ill., and New Orleans, La., via the Illinois Central railroad, were established; total distance, 3,766 miles.

Additional railway post offices were authorized on the New York Central, Boston and Albany, New York, New Haven & Hartford; Pennsylvania Company between Pittsburg and Chicago, on the Baltimore and Ohio and several other railroads, which are embraced with others in the increased mileage given below.

The statistical record of the eighteen and a half months of Mr. Bell's administration as General Superintendent is about as follows: When Mr. Bell assumed charge, March 20, 1889, the

number of clerks employed were about	5,348
When he retired, October 3, 1890, there were about ...	5,930
An increase during the administration of about	582
The miles of railroad upon which mail was carried, March 20, 1889, was about	148,530
When he retired from the office, October 3, 1890, it was	155,913
An increase in the eighteen and a half months of......	7,383
The annual mileage on March 20, 1889, was	198,963,182
When he retired, October 3, 1890, it was	218,692,505

An increase for the eighteen and a half months of.... 19,696,323
And an average annual increase of 12,775,992
Pieces of mail distributed, fiscal year ended June 30, 1889 7,043,838,598
Of which there were distributed between March 20 and June 30 1,817,751,249
An increase over the same period of 1888 of 4,792,224
And for the whole fiscal year of 497,962,396
The errors in distribution for the whole fiscal year were 1,808,825
And for the period between March 20 and June 30, 1889 466,791
Being in both instances one error to each 3,895
Correct, an increase to each error of 251
Pieces distributed during fiscal year ended June 30, 1890 7,865,438,101
Errors in this distribution, same period 2,812,574
Being one error in the distribution of each 2,797
A decrease in pieces correct to each error of 1,097
And an increase of pieces distributed over 1889 of 821,599,503
Pieces of mail distributed from June 30 to Oct. 4, 1890 2,212,431,912
The errors made in distributing the same numbered.... 527,526
Being one in the distribution of each 4,193
An increase of pieces correct to each error for 1891 over 1890 of 1,396
Pieces distributed during the whole fiscal year 1891.... 8,564,252,563
The errors made in this distribution amounted to 2,042,049
Being one error in the distribution of each 4,193
An increase of pieces correct to each error 1891 over 1890 of 1,396
An increase in the number of pieces distributed during the whole fiscal year 1891 of 698,814,462
And an increase June 30 to October 4, 1891, over same period 1890 of 176,582,150
The increase for the eighteen and a half months of this administration was 832,037,326
And the increase in errors for the same period was 830,237
Average pieces correct to each error for the whole period, about 3,628
Being a decrease in pieces correct for each error of about 267
No. of case examinations, permanents, March 20 to June 30, 1889 1,403
Cards handled 1,537,715
Correctly handled 1,408,030
Average per cent. correct 91.57

No. of case examinations, probationers, same period... 1,873
Cards handled 1,226,476
Correctly handled 985,458
Average per cent. correct 80.35
No. of case examinations, permanents, fiscal year 1890 8,959
Cards handled 10,936,679
Correctly handled 10,296,073
Average per cent. correct 94.11
No. of case examinations, probationers, fiscal year, 1890 7,125
Cards handled 6,861,471
Correctly handled 6,763,741
Average per cent. correct 84.00
No. of case examinations June 30 to Oct. 3, 1890, of
    fiscal year 1891, permanents 2,715
Cards handled 3,217,668
Correctly handled 3,138,629
Average per cent. correct 93.81
No. of case examinations, probationers, same period.. 927
Cards handled 867,714
Correctly handled 755,763
Average per cent. correct 88.87
Increase per cent. correct made by permanents during
    the eighteen and a half months 2.24
Increase per cent. correct made by probationers, same
    period 8.52
Pieces of mail separated for immediate city delivery, by
    carriers, in railway post offices from March 20, 1889,
    to Oct. 4, 1890, eighteen and a half months 333,589,511
        Being 43,024,209 for the period from March 20
        to June 30, 1889, and 226,429,575 for the fiscal
        year 1890, also 64,135,727 for the period June
        30 to October 4, 1890, being part of the fiscal
        year 1891.
This shows an annual increase during Mr. Bell's ad-
    ministration of about 60,000,000
The number of registered packages and cases, through
    registered pouches and inner registered sacks han-
    dled by the railway mail service during the eighteen
    and a half months of Mr. Bell's term as General Su-
    perintendent was 27,051,965
        Being 4,722,627 for the period from March 20
        to June 30, 1889, and 17,714,501 for the fiscal

year 1890; also 4,614,837 for the period from
June 30 to October 4, 1890, a part of the fiscal
year ended June 30, 1891, an annual increase
during Mr. Bell's administration of about. . . .   698,256

Mr. J. Lowrie Bell was appointed Second Assistant Postmaster General, October 3, 1890.

JAMES E. WHITE

became General Superintendent, by regular promotion, October 4, 1890. He was appointed a route agent on the Chicago and Northwestern Railway between Cedar Rapids and Boonesboro, Iowa, March 5, 1866, at $800 per annum; transferred to the Clinton and Boone railway post office in September, 1866; promoted to class three at $1,000 per annum, and assigned as head clerk. Transferred to the Chicago, Ill., and Cedar Rapids, Iowa, railway post office, at same class and assignment, early in 1869. Transferred to the Chicago, Ill., and Iowa City, Ia., railway post office at same class and in same assignment soon thereafter, cause change in the routing of the overland letter mail. Transferred to the Omaha, Neb., and Ogden, Utah, railway post office (Union Pacific Railroad) April, 1870, and promoted to chief head clerk, headquarters Omaha, Neb., at $1,400 per annum. Promoted to Superintendent railway mail service at Chicago, Ill., November 21, 1871, of the division then known as the Fifth, afterwards as the Fourth, and later, and now as the Sixth, the number changing with territorial reorganizations of the service. Promoted to General Superintendent railway mail service October 4, 1890, headquarters Washington, D. C. Resigned February 4, 1907, cause ruined health. Served in the Civil War—1861 to 1865—four years and two months. Entered the army as a private in May, 1861; honorably discharged as a captain in 1865. Wounded.

I cheerfully divide the credit for the success of my administration with everyone connected with it in any capacity, who was faithful, efficient and loyal; doing his duty as he was given to see it but in the interest of the public always. It could not have been the success it was but for the able division superintendents who gave me their earnest support during the seventeen eventful years it covered. They were, as a rule, men who had been promoted to that office after many years of experience in all subordinate positions and this long and effective service made them almost invaluable. Behind them stood a body of chief clerks who were being prepared for further advancement as emergencies arose. In fact the whole service was permeated with healthy ambition and was progressive individually and collectively.

CAPTAIN JAMES E. WHITE
Ninth General Superintendent R. M. S.

REMINISCENT.

Previous to the breaking out of the Civil War, I had acquired sufficient knowledge of a trade to insure me a good living, if not a competency, during a fair span of life, after reaching the age of twenty-one, if my health remained good and my body sound, but the war came on with a rush and I went to the front when eighteen and served more than four years, in the 3rd and 13th Regiments, Iowa Infantry, returning to my Iowa home in August, 1865, disabled permanently, and with hardly any income.

It therefore became necessary for me to prepare to earn my living, and more, if possible, through some avenue not yet considered, and after mature reflection I concluded to enter school and remain there until I had acquired a fair education, and then to study law until qualified to enter upon its practice. Accordingly, I entered our high school and came to an understanding with Judge Conckling—one of the leading jurists of Iowa—to enter his office as a student as soon as my school days were over. Another case of "Man proposing and God disposing," as is shown by what follows.

One afternoon, early in March, 1866, on my return from school, my uncle, with whom I made my home, handed me an appointment as a route agent on the Chicago, Iowa & Nebraska R. R. (now the Chicago & North Western R. R.) between Cedar Rapids and Boonesboro, Iowa, vice P. W. Randall, resigned.

I knew nothing of the railway mail service, had never seen a mail apartment and had not made application for appointment to it, or to any other service. I had determined to be a first-class lawyer, and so I expressed surprise that an appointment should be sent me unsolicited, and found that Judge Conckling and my kinsman had requested the Hon. J. B. Grinnell, of the House of Representatives from Iowa, to secure it. I said to my uncle that I knew nothing about the requirements of the office, but as my wrist was still suppurating and abscesses were forming occasionally, and I could not turn the palm of my left hand upwards, I did not see how it would be possible for me to handle the mails, but, under the circumstances, I would go down to Cedar Rapids, examine the work, see the route agent, and if I found there was a probability of my being able to do it, would qualify and remain.

Upon reporting at the postal apartment I found that the retiring agent had been absent for some time; that he was represented by a substitute named Coulter—a most excellent gentleman—who was expecting the appointment himself. After expressing my regret that he was disappointed, I explained the situation to him and said I would qualify and assume charge of the run; that if he would remain with me two weeks, giving me instructions, and provide me with a list showing the disposition to be made of local mails and those foreign to the line as well, I would allow him the salary for that period and twenty-five dollars additional, and if I could not fill the position properly at the expiration of that time I would resign in his favor and request my friends to endorse him for the vacancy.

This was agreeable to him, and he did his part pleasantly and efficiently, and at the end of the two weeks I did not find it difficult to perform the work properly. The distribution was simple, because in the beginning of my service it was purely local. There were no cross lines, the bulk of the mail was received, made up, and we assorted the packages and dispatched them to the head, terminal and intermediate offices. Those that were received from these offices not prepared for delivery we distributed and dispatched to the same offices, in the aggregate, to be delivered to their patrons or to be forwarded by the star routes indicated.

The largest portion of the mail handled by the route was made up in the Chicago D. P. O. and in the Chicago & Clinton R. P. O., until our line was extended eastward to Clinton, on the Mississippi River, and designated the Clinton & Boone R. P. O.

The car to which the post office apartment was assigned was occupied principally as a smoker. A space about 7x10 feet in dimension was allotted to the mails and opened into an alley, on one side of the apartment leading from the outside platform at one end of the car to the smoker which occupied the full width of the car. A sliding door opposite the one opening from the apartment into the alley enabled the agent to exchange mail with the offices on one side of the track, and a similar door in the other side of the apartment provided for exchanges with offices on that side.

The "go-back" was exchanged as a rule at the meeting point by the west bound route agent who carried his return across the open space between the trains and delivered it to the east bound agent, receiving from him the east bound return. The alley side of both apartments usually faced south, so that the agent making the exchange left his by the door on the north side after slipping the bolt in the door opening on the alley. This facilitated his movements and protected the mail during his absence; it also enabled him to throw the mail into the car as he approached it on his return and by grasping the perpendicular iron rods on either side of the doorway and placing one foot on the rod, hanging ten inches or so below the car at that point, follow it in without letting it out of his sight a moment.

A case of boxes, each about a foot square on the face, was fastened to the partition separating the post office apartment from the smoker, a distributing table, upon which the pouches and sacks were emptied, extended the full length of the case, and on one side was a letter case also provided with a distributing table and facilities for postmarking letters and cancelling stamps on those mailed at the car. Under the table were two or three drawers in which valuable matter could be placed and locked up. In those days this space and the facilities were ample to accommodate the mail received and the distribution. One route agent could perform all the duties of the run without much exertion and have time to look at that magnificent prairie country, and to think of things pertaining to his occupation and otherwise.

The light furnished was wretched. Old dingy oil lamps were attached to the sides of the apartments, as near the cases as possible, and gave out about as much light as a tallow dip of the third magnitude, with an eclipsed moon for a shade. Fortunately when the trains were on time not much artificial light was needed. At this time Iowa was sparsely settled and the railroad mileage limited. I am quite sure that the Chicago, Iowa & Nebraska R. R. had reached the most westerly point of any under construction in the state and it was in operation to Boone only. Stage coaches that were forerunners of the approaching trains connected with them and carried travelers and mail on toward the setting sun under the crack of the whip and the sting of the spur night and day as fast as hardy animals could haul and carry them.

Soon after assuming the entire duties of my run I got out of the post office apartment one day to exchange return mails at the meeting point as I had done times before without incident; this time the train started west before I reached it and I made a dash for the front platform, throwing the mail through the open doorway as I passed it, mounted the platform and entered the alley rapidly, tried the door to the apartment and then remembered I had bolted it before leaving the car. New in the service, not well acquainted with the trainmen and sensitive, it flashed through my mind if I pulled the bell cord and stopped the train it would be a violation of the rules of the company and undoubtedly offend the conductor.

These reflections stung my pride and I made a dash for the platform again, swung off the steps and as the car came on reached up

high above my head, grasped the iron rods on either side of the doorway, climbed in and unbolted the door, but could not resume work for
some moments. The conductor came forward shortly, looked in and
noticing that I was unstrung asked what was the matter, and I
told him; he asked why I had not pulled the bell cord and I told him
and added I did not want it known I had locked myself out. He said I
was too sensitive, that emergencies sometimes arose which justified
the violation of a rule and if I was similarly situated on his train again
to pull the bell cord.

Mr. Eddy, who was the senior route agent, and myself took care
of the route from Cedar Rapids to Boonesboro until the fall of 1866,
when it was extended eastward to Clinton, Iowa, on the Mississippi
River, and its designation changed to Clinton & Boone R. P. O., then
an additional crew of one clerk and a helper were appointed to it.
The character of the work was changed to a higher grade, became
more extensive and complicated, and the salary was increased from
$800 to $1000 per annum.

Doctor Mathews, of the Chicago & Clinton R. P. O., a thoroughly
good man and an efficient officer, patient and kind, was detailed by
Mr. Armstrong to instruct us in railway post office work. It seemed
to me that I was not progressing as fast as I ought, and one night,
when we were alone in the apartment, I said to him I did not think I
was making satisfactory progress; but he very kindly said I was
among the "flyers," and would go into the home stretch with the best.

This encouraged me, and I began to search with renewed energy
for information respecting distribution—material for the building of
schemes—Chicago standpoint, and to print it with pen and ink as fast
as I could marshal it in order, in a book especially provided for the
purpose. I had much information and many schemes, general and
standpoint, in this book, but it did not quite suit me, so I commenced
on a more elaborate one, better suited to the class of distribution I was
learning and making voluntarily. This was completed in 1868-1869,
and I presented the first book to our helper, Mr. Frank M. Journey.
The one I retained embraced ultimately all the schemes used in the
Clinton & Boone, the Chicago & Cedar Rapids, and the Chicago &
Iowa City R. P. O.'s. I also made a separate scheme of everything
west of the Missouri River and, when assigned to the last mentioned
route, distributed it.

In connection with the above it will be well to remember that
no schemes were printed until late in 1868, and that not much progress
was made in that line until in the seventies. Thus it will be seen that

to be counted worthy one found it important to mould his own schemes out of material collected by himself, or to secure assistance from the more studious and determined.

The Ward mail catcher service was established early in 1869. Previous to that time the catching, when the train was in motion, was done with the arm, and the person who acted as the "crane" held the pouch perpendicularly in such a way that the route agent or clerk might pass his arm around the pouch and close in on it as the human crane relinquished his hold. It was not difficult in the early days to do this if the person holding the pouch used judgment and held it right, and the engineer slackened the speed of the train; sometimes, however, the pouch was held wrong and a failure to catch was the result. I remember one such case on my own run. A post office named Cedar Cross Roads—now known as Lamoille—had been established on a farm a few miles west of Marshalltown, Iowa, just at the point where the west-bound train commenced to climb the hill to State Center, and the farmer, who was an elderly gentleman, had been appointed postmaster. After receiving the appointment he came to the train at the depot in Marshalltown to ascertain how to hold the pouch and to arrange for his first exchange with me on my next west-bound trip. I showed him how to do it, but his heart must have failed him, for he placed the pouch on the end of a long pole and stood back as far as the pole would allow and held the pouch up to the side door. I did not attempt to make the catch, but wrote the postmaster a note explaining the matter further and provided him with a diagram.

When I came west next he was standing on an improvised platform not far from a post he had sunk in the ground and through the top of which he had bored a hole parallel with the track and driven a smooth stick so that one end of it stuck out a foot to the east and the other about the same length to the west. It was his intention to hang the pouch on the west side of the post for the west-bound exchange and on the east side for the east-bound exchange. As I approached the arrangement I could see that a catch could not be made without encircling the pouch and the post with the arm, and as I did not want to enter the Kingdom then I shook my head and wrote him a third note. When I went west next he stood on the platform holding the pouch so nearly correct that I thought I could make the catch. It was not quite right, however, his arm did not clear the pouch, as it should, and just as I was in the act of encircling it the car swung slightly to the right, and I closed in on the pouch and his arm, lifted him from the ground, and let him drop in a ditch by the side of the track. If I could have selected the spot and held on to him until the train reached it, I could not have found a safer place to drop him and save myself. After that his daughter attended to the exchange and the trouble was reduced to the minimum.

The Chicago, Iowa & Nebraska R. R. was completed to Council Bluffs in 1867, I believe, and made connection with the Union Pacific railroad at that point. The overland mails were dispatched by the C. I. & N. R. R. after that date, and a line of full railway postal cars was established between Boone and Council Bluffs in which to distribute the mail east and west-bound. Experienced clerks were transferred from other lines farther east to equip it efficiently.

For two years and a half after the Clinton & Boone R. P. O. was ordered I ran in it and made my home in Clinton, Iowa. I often came in contact with the clerks in the Chicago & Clinton R. P. O., and through them with the most expert clerks assigned to railway post offices centering at Chicago. From them I gathered information that I utilized then and subsequently in compiling schemes that were very useful to me then and later, and the practical railway post office work we were taking up as fast as our minds could hold it was fitting us mentally and physically to give a more correct and complicated distribution of important mails that were increasing in magnitude rapidly.

We no longer threw mail needing distribution to advance it into our head and terminal offices for them to dispose of through distributing post offices, railway post offices, and route agencies. We were beginning to distribute our own mails from our own standpoint, and those that were not local we gave in the main a mild general distribution. We received massed instead of made-up mail, and dispatched made-up instead of massed mail to a considerable extent, and now, early in 1869, it was announced that the three R. P. O.'s of this line, viz.: The Chicago & Clinton R. P. O., Clinton & Boone R. P. O., and Boone & Council Bluffs R. P. O., would be reorganized into two and be designated the Chicago & Cedar Rapids and the Cedar Rapids & Council Bluffs R. P. O.'s, and I was assigned to the former, but only for a brief time; the Chicago, Rock Island & Pacific R. R. immediately began building a line of railway post office cars expressly to accommodate the distribution of overland letter mail moving in both directions, and the Department accepted them and designated the route the Chicago & Iowa City R. P. O. Some of the clerks who had been handling these mails in the Boone & Council Bluffs R. P. O. were transferred to this line; some were transferred to it from other lines. My transfer was from the Chicago & Cedar Rapids R. P. O. During the time I remained upon that line, and after reporting to the Chicago & Iowa City R. P. O., I spent part of my late afternoons and early evenings in Chicago, where I came in contact with so many clerks who had benefited by considerable experience in the Chicago D. P. O., and in the first railway post offices inaugurated, that I found that all one had to do to become acquainted with the distribution was to ask questions, to note down the answers, and to verify their correctness. This I did, and entered them in my book to refer to afterwards.

The Chicago & Iowa City R. P. O. commenced service early in 1869, and the force of clerks selected to equip it was on hand in advance. Mr. Walter L. Hunt—afterwards superintendent of the Seventh Division and the first to place an "iron bag rack" in a postal car—was my assistant, and I was very fond of him; he was a bright, studious, and competent clerk, and an attractive and agreeable companion. In fact the line with few exceptions was equipped with clerks carrying full cargoes of sand and they were boiling over with vigor. The large number of letters received per clerk fell into order in the distributing cases under the educated and systematized mental and physical manipulations of these artists in a way that never failed to have them ready for dispatch before our western terminus loomed up by the side of the track in the blackness of the night. They did splendid work and lots of it, but as compared with the work of to-day, regardless of the improved facilities now provided and the years of education and discipline through which the backbone of the service has passed to reach its present efficiency and expertness, it is believed that the clerks on the best lines of those days did as much per clerk as those on the best lines of these later days, but it was not so diversified, nor so generally useful to the country as a whole or of so much importance to business and professional interests.

No city distribution was made in railway post offices then and registered mail was handled in a very simple manner. These two innovations have been of great benefit to the public, have increased the work of the clerks and made the growth of the force more rapid than would have been necessary otherwise. In fact the service has been forced with the speed of a race horse ever since 1869, when it was first given an organization; that organization had to be educated and developed, and the supervision increased, and that too developed before flesh began to form on the skeleton and muscles and strength began to show in the long strides it has been making for many years.

I remained in this R. P. O. about one year and was then transferred to the Omaha & Ogden R. P. O., and assigned to duty as chief clerk, R. M. S., headquarters at Omaha, Neb., and with an increase of salary from $1000 to $1400 per annum. The Omaha & Ogden, the Burlington & Council Bluffs, the Council Bluffs & Kansas City, the Kansas City & Denver, the Cheyenne & Denver and the Missouri Valley & Fremont were assigned to me, and, as I did not have an assistant and was introducing a new system and correcting the evils of the old, and disciplining and educating the employees, especially in the Omaha & Ogden R. P. O., I was in active service all the time.

I had a family to support, and was not allowed, as chief clerks have been for many years, necessary traveling expenses. All I received was a salary of $1400 per annum, so that when I left Omaha in November, 1871, I owed $500, borrowed money, which had been expended in traveling expenses and in providing my family and myself with the absolute necessities of life.

The train which carried me to the Union Pacific Transfer, Iowa, opposite Omaha, Neb., one pleasant day in April, 1870, landed me close to a carnival of mud and profanity, such as the Missouri river only can produce when "Old Sol" has liquified the ice and snow in the mountains around Fort Benton and to the south, and sent it rushing down from the zone around that old military post, and from the country contributary to its tributaries, boiling and crashing through villages, driving steamboats upon the land; destroying railroad tracks, drowning horses, cattle and other farm stock within its track. A mighty torrent headed in a primeval wilderness, at war with civilization, and the inventive genius of man, through whom the elements of nature are subdued, and made subservient to progress and development, instead of continuing on its course of destruction and desolation.

I found the mail messenger loading the mail for Omaha and the Omaha & Ogden line (U. P. R. R.) on his wagons preparatory to transferring it across the river, and the transfer clerk watching him with that smile of confidence playing over his classic features which afterwards became as noted the world over for "taking them in" as the one we know as the "childlike and bland" brand. When the wagons were loaded and the transfer clerk ready I accepted the entourage as a convoy and arrived in Omaha without paying tribute to either "The First Chance" or "The Last Chance," or going into a strange land with the scent of whiskey on my breath.

After breakfast I called on the postmaster, at the post office, and inquired for the office of the chief clerk of the R. M. S., and was directed to the second floor back. The back room on the second floor was quite large and rather dark, and without furniture to speak of.

At the time of my first call my predecessor was not in, so I introduced myself to the agents who were assembled and there were quite a number; many of them were bright, active, earnest-looking men, as well put up and with as agreeable features and pleasant manners as clerks in other centers. Others there were who had passed the period in their careers when one in charge, who could not keep his eyes on them most of the time, could not hope to compete successfully with the d—i for their salvation; so as time moved on it was found best not to let them embarrass the service and annoy the business public any longer.

I introduced myself, as I have written, and fastened to one of the walls of the room a greeting and an announcement of assumption of command which began with the salutation, "Gentlemen.—"

I then stepped back, sat down and waited for the next move. In a moment Captain Smith—who had been an officer in the regular army, was well educated, a polished gentleman when himself, and a good clerk under the same conditions—took a position in front of the manifesto and began to read it.

When he reached the word of greeting—"Gentlemen"—he repeated it, and said, "Well, well, we're gentlemen, are we? The transformation is sudden, wonder if it will last?" I said, "It rests with you men; suppose you try, captain." In the conversations that followed I tried to impress upon the captain and all the others, that it was not hard for any one to be a gentleman; that it ought to be easy for one who was born and educated among those who had been counted as such from infancy to the grave, and who had served in a profession none but gentlemen could enter or remain in. All that was necessary was to be courteous and kind, sober and industrious; well-behaved, prompt in reporting for duty, obedient, law-abiding, studious, energetic and active; that no one who could not fill all these requirements after a fair and reasonable trial could remain in the railway mail service, because he would be worthless.

I said I would help them all I could; that I would compile and have printed for their use books of schemes of all the states and territories west that required distribution at their hands, and one also of such eastern states as must be distributed before reaching Chicago to insure their dispatch from Union Pacific Transfer without delay. The Department had authorized the expenditure of a sum of money for printing for the R. M. S. at Omaha. I found that $300 of this was unexpended and I expended it for the schemes mentioned.

The compiling of these schemes was a difficult work, so far as the states and territories were concerned. I had much data on hand;

the scheme I made and used while assigned to the Chicago & Iowa City R. P. O., a post route map, and star route lettings. I spread the star route maps on the floor in our sitting room and placed a book of lettings within reach, then laid down on the map and examined the data I had received in answer to inquiries, compared it with the lettings and the map and then made my notes preparatory to the final compilation, but in many instances the same routes were scrutinized carefully two or three times, and the same postmasters were written to again for further information. The work was long and tedious, but when it was completed and the schemes were in the hands of the agents we were all—including Superintendent Bangs—very greatly pleased.

Before leaving Chicago for Omaha Mr. Bangs and I had a comprehensive conference respecting the policy I should pursue in the management of the employees who were to be under my supervision. He said his information was that discipline was very lax at Omaha; that the clerks did about as they pleased—drank firewater of the hottest kind, gambled, shocked the moral sentiment of the community by crucifying all decency, etc., but he thought I had best not put any restraint upon them for a month or so, but keep my eyes open, note their misconducts and after that time handle the cases as in my judgment seemed best, making, when I was ready to act, such recommendations as the merits of the cases demanded. If the case was so grave as to indicate immediate action, I was to suspend and recommend removal, etc.

I found by keeping my eyes open that the Union Pacific R. R. was in more ways than one a ward of the nation, that every law-maker of the republic who was not barred from participating in patronage assumed that he had a right to be represented in the mail service on that line, because it ran through territories, except so far as Nebraska was concerned, and was not protected by the wise features of the present splendid civil service laws and regulations. Under these conditions it had become a dumping ground for those in remote states, and some not far away, whose demands for appointments had become so importunate, and who from a political standpoint were so valuable as working constituents, that on their own account and that of their friends they could not be ignored. Yet they could not be provided for in their own congressional district or state without offending some-one, and his friends, whose combined influence was more necessary to the success of the member, therefore the individual most undesirable for home consumption was made to see that "Westward Ho" should be his cry, and "Westward Ho" it was; with the result that among a large number of good employees there was much more than the usual per cent. of worthless and demoralized ones, and it was necessary to weed these out in order to build up an efficient and respectable service, and this was done without much delay.

It affords me pleasure to write now that I have never seen clerks improve more rapidly than those did who survived the winnowing. The line moved upward in the scale of efficiency day by day as the clerks took root in the knowledge of distribution, and the strife to excel in making up the mail in a neat and secure manner, to keep their cars tidy, and to maintain a clean and pleasing personal appearance grew constantly and was gratifying.

Occasionally a sluggard—unmanned by whiskey—would show up on his run, peevish and complaining that the work was greater than should be required of him; but as a rule these men were not of that character. I remember one case that illustrates forcibly how little value such men are to the service. A large, strong-built man from one of the large rock-ribbed Eastern states was appointed to this line because he was a kinsman of a gentleman of great political influence, and when the line was made a full railway post office he was made a clerk in charge for the same reason, but he could not maintain himself and was reduced. I visited the railway post office at the depot, one evening in Omaha, as I often did before the train started on its run of more than a thousand miles, to see if the crew was on hand and everything in condition. I found the crew there and a very large mail; the clerk of whom I have been writing was in charge of the paper mail, and as soon as he saw me he announced that the mail was so large that it would be impossible to distribute it all before reaching Ogden, Utah. I looked it over and said he could finish it by the time the train arrived at Cheyenne, but he protested that it was impossible, and finally I said to him that I would go out with him and would guarantee to distribute the mail before reaching North Platte, Nebraska, if he would keep the case tied out and bring in and dump the mail on the table. He agreed to this, and I sent a note to my wife telling her I would not be home until the next evening, and why.

We started out and I buckled down to the work. The lights were inferior, but my eyes were splendid, and I kept at the paper case all night, and in the morning as the sunbeams were playing on the water under the bridge over which we passed to enter North Platte, I threw the last piece of paper matter in the case. That settled the question as to how much mail could be worked on the run, for North Platte is only about one-quarter of the distance to Ogden.

I had kept fully posted on the distribution from the beginning so that I could enter a postal car anywhere on the line and examine mail made up by the clerks, and at the same time ascertain if the clerk whose mail I examined kept his scheme corrected to date. It was my custom to enter the car when and where I was not expected, to call upon the second clerk to bring in and dump on the table the mail he had distributed (his scheme and my own were placed at hand), and as I took up this mail piece by piece I redistributed it into the boxes and sacks and threw out before the clerk the errors I discovered, and asked him where they belonged. If he answered incorrectly, I would ask what his scheme said, and look at his book; if the book did not agree with mine it was corrected at once and the clerk admonished that a failure to obey instructions on this point would result in a record that would oust him from the service.

I took this action on those runs whose crews I had reason to believe were filled, in part, with members who were not up-to-date in their work, and who were defective in memory and too inert mentally and physically to make an effort to do a man's part to earn the salary paid; men whose days of usefulness had passed and who had not sufficient pride of birth or respect for their families to do their own part well and faithfully.

In order to keep myself thoroughly posted on the schemes I finally went to the Union Pacific R. R. shops and showed Mr. Stevens—the master car builder—a diagram of a model examination case, as I named it, and asked him if he would build it without cost; he said he would, and did, out of black walnut. I then bought some cards, such as we use to-day, addressed them, and after taking the case to my house began using it—once daily, except Sundays, when at home, and finally I examined some of the clerks on it, and when I was placed in charge of the division with headquarters at Chicago, took it with me and began using it about January, 1872.

UNION PACIFIC R. R.

The Union Pacific R. R. was not completed to Ogden, Utah—a distance of 1,029 miles—until 1869, though its construction was commenced in 1863. The building of the first forty miles—Omaha to Fremont, Nebraska—was slow and was not finished until 1865, but thereafter it was built with remarkable rapidity; 265 miles in 1866, 245 miles in 1867, 350 miles in 1868, and the remaining 129 miles in

THE EXAMINATION CASE

1869, when connection was made with the Central Pacific R. R., and a through all rail route established between the Atlantic and Pacific oceans.

During most of this time the worst elements of our population flowed westward in the wake of the construction trains of the Union Pacific, and towns sprung up in a night, wherever the temporary western terminus happened to be located, made up almost wholly of saloons, gambling hells, brothels and shacks in which all known immorality was practiced and crimes—from petty larceny to murder—were committed.

Railway mail service was authorized on the line as fast as changes in location of the western terminal occurred, and the route agents who were appointed to handle the local mails and those made up in the Boone & Council Bluffs and the Chicago & Iowa City R. P. O.'s were subject to great temptations because they were in these cesspools of wickedness, were associated with vice when not on duty in their cars, and too often this familiarity with it lessened their fear of its influence upon their morals and in many instances it became a potent factor in their downfall.

I think I may say that my disposition is sympathetic. To the best of my recollection I never disciplined a subordinate for misconduct or disobedience of orders or violation of regulations, either in the civil or military service of our government, until he was found guilty of the act for which he was disciplined and an effort made to reform him by moral suasion. I believe in punishment after a hearing, if guilty, not before, and in rectifying injustices as soon as discovered. So in the management of the service on this great overland route I moved with extreme caution, seeking to know the men and to gain their confidence.

Experience inclined me to the opinion that the young men who were somewhat wild—full of pranks, restive under the restraints of good government, champed on the bits and "kicked against the pricks" —when they entered the service were so because of a superabundance of vital force, energy of mind and body, and in most cases if they were not vicious and survived the weeding out process incident to passing under the influence of a systematic and equitable discipline, became excellent clerks and agents; just as observation inclines me to believe that one whose "family tree" shines with some illustrious names but has an occasional d—l perched on its branches has more to be proud of than one whose tree is full of sluggards and imbeciles.

The success of the service is due to red blood and vital energy and lots of it.

In the days of which I write men who would not now be eligible for appointment on account of age, physical infirmities, mental shipwreck and moral insolvency were not barred; there were no civil service laws and rules guarding the portals of entrance to the public service, therefore it not infrequently happened that the employee who had demonstrated positive fitness for the position he held passed out through the portals as his successor, upon whose face and form was stamped the inevitable signs of physical and mental decay or moral degeneracy, passed in. It was too early in the life of the service then to charge this destructive procedure to the dogma "to the victors belong the spoils," for the first railway post office was not inaugurated until three years and more of President Lincoln's first administration had expired, and the party he represented so gloriously continued to administer the government for more than twenty years afterwards; again, when President Lincoln was inaugurated there were all told but 427 employees in the whole railway mail service, and only 22,018 miles of railroad upon which mail was carried, and not one railway post office clerk or railway post office car. When the party was defeated and passed out of power the first time there were 4,387 employees in the service, all known as railway postal clerks—all other designations having been abrogated by Act of Congress effective July 31, 1882—and 121,032 miles of railroad upon which mail was carried.

The facts are, the Jacksonian cry lost its party significance for twenty-four years, because the same party administered the government and dispensed the Federal patronage all that time, but it remained of national importance, for the "tenure of office" became to some extent a personal matter between the employee and his friends, and the member of Congress and his friends, if both were of the dominant party; and the effect upon the service and the business interests of the country was of the same character, only less baneful because being of the same political faith, the incentive to demand removals was not acute unless the employee favored the nomination of some one else for the seat and that some one else failed to secure it, or criticised the member in abusive and disrespectful language or brought false charges against him, etc. The fact that a clerk or agent was subject to removal on the demand of his congressman and that the same gentleman could name his successor kept all of us in a state of unrest and made the success of the service problematical until President Grant issued his executive order of 1872, carrying into effect the civil service rules drafted by the commission appointed by him in pursuance of the Act of March 4, 1871.

The order and rules provided for a "tenure of office" based on "good behavior and efficiency," but did not deprive the members of Congress of the privilege they had enjoyed from the beginning of naming those to be appointed to vacancies and as additional clerks and agents. The order allayed the unrest very materially and was of great assistance in developing the service, but it fell far short of the civil service methods that have prevailed since 1889, of which mention will be made later on.

It may not be known that the noble red men disapproved of the building of the Union Pacific railroad and, assuming that the great plains and the foothills and mountain ranges back of them were their game preserves and that those employed in constructing the road were trespassers, they protested, but it was not heeded, and they undertook to enforce it by obstructing the track and lassooing the engine. The result of the lassooing was a whole string of Indians sailing through the air, their heads and legs cracking like whip cords while their whoops of astonishment showed that the iron horse was a revelation to them; the obstructions, however, ditched the train, some of the equipment was burned, some of the passengers killed, others injured, and the conductor was scalped, but recovered and resumed his duties, remaining on the line for many years. I believe his name was John Calhoun.

About the time this tragedy occurred an ex-clergyman was appointed from Ohio—I think—a route agent on the Union Pacific railroad, and reported for duty at Omaha, Neb. The officer in charge at the time assigned him to a crew that, with others, had been trying to secure an appointment for a young man named H——, then a resident of Omaha, but who had been a clerk in the Cairo, Ill., post office, and was bright and energetic. They concluded that the time was opportune for them to make a telling stroke for H——, so when the clergyman reported at the mail apartment he was informed that the Indians had been so troublesome of late that one member of each crew was required to sit at the open doorway all night, with a musket in his hand or lying across his lap, and a revolver by his side, watching and listening to outside movements and sounds in order to give the alarm in case of an attack, and to protect the mail and the members of the crew who might be sleeping until they could be aroused and made ready to aid him; that they had been doing this night duty and working daytimes so long that they were tired out and as he was fresh he must do the guard duty that night. They placed a chair by the open doorway, gave him a musket and revolver and, cautioning him to be very vigilant, after the train pulled out, returned to their cases and resumed work. In a short time B—— dropped in and, speaking loud enough to be heard by the clergyman, said to the agent in charge that he had just visited the railroad office, where he had been informed that the Indians were on the war path again—burning, plundering and killing—and that undoubtedly they would attack the train that night somewhere up the road; that they had asked him to visit the outgoing train and to put the agents on their guard and see that they were properly armed. Being told they were short he handed his own revolver to the agent, telling him to take it along. A little later C—— looked into the car, told about the same story and donated his gun. Then came D—— with a more startling story of outrage and the tender of his gun was accepted.

All this time our clergyman was drinking in these blood-curdling and nerve-racking tales, but he remained at his post through all the night like a gentleman, and when he returned to Omaha, he resigned, and the service knew him no more forever.

When it is remembered that the whole stretch of country from Omaha to Ogden, 1,029 miles, through which the Union Pacific R. R. runs, was practically uninhabited by civilized people, except those engaged in the construction of the road, and the offscourings of all creation who had fallen from that high estate and were using every means known to the vile intriguer to debauch and ruin those who were thrown in their way; that the greatest Civil War of all times was swallowing up the best blood of our country and that the whole population of the United States numbered not more than 35,000,000; that the aggregate population of Nebraska, Wyoming, Colorado, Utah, Idaho, Montana, Neveda, California, Oregon, and Washington— the mail for which passed over this great overland route—was but 978,000, and that there were about 14,000 Indians in and close to these plains who were hostile to the project and 37,000 more roaming over the upper Missouri country ready to reinforce them at any time, we wonder that it was built with so few mishaps, in so short a time, and so substantially.

Since then and as a result of the success of this great undertaking, and of others that followed after the way had been made plain, the development of this vast territory has been phenomenal in all respects except crime, immorality and hostility of Indian tribes; in these respects there has been a decrease in proportion to the increase of population. This has increased from 978,000 to more than 5,000,000, and all the tracts of land then known as territories have become states, and the population of the United States has grown from 35,000,000 to more than 88,000,000. The increase in the weight and number of pieces of mail handled and transported on railway routes has been greater than the increase in population.

Much more of a reminiscent nature might be written respecting my experiences in the railway mail service prior to November, 1871, but I deem it unnecessary, except to state that my experience includes some of the work of a special agent and as acting postmaster at Cheyenne, Wyoming, during the time the postmaster was held in duress pending the settlement of a defalcation case and the appointment of one of his bondsmen as postmaster.

Before the city of Chicago, which was almost swept out of existence by the great conflagration of October 7th to 9th, 1871, both inclusive, had become a smouldering ruin, I was called there by General Superintendent Bangs, who had, come on from Washington to assist in restoring order to the postal service of the city, and, pending its full rehabilitation, to provide some way by which the post office force could take care of the mails for city delivery, and arrange to distribute the greater part of that which originated inside the city for outside addresses independent of the post office. This was accomplished by establishing a temporary office in a car barn on State street, and stationing relief railway post office cars at different points in the city, calling in the clerks who were off duty, and sending to the cars for them to distribute the mail which was ordinarily distributed in the post office; provision was also made to pass the outside mail, moving in all directions around the city from one railway line to another, thus avoiding a blockade at that point and keeping the mail moving toward its final destination with the least delay possible.

I spent one day with Mr. Bangs and then returned to Omaha. This was but a brief time before I was promoted to the superintendency of the then Fifth Division, with headquarters in Chicago, but he did not indicate in any way that a change was contemplated, and I had not thought of it.

I resumed duty and moved along as usual until the 21st of November, 1871, upon which day E. L. Alexander, who had been a clerk in charge in the Chicago & Iowa City and the Boone & Council Bluffs R. P. O.'s, and was then chief head clerk at San Francisco, called upon me. We remained in each other's company all day and toward evening went to my home where I usually remained—when not absent from the city—until morning, but we concluded to go down to the post office after dinner and, being there, went to my letter box and found in it a telegram from Mr. Bangs informing me that I had been appointed superintendent of railway mail service at Chicago, and that he wished me to report there as early as possible and to take the oath of office and assume charge of the division immediately on my arrival.

I did not know what to do; did not feel confident that I could discharge the duties of such a responsible office satisfactorily at that time and said to Chief Clerk Alexander that I would wire Mr. Bangs declining the appointment. He expressed his views of such a proposition very freely and forcibly and I concluded to telegraph an acceptance, which I did, and commenced to prepare for the trip to Chicago at once. In the morning the ice was running in the river so thick and strong that it was considered unsafe to attempt to force the steamboat through it. This condition continued until the 24th, when the pressure to cross was so great that the company concluded to risk their property if we would risk our lives. We crossed safely and I arrived in Chicago that night long after dark, but I obeyed Mr. Bangs' instructions, hunted up a notary public, took the oath of office and took active charge of the division on the morning of the 25th of November, 1871.

CHICAGO POST OFFICE FIRE.

As I have said in another part of these reminiscences, immediately after the great fire of October, 1871, the Chicago post office and the office of the superintendent of railway mail service were located in a car barn on State street. They occupied the second story of the building, which consisted of a very large room known as Burlington Hall. The furniture and fixtures placed in this hall for post office purposes were very ordinary—such as had been discarded by other offices in the main, or put together rudely for temporary use only. No attempt was made to give the interior arrangement of this improvised office an artistic touch because business urgency and the economizing of time did not permit it; besides it was a "make-shift," only intended to last until a more suitable building could be fitted up for more permanent occupancy.

Both offices were without homes. Chicago was the chief sufferer by the destruction of its facilities for handling the mail addressed to its citizens, from without and within, and that addressed by the same citizens to their correspondents without. It was realized that whatever building was selected in which to perform the postal service of that city more permanently would be occupied almost wholly by the local post office. One modest sized room, or at most two, would accommodate the headquarters of the railway mail service at that time and in the near future. But in those days all the work of the

Chicago post office, and all the employees engaged upon it, were housed in one building and were in view of the postmaster at all times. Branch offices and postal stations were then unknown.

The general business of the office before the fire was only surpassed by the offices of New York and Philadelphia, while in the number of letters received and mailed New York alone exceeded it; and yet the population of Chicago was then but 334,270; it is now between two and three millions. It will therefore be seen that it was of paramount importance to secure a home for it at once, to equip it for the transaction of its regular business in the shortest time possible, and to resume work in the meantime in Burlington Hall to a moderate extent with the primitive facilities provided.

In the interim the railway mail service assumed the separation, distribution and dispatch of the greater part of the mail originating within the city. This it could do because it was not centralized in one locality or building. Its organization is as broad as the country; each integral part of it being as complete as a whole, and movable; each postal car, with its crew of clerks, is an integral part of the system and each integral part is capable of duplicating the work of the others. So that in stationing the relief cars at several points in the city, placing the clerks "lying off" on extra duty, and sending to the cars the greater portion of the mail usually handled in the post office and making the diversions heretofore mentioned, the troubles and delays anticipated were minimized.

In the emergency then existing it was not absolutely necessary that the headquarters of the railway mail service should have a room in any building, provided records of the superintendent's official actions were allowed to lapse temporarily. The superintendent and chief clerk could have stood in the open air, "scratch block" and pencil in hand, and sent by messenger to any railway post office, publishing house, railway company, the post office or the mail messenger, such orders, instructions and requests as the changing conditions indicated; or they could have occupied "standing room" in one of the relief cars and directed the movements of the service therefrom. In fact, the superintendent could have handled the service in and around Chicago much as a general handles his army when manoeuvring for position or launching its battalions against the enemy in a great battle; namely, stand in the open under the broad expanse of Heaven and direct its operations through aids and orderlies, personal observations and visitations, and the word of mouth. Therein consists one of its values over any other arm of the postal service; it has many more, and when all are considered and comparison made it stands out pre-eminent; it is always ready for any emergency, and thus far has coped successfully with all that have arisen. The self-sacrificing men who have assisted in building up the service from the beginning have always placed in the balance against failure to protect and enhance the interests of the public—whom they serve—their own interests, rest and comfort, enjoyment of wife, family, kindred and friends, those sports and recreations so dear to men of their caliber in other pursuits of life, and crowned all this possible discomfort, deprivation and sorrow with the jeopardy of their lives and limbs.

When I entered Burlington Hall on the morning of November 25, 1871, to assume the duties of my new office, Mr. William P. Campbell, who had served as chief clerk under Colonel Armstrong, Mr. Bangs and Mr. Wood, and who was a very bright and competent officer whom I was fortunate in retaining and attaching to myself during the greater part of my official career as a commissioned officer, met me with a hearty shake of the hand, sparkling eyes and a winning smile. After extending his congratulations and assuring me of his earnest assistance he handed me some letters which Mr. Bangs had telegraphed I would find on my arrival at Chicago, and which would explain the urgency of the situation. These letters I need not say I studied carefully and then had a long conference with Mr. Campbell, during which he gave me some valuable information, and I may as well say now as later that he never failed to give me loyal and helpful support during the time we were associated together. Mr. Campbell introduced the facing slip in the LaFayette and Quincy R. P. O. in 1869—this was to ascertain if the clerks in that office missent matter, as claimed by the Chicago and Centralia R. P. O. It uncovered many errors, and who made them. Better work resulted until a lapse came, when those offending were called to judgment and saw "the handwriting on the wall." The work improved continuously thereafter, and it was ordered into general use.

During the time we were in Burlington Hall the post office was embarrassed in every respect, and the work of my office and of the employees of the service centering at Chicago was very exhausting, but all were comforted with the knowledge that another building was being remodeled and enlarged and the interior made suitable for the work which was to be performed in it. This building was the Methodist church, corner of Wabash avenue and Harrison street. Its trans-

Hon. William P. Campbell
Ex-Assistant General Superintendent R. M. S.

formation was pushed with great energy and the post office and railway mail service moved into it about December 20, 1871, and remained there until July 14, 1874. Our office was assigned to the annex to the main building, and consisted of two rooms and a dormitory, one on the south side of the hall that divided it, and the others on the north side. The one on the south was light, those on the north dark. At first Mr. Campbell and I constituted the whole force of the office, and we took the south room. The north room was fitted up with a letter case and very soon it was assigned to the handling of error slips, etc. In a very short time this room, as I remember it, was placed in charge of Mr. John A. Montgomery, who remained with us until 1889, when he was made superintendent of mails in the Chicago post office. He had excellent qualities, was resourceful, energetic and somewhat diplomatic in temperament; he served many years with ability in the postal service, filling every position he held with credit, and was always loyal to his superiors; but his services as a brave and faithful soldier during the dreadful years of the Civil War, and his labors in the postal service thereafter, weakened his vitality and when he should have been in the prime of life his soul had returned to its Maker "Peace to his ashes."

As soon as we were settled in our new quarters the work of re habilitating and improving the service began. It was realized that before it could reach a point in its progress where eternal warfare upon it would cease, a vast expenditure of energy, stamina, inventiveness, discrimination and judgment would have to be made in demonstrating that it could do all that was claimed for it; that it was a meritorious system and not unreliable and extravagant, and so the work commenced on that line and the service was ready to prove when the final struggle came that those who had been assailing it did not comprehend its organization and capacity. The then postmaster at Boston—sometimes called ironically the "Postmaster-General of New England"—had a wire strung from his room into the office of the superintendent of the First Division, railway mail service, located, then as now, in Boston, and had a bell attached to the end in the superintendent's office. One day he rang it, and Superintendent Cheney, "our Tom," grasped the whole situation, immediately realized that upon his action then depended whether as a useful officer of a cooperative, but independent service, he was to "Sink or swim, live or die, survive or perish," and he looked up at the bell with a smile and kept on holding down his chair. The bell rang again and again and then a messenger from the postmaster appeared in the superintendent's office and asked him if he had not heard the bell ring. Mr. Cheney said, "Yes, what of it?" The messenger answered, "The postmaster rang it because he wants you to come to his room; he wishes to see you on business." "Tom" told him to go back and tell the postmaster that he was in his room and that, "the bell is on the wrong end of the wire."

Scheme building, which had made very little progress, because it had been largely an individual matter with the employees, was centralized in the office; some of them were built by myself as late as 1876, and all of them were printed. I remember that with the assistance of Mr. S. L. Foster, who was my secretary then, I built a scheme of Iowa—county and exception—in 1875, or 1876, and had it printed; I had built one, in my scheme book, of the state by county and exceptions, and from it one by office in 1868. The boys, as they dropped into the office, were informed that they would be called upon in a short time to be examined upon it. It was a sheet scheme and as compared with others issued at a much later date was small, but all seemed to think that in requiring them to memorize it I was subjecting them to unnecessary hardships, and some said no clerk could pass a creditable examination upon it. One day several of those who felt that way were in my office, and I said to them, "Boys, I must leave for the upper peninsula of Michigan to-night and will be absent for a week. I will put one of these schemes and a schedule in my pocket, and you may name a committee to examine me on it when I return. If I cannot distribute 95 per cent. of the cards correct I will not ask you to try it."

I returned in the time stated; the committee, case and cards were ready in due time, and I distributed the cards, making 96 per cent. correct. That settled it; nothing more was said, but the clerks who worked Iowa by that scheme passed creditable examinations on it. Afterwards I learned Illinois while on a pleasure trip around the lakes from Chicago to Ogdensburg, New York, with Mr. Bangs, ex-Governor Stewart and Mr. Vail—the latter leaving us at Cleveland, Ohio—but I did not deem it necessary to pass an examination upon it. I learned it for the use it would be to me in correspondence and on tours of inspection.

In January, 1872, we began case examinations at Chicago. At first they were made in a case which the master car builder of the Union Pacific R. R. built for me at a time in 1870 when he was completing the construction of a line of full cars authorized by the Department. I made many examinations on this and other cases. The system of case examination has spoken very effectually for its efficiency as a developing medium since that year. It is the most important educational method in use in the service. In 1872 I detailed Mr. C. G. Weirrich from the Chicago & Iowa City R. P. O. to my office as chief examiner; he had a wonderful memory, and kept the cases busy all the time; so did the chief clerks, as far as possible.

ILLUSTRATION OF THE ORIGINAL SCHEDULE OF MAIL AND
EXPRESS TRAINS AT JUNCTIONS.

JUNCTIONS		MAIL	EXPRESS
BURLINGTON, IOWA.			
Chicago & Burlington, R. P. O.	Leave	7.00 A.M.	9.00 P.M.
	Arrive	7.20 P.M.	6.25 A.M.
Burlington & Council Bluffs, Agent	Leave	6.45 A.M.	7.40 P.M.
	Arrive	8.40 P.M.	6.45 A.M.
Burlington & Keokuk, Agent	Leave	7.20 A.M.	7.30 P.M.
	Arrive	6.35 A.M.	7.10 P.M.
Burlington & Quincy, Agent	Leave	7.05 A.M.	
	Arrive	7.05 P.M.	
Burlington & Laclede	Leave	6.00 P.M.	
	Arrive	9.50 A.M.	
Albert Lea & Burlington, Agent	Leave	6.45 A.M.	7.30 P.M.
	Arrive	11.10 P.M.	9.45 A.M.
Burlington Br. T. P. & W. R. R.	Leave	4.25 A.M.	2.30 P.M.
	Arrive	7.25 P.M.	1.50 P.M.
WEST LIBERTY, IOWA.			
Chicago & Iowa City, R. P. O.	E.	5.50 A.M.	6.47 P.M.
	W.	8.20 P M.	8.50 A.M.
Davenport & Council Bluffs, Agent	E.	6.47 P.M.	
	W.	8.50 A.M.	
Albert Lea & Burlington, Agent	N.	9.28 A.M.	10.30 P.M.
	S.	8.20 P.M.	6.32 A.M.
CEDAR RAPIDS, IOWA.			
Cedar Rapids & Council Bluffs, Agent	Leave	7.05 A.M.	8.30 P.M.
	Arrive	8.30 P.M.	5.45 A.M.
Cedar Rapids & Holland, Agent	Leave	7.15 A.M.	
	Arrive	7.05 P.M.	
Chicago & Cedar Rapids, R. P. O.	Leave	5.55 A.M.	8.35 P.M.
	Arrive	8.00 P.M.	6.45 A.M.
Farley & Cedar Rapids, Agent	Leave	4.45 P.M.	7.00 A.M.
	Arrive	11.50 A.M.	6.30 P.M.
Albert Lea & Burlington, Agent	N.	11.35 A.M.	12.35 A.M.
	S.	6.30 P.M.	4.35 A.M.
Postville & Cedar Rapids, Agent	Leave	1.15 P.M.	4.40 A.M.
	Arrive	11.00 A.M.	7.40 P.M.

About a year after we commenced case examinations we began to keep a record of all errors noted on facing slips returned. A book account was opened with each clerk who used slips and the errors entered in the book were charged to the clerk who made up the package in which they were found. The name of the office, county, state and where sent, and proper destination each occupied a column, but before these entries were made the alleged errors were carefully examined by an expert. If they were errors they were charged as stated; if they were not they were charged to the clerk who noted them on the slip; and a doubtful check was referred to the clerk against whom it was charged, and if he could show that it was an unjust charge he was given credit for it; if not it was held against him.

In March, 1872, I arranged and compiled, and had printed in the *Chicago Postal Record,* the first "Schedule of Mail and Express Trains at Junctions" ever issued. It was for the state of Wisconsin and was in sheet form. This was followed month by month with schedules of other states until all in the division were provided for; and thereafter a schedule in sheet form of all the states and territories in the division was issued monthly. The first schedules had foot notes explaining how they were to be applied and examples illustrating the application.

This schedule was immediately approved by General Superintendent Bangs, who predicted that it would become of inestimable value, and he directed its use throughout the service. It would be impossible now to handle, distribute and dispatch the mails correctly without a schedule of connections. This schedule was improved upon afterwards by Mr. French and has been greatly improved in many respects since.

The mission of the schedule was to enable the clerks in railway post offices and large post offices to determine by which route, offices, and lines that could be supplied by two or more routes should be dispatched in order to arrive at destination at the earliest hour possible.

It was found that offices located on three-times-a-week star routes running from an office on one railway route to an office on another railway route, up one day and down the next, could be supplied six times a week if the mail addressed to them was dispatched by one route to-day and the other to-morrow; so, too, some railway routes were crossed and connected with at different junctions and termini—by several railway post offices heading from a common junction of great commercial importance. A portion of the route so connected could be supplied quicker and at less expense by one railway post office than by the others. By the schedule the clerks centering at the common junction were shown how to distribute or dispatch the mail for this line so as to give all the offices supplied by it and all its connections quicker supply than would have been possible if all these railway post offices had distributed the mail for one connection, ignoring "subdivisions as between junctions."

Again sometimes a line located a great distance from an important supply, it was found, could be reached best by sending the mail for it over two or more chains of routes, none of which were full railway post offices. Sometimes one of these chains reached the route at a point which enabled it to supply all the offices on it quicker than the others could any of them.

Such routes as those mentioned I studied and tested thoroughly while working out the schedule, and it was to place in the hands of the clerks information that would enable them to work the schemes to the best advantage that I built the original "Schedule of Mail and Express Trains at Junctions," and also to point out to them, to the transfer clerks and the mailing divisions of large distributing post offices, how made up and pouched mail should be dispatched to reach destination without loss of time.

When I became superintendent of the Fifth Division—now the Sixth—it comprised the states of Illinois, Iowa, Missouri, Arkansas, Minnesota, Wisconsin, Nebraska, the upper peninsula of Michigan and the line of the Union Pacific railway.

The Fourth Division, headquarters Indianapolis, Indiana, comprised Indiana, Michigan—excluding the upper peninsula—Ohio, Kentucky, Tennessee and West Virginia.

Soon after this time the San Francisco division was designated the Fifth instead of the Sixth; the Fifth, or Chicago division, was designated the Fourth, and the old Fourth was divided between the Second, Third and new Fourth divisions. West Virginia went to the Second; Kentucky and Tennessee to the Third; Indiana, Ohio, Michigan, and the mails passing through Canada, over what was then the Great Western and Grand Trunk railways, to the new Fourth. There was also added to it Kansas, Colorado, Indian Territory, New Mexico, Dakota and Wyoming, so that early in 1872 the Fourth Division comprised Arkansas, Illinois, Indiana, Iowa, Kansas, Michigan, Minnesota, Missouri, Nebraska, Ohio, Wisconsin, and the territories of New Mexico and Indian, Colorado, Dakota, the through line of the Union Pacific railway, and the mails passing through Canada.

It was an enormous territory to cover, and it kept me traveling most of the time, and yet there were but about 1,500 employees in the railway mail service then. How many of these were assigned to the new Fourth Division I have not the data at hand to tell, but as there has been taken out of it since the whole of the Seventh Division, all of the Ninth, except the New York & Chicago R. P. O. between New York and Buffalo, all of the Tenth except Montana, Arkansas and Oklahoma of the Eleventh, and Ohio and Indiana of the Fifth, it could not have been much less than half.

I remember receiving instructions from Mr. Bangs early in 1872 to assume charge of Indiana, Michigan, Ohio, and the Baltimore & Ohio R. R. to Grafton, West Virginia, with authority to detail a clerk as chief clerk at Indianapolis. I detailed James Kerr, who was afterwards chief clerk at Fort Scott, Kansas, and later a distributing clerk in the Chicago post office. He was a red-headed, sandy-complexioned, sturdy-built man, true as steel, determined, capable, outspoken, fearless, on deck all the time—an old Roman centurion. As soon as he entered upon his assignment he notified me of the fact and said he had been given a room in the Indianapolis post office building; that it was furnished with an old table for a desk, a candle box for a chair, and a candle for a light; that the officer who had been relieved was too busy following Senator ——— around to turn anything over to him, but that he would do the best he could; would look after the lines and clerks placed under his immediate supervision and start a fire under the "sweat box." Mr. Kerr was comforted; in a short time his office was equipped as well as that of any chief clerk in the west at that time, and that is not saying much for it.

Captain Maurice J. McGrath ran into Chicago when I did. He entered the service fourteen months after I did, May, 1867. He had been a soldier in the Civil War, and came out of it with a record for courage and endurance unsurpassed. Like many others who sought appointments in the railway mail service at that time, he did so because he was out of touch with trades and business pursuits—physically and temperamentally.

The occupations that were congenial to him and to many other young men in the comparatively placid and uneventful years preceding the war, became irksome after passing through scenes of carnage and strife which infused in their earthly tenements a more fiery, determined and ambitious spirit on the battlefields where contending hosts struggled for supremacy. The Captain was a positive character; a determined student of the practicability and possibilities of whatever he engaged in; there was nothing superficial or unstable in his make-up. His best understanding and energy was devoted to the postal service after he became associated with it, and as a natural result he rose, as the railway mail service grew, from one position to another until he became, in the order named, assistant superintendent, railway mail service, superintendent of mails, and superintendent of free delivery service, then superintendent of mail again in the Chicago post office, which latter office he held when summoned to the Great Beyond. "May he rest in peace."

As superintendent of mails, Captain McGrath carried into that office the methods he had been taught as a clerk and assistant superintendent of our service, thus insuring harmony in the handling of the mail in that great centre and more rapid progress in the development of the railway mail service, and he unquestionably was entitled to the credit of compiling and arranging the first county and exception scheme of a state ever printed; and the state was Illinois.

Colonel James E. Stuart entered the service in the fall of 1866 as a route agent on the Wisconsin division of the Chicago & Northwestern railway between Chicago, Ill., and Green Bay, Wis. He was young, active and full of vitality. He had been a soldier from Wisconsin during the Civil War in a regiment assigned to the "Iron Brigade," which participated in some of the most desperate battles of the war, and I have been told that Stuart was always in the "mix-up" when Greek met Greek.

He has lived quite largely in a military atmosphere almost all his life, and could not resist the impulse to participate in the Spanish-American War, which drove the Spanish Government out of Cuba and away from this continent.

After serving on the Chicago & Green Bay route a year or more he was transferred in September, 1867, to the Boone & Council Bluffs R. P. O.—a line which had just been established to handle the mails passing to and from the vast territory lying between the Missouri River and the Pacific Ocean. Colonel Stuart and the other employees who were assigned to this railway post office were selected by Colonel Armstrong on account of their fitness, or prospective fitness, for the work that was to be performed therein. They made good the confidence reposed in them and when this mail was transferred to the Chicago, Rock Island & Pacific R. R., the Chicago, Ill., & Iowa City R. P. O., Colonel Stuart, with others of the Boone & Council Bluffs railway post office, was transferred with it. As I remember the organization of this line the crews were as follows: E. L. Alexander, head clerk; C. G. Weirrich, clerk; James E. Stuart, head clerk; "Shorty" Gates, clerk; Mr. Brooks, head clerk; ——————, clerk; James E. White, head clerk; Walter L. Hunt, clerk.

Colonel Stuart remained on this line until it was discontinued, which was after full railway post office service was organized on the Union Pacific railway between Omaha, Nebraska, and Ogden, Utah, in September, 1870. I do not remember the date of its discontinuance, but know that after I was stationed at Chicago as superintendent, Stuart was one of my chief head clerks, with headquarters at Iowa City, Iowa. After serving some time as a chief head clerk he was promoted to be a special agent of the Department, and later to be post office inspector in charge at Chicago, and is still in that position. For the splendid services he rendered our government as a soldier in two wars, and the equally valuable services performed for it in the postal service, he deserves all the consideration it can give him. May his days be long, and life pleasant to him.

Mr. Edward W. Alexander was one of the early appointees of this service. He, too, was a splendid soldier in the Civil War, and was a very capable railway postal clerk.

I detailed Alexander to my office in 1872, and afterwards made him chief clerk at Lafayette, Ind. He was transferred thence in the same capacity to Indianapolis, after Indiana was taken from my division, and then became assistant superintendent, R. M. S., under the immediate supervision of General Superintendent Vail and afterwards was appointed superintendent of mails in the Philadelphia post office, where he has served, as in all other offices he has occupied, intelligently, efficiently, modestly and cleanly in every respect.

There were other excellent clerks whom I brought into my office, or assigned as chief clerks as the work of the service and the development of its organization increased; of these I will speak later on.

I had, as will be seen, associated with me in my office, and as chief clerks, within two years after we moved into the Wabash Avenue Methodist church, some of the brightest lights in the service, and among them J. B. Harlow and J. Stearns Smith, and had a valuable ally in Captain McGrath. All of these men save one had served in the army during the Civil War; they knew from experience how important to the successful accomplishment of any undertaking in which a body of men is engaged is discipline, and most of them were disciplinarians of good quality; they were accustomed to obey and they exacted obedience from their subordinates; they had endured hardships in all forms for years without flinching. With empty haversacks they had marched with heads erect, sparkling eyes, and unfaltering footsteps in the pathway of "Old Glory." They had faced death and disability on every battlefield of the republic; they were willing to face hardships and hazards in building up this service, and they did. I ask, where in the world could have been found men as capable of raising from its low estate to its present exalted condition a service so full of benefits and blessings to mankind and so laden with hazard and death to them?

Notwithstanding the impulse given the growth of discipline and efficiency in the service by the introduction of the war element, printed official schemes, case examinations, schedules of connections, lists of night offices and time of closing, facing slips, lists of exchanges at termini, trip reports, President Grant's celebrated civil service order of 1872, the probationary feature which enabled the officers of the service to ascertain whether the habits, morals, memory, physical and intellectual capacity of a clerk were such as to justify his being given a permanent appointment, and, as a rule, basing promotions on merit alone—though exceptions were made—the effort to secure the discontinuance of the railway post office system and the restoration of the distributing post offices grew more aggressive each year under the manipulations and misstatements of the postmasters of some of the larger post offices whose opposition was founded, as one editorial writer stated, "in the fact that it swept away from them very much of the political power which they possessed under the old system. The postmasters at ———— ———— ———— then had hundreds of clerks to appoint; they now have but scores, as the labor of distribution is now done while in transit, instead of at the great distributing offices. An effort is now being made by these central powers to reinstate the old methods and again permit us to 'wait a week' for replies to our letters from New York," etc.

This effort culminated in a fierce and unwarranted attack upon the railway post office system during the closing months of 1873 and the beginning of 1874. The principal assault was delivered in the *Boston Morning Journal* of January 16, 1874, and a copy of the paper was sent to me. I saw at once that it was calculated to injure our service very materially if its misstatements were allowed to go unchallenged, and this view was confirmed by the announcement made in the public press, "that the Senate appropriations committee will propose the abolition of the postal car system on railroads, and of the free delivery of letters, hoping thereby to cover the $7,000,000 deficiency in the postal department. As to the free delivery, we have little to say, though the letter receivers would be very loth to have the act repealed; but as to the postal cars, their abolition, and a return to the slow and uncertain method of 'distributing offices,' is something that the business community would not put up with."

The criticisms made upon the service in the west were not serious; all but two or three of the larger offices and the press and enlightened men generally were its friends and helped fight its battles. I made a study of the article which appeared in the *Boston Morning Journal*, and, as no answer had been published, concluded to answer it myself, and did so in the *Western Postal Record,* for the month of February, 1874, published in Chicago.

The article published in the *Boston Morning Journal* was headed, "The Railway Mail Service and Postal Cars," and read:

(From the *Boston Morning Journal.*)

THE RAILWAY MAIL SERVICE AND POSTAL CARS.

During the last fifteen years there has grown up in this country, in England and upon the continent of Europe a system of mail service which has been performed upon the steam railroads in the cars while in motion, which is known as Railway Mail Service, or the Postal Car Service, and this service has been increasing on all the lines of the railway until it has substantially absorbed all other mail transportation on the lines where it has been adopted. It was deemed the most perfect system that could be devised. It expedited the mails, and the Government has felt justified in expending enormous sums to perfect and extend this service; but while it has thus been perfecting itself, the growth of railway transportation and the means of supplying the public wants of travel have caused a corresponding increase in railroad facilities, and we are to-day, on all the principal lines of road between Boston and New York, between New York and Washington, New York and Albany and Buffalo and Suspension Bridge, in a condition where postal car service has entirely fulfilled its mission, and seems ready to give way to a better and more intelligent service, which can be performed at a more reasonable expense.

Whether upon the cars or elsewhere the postal service is not an independently sustained service, but is dependent and secures its accommodation through alliances with existing means of transportation. Moreover, the volume of mail matter has so rapidly increased, and has grown to be of such enormous amount, that it is no longer possible to accommodate it upon any one train, although occupying an entire car. It is as idle as it would be to require all the passengers, who now fill a dozen succeeding trains on each of our lines of road, to occupy one train and be drawn at the time by the combined locomotives of the several trains that now draw them. We have between Boston and New York two postal cars daily each way, and when they were established, they were run upon what were called express trains, meaning thereby the fastest trains that ran. But this is all changed. The postal car which leaves Boston at 8 :30 a. m. is, to be sure, an express train, but it is not either the fastest express train or the only one that would accommodate this service, and Boston is in a condition to-day of being deprived of mail facilities through the fact that these postal cars are run. If we had no postal cars, the mail would be made up in Boston, not only for the 8 :30 train for New York, but also at 10 o'clock for New York, the 11 :10 Short Line for New York, both of which last mails are now delayed for points beyond New York twenty-four hours. Mails could be collected in Boston from a circuit of country of fifty to one hundred miles in season for the 11 :10 a. m. train. These mails could reach New York in season for the night mail train for Washington. Now they are delayed for the night mail from Boston, which reaches New York in the morning, leaving there at 9 o'clock a. m., and reaching Washington the next night, letters destined for business houses and delivery by carriers not reaching their destination in Washington until the following morning.

What we require now is this: Separate the large mails which lumber up a single train and forward them on every train that leaves Boston. Let the first mail from Boston for every city on the line of the Boston & Albany Railroad leave Boston on the 5 o'clock morning train. At half past eight o'clock let the mail leave for New York and intervening cities. At 10 o'clock a. m., at 11 :10 a. m., at 3 p. m., at 5 p. m., and at 9 p. m. let the mails for the same places be made up and sent without a postal car, and in addition to this let there be placed upon the local train leaving Boston at 7 o'clock in the morning a car to do the local service between all the offices along the line of the road. The local service is entirely independent of the great through service which now overshadows everything. The same thing is required upon the New York Central Railroad. It is no benefit to anybody that they should carry postal cars on such express trains as they now do. Through mails for every city on the line and for every city beyond should be made up in New York and dispatched upon each succeeding express train from 8 o'clock in the morning until 11 o'clock at night. This, especially for the through letter mail, would secure greater dispatch and would prove no incumbrance whatever to the trains themselves. All the letters that would be required to be sent on each train would not be equal to the Saratoga trunks of a single female passenger in the fashionable season.

It now costs the Department six hundred dollars per mile, per annum, for the service on these routes, which indicates partially the enormous expenditure for this service, and even this amount paid is entirely unsatisfactory to the railroad companies, and upon examination probably will prove entirely inadequate to the service required. Between New York and Washington a still worse system of things exists. The mail leaves New York for Washington at 9 o'clock in the morning, although trains leave three hours in advance and reach Philadelphia before the postal car starts from Jersey City. From Philadelphia to Washington no mail is furnished until this postal car comes from New York, and a city of a million inhabitants, and one hundred and thirty miles only from the capital of her country, has no mail communication during the day that reaches Washington in season for the same day's delivery, while from Boston we are able to send a postal car that reaches Albany, a distance of two hundred miles, at noon, and Philadelphia has no mail that reaches Washington, a distance of one hundred and thirty miles, until night, and this is delivered the following morning.

Another difficulty with the postal cars is this: They furnish substantially, with all this expense, but one mail a day between these principal points. Between New York and Washington a day line is of no advantage to business men at the terminal points, and the letters by the day line arriving at either terminus are not delivered any sooner than those starting at night, making but one mail a day each way. Still another difficulty with the postal cars is that the mails being made up on cars running between New York and Washington for postal cars running between New York and Boston, and vice versa, any failure to connect renders the whole distribution of the mail for the day useless, and the mail arriving from Washington in New York in the morning too late for the postal car leaving for Boston, cannot be forwarded on the express train at 10 o'clock, as it would be if made up for each city on the line, and for the terminal cities, but it must lie over the entire twelve hours in New York and go on in the postal car at night.

The remedy for this at the present time is inexpensive and efficient. All these lines of road run five or six and some eight or ten express trains daily, upon which, as the presidents of the different lines have frequently stated to the Post Office Department, they are perfectly willing to carry the letter mail for all the cities on their lines, and in many instances they have offered to carry it for nothing. It is stated that one of the leading railroad presidents offered to carry the mails out of the postal car in this way on his line without any compensation. The same system of dividing up the mails and carrying them in an inobtrusive and at the same time efficient manner, has been established to all points on the horse railroads out of Boston. Instead of carrying them as formerly with teams, at fixed hours three or four times a day, they are now sent every hour for ten hours per day, thus keeping the central office free from accumulating mails and enabling the officers receiving them to be constantly employed. There are over two hundred such mails sent from the Boston office regularly, daily, none of them reaching a point more than three miles from Boston. On holidays these mails are not forwarded in this manner, and on the succeeding morning it frequently requires two-horse wagons for them, and when placed in the horse cars the mails load them down to the exclusion of passengers. A constant running stream draws off what would otherwise accumulate into an overpowering torrent. The same common sense must be applied to the transmission of our enormous mails upon the lines of railway. With eight express trains in each direction between Boston and New York daily, there is certainly no need of keeping an entire car upon any one train to the exclusion of the others.

Another very important item to the Department would be also a saving of expense in the employ of postal car clerks. These employees are paid nearly double the average paid for the performance of the same service in the office, and they perform about half the amount of work. Postal car clerks between New York and Boston run every alternate week and make one trip only each day. They work only one-half the time; or, in other words, the actual cost to the Department for doing the same work is four times what it would be if performed in the post offices, and this certainly can only be justified on the ground of great expedition, which we have shown above is not secured by the postal car service.

But there is still another aggravated expense. In any delay of mails upon the railroads—and these delays occur constantly from accidents both to freight and passenger trains, obstructions of bridges, delays by snow and flood—the entire mail is thrown upon the offices at the termination of the routes, and those offices must necessarily be supplied with sufficient clerks to meet any such emergency. Were these distributions performed regularly at the offices, and lock-bags sent to every principal office, and not opened at any intervening office, and were the mails sent directly from railroad station to railroad station in the cities, more time would be saved than all that is now secured upon the postal car trains. The running time required between New York and Boston is eight or nine hours, and yet the postal car arriving in New York at 5 a. m. remains with its mail until 9 a. m. before leaving for Washington, one-half the time required for the whole transmission. This extraordinary and expensive work is performed in this extraordinary and expensive manner, not to make close connections, since the connections that have been permanently arranged are disconnections.

The same is true of the day mail arriving in New York at 5 p. m. It does not leave for Washington until 9 p. m.—an abundance of time in the New York office to distribute the entire mail. If this postal service was being performed by the railroads in a manner that was acceptable to the Department and for a compensation that was mutually satisfactory, it might be permitted to rest for awhile, but even then it can do its work only for a few years longer. But the railroads are dissatisfied; the Department is dissatisfied. The expenditures for this service to-day amount to millions of dollars annually, and these are some of the results. The appropriation for the Post Office Department, we venture to say, can be reduced three million dollars this year and better service secured for the public, more satisfactory service for the railroads, and the inauguration of a plan for the future transmission of the mails on these crowded lines of railway that will meet the approbation of everybody, and would expand indefinitely with the growth of the roads.

It may be said that this service is more for the intermediate portions of the lines that this expense is incurred. This is true. We have four postal cars between Boston and Springfield, a distance of one hundred miles, and yet between Boston and Providence, New London and New Haven, a line of cities and business of equal importance with any, have no postal car service, and between Boston and Providence not even a route agent runs upon the road. The mails are all made up and dispatched from the terminal offices, and yet there is no distance in New England where there is more passengers or business travel, or where there are more intimate financial and business operations than between Boston and New York and the cities along the Providence line.

At all events this subject, in these days of retrenchment and reform, is one that will bear scrutiny, and if we are doing what is not the best, but which costs us most enormously, we ought to survey the whole field, and if possible test by experiment some change.

My answer was headed:

"R. M. S."

"The Railway Mail Service as Compared with the Route Agent System of Distribution."

and read:—

(*Western Postal Record*, Feb., 1874.)

The *Boston Morning Journal*, of January 16th, 1874, contains an article of nearly a column and a half in length, upon what is known as the Railway Post Office Service. The tone and general style of the article indicates that it was written or dictated by some one connected with the postal service of the United States, and as it abounds in erroneous statements, and is predicated upon a state of things that does not exist, it is but fair to conclude that the author is ignorant of the true object of the service—does not realize what it is accomplishing—or else, knowing its object, and realizing the work it is performing, he, for reasons of his own, chooses to place himself in a position of antagonism to it; and when we come to consider that it appeared originally in a Boston paper, and that there is, perhaps, but one person in Boston, or New England, who has felt it incumbent upon him to oppose this service upon every occasion, both in his official and private capacity, and that this person is shorn of political power and patronage that he previously possessed, and would now possess and control were it not for this service, it will be seen at once that it does not require the gift of omniscience to name the writer, or to reveal the motive which impels him to this antagonism.

*   *   *   *   *   *   *   *

We maintain that the railway post office service is far from having "fulfilled its mission," and also that there cannot be "a better and more intelligent service" established either at less or greater expense to the Government, and we expect to demonstrate this fact before this article is finished.

The gentleman will not contend that any system of distribution or transportation could be organized, that would give to the mails any better advantages, as to time in transit, than is enjoyed by first-class passengers; the system advocated by him will not do this, while the railway post office service is intended to, and does accomplish this result everywhere where it has been established west of New York and Washington, and in some cases it accomplishes more than this: it has a quicker transit between certain points on all trunk lines than first-class passengers, and this is accomplished through the assistance of what is known as "Ward's Mail Catcher," which is auxiliary to the railway post office and operates in conjunction with a "crane."

*   *   *   *   *   *   *   *

Here, in the west, all of our railway post offices are run upon fast express trains, which do not stop at many of the small way stations; hence a person desiring to take passage from one of these way stations for some distant point is compelled to start from his home on an "accommodation train," several hours, perhaps, in advance of the arrival of the through fast express, and ride to some station where the through express does stop, and there change from the one train to the other; whereas, a letter or paper may be deposited in the post office at the station from which this person started, addressed to the place of his destination several hours after he has taken passage, and arrive at the objective point as soon as he, because it will be placed in a pouch by the postmaster, and just before the through fast express train is due, the pouch will be suspended upon the crane so as to be caught by the catcher, and be taken into the railway post office, as the train passes, opened and the contents distributed; which means that the letters and papers, in passing through the hands of the head clerks and clerks, will be so disposed of as to keep them in motion until they arrive at the office of destination.

The accommodation trains are run without reference to connections at terminal points and junctions, being intended to transact the local business between station and station on the line, and any business man who ships goods or takes passage on one of these trains, for any place not on the line, in the expectation that he or they will arrive at the point of destination in time to transact business, or to realize on the goods within the first thirty days after shipment, is as certain of being a bankrupt as he is of any thing this side of eternity.

Under the system advocated by the gentleman from Boston, mail matter, say for the state of Illinois, mailed at offices on any of the lines of roads centering at Boston, from the north, would be forwarded from the mailing office to the route agent running upon an accommodation train, and be, by him, massed upon the Boston office, and be there held for distribution. In making this distribution the Boston office would mass a portion of the state upon each of the following offices: Cleveland and Cincinnati, Ohio; Indianapolis, Ind.; Cairo and Chicago, Ill. This massing involves a delay of twelve hours for all the larger or "night offices," and twenty-four hours for those not exchanging pouches with these distributing offices by night express trains, at each of the offices named. Take for instance, three letters mailed at some point on the "Eastern & Maine Central R. R.," one addressed to Geneseo, one to Colona, and one to Mokena, Ill. The former is a "night office" on the Chicago, Rock Island & Pacific R. R., and is supplied with eastern mail twice daily; once by the railway post office departing from Chicago at 10:15 a. m., and once by through or "night pouch" leaving Chicago on express train at 10:00 p. m. in charge of train baggageman. Colona is a station on the same line, and also receives its eastern mail twice daily, but in a different way: once by the railway post office, and once by means of what is known as an "express mail." Mokena is also a station upon this line, but as it is neither a "night office," nor comes within the scope of an "express mail," it receives its eastern mail but once daily. These three letters having been placed in charge of the route agent by the postmaster of the mailing office, would be massed, with other letters addressed to offices in the western states, in packages, and on arrival of the agent at Boston, would be sent to the Boston office for distribution. Here, in the west, all of our railway post office trains run to make eastern and western connections, and to make the illustration hold good we will assume that the same system obtains in the east. Working upon this hypothesis, we will say that the accommodation train upon which this agent arrived at Boston, arrived there in time for the passengers to make connection out of Boston by the 5:00 p. m. train for the west, (In this connection it is proper to state that, under the route agent system, it makes no difference whether these letters arrived at Boston on an accommodation or a fast express train, the illustration holds good in either case,) but this mail could not, for the reason that it must lay in the Boston office for distribution, and as it has missed the 5:00 p. m. connection, it may as well lay there until the 8:30 a. m. train departs, because, if sent out by the 9:00 p. m. train, the letters will arrive at Chicago 40 minutes after mail dispatched by the 8:30 a. m. train. This makes a delay of $15\frac{1}{2}$ hours at Boston. These letters will arrive at Chicago at 9:00 p. m., Chicago time, and as the mail with which they are massed, cannot be taken to the post office, be distributed and taken to the Chicago, Rock Island & Pacific depot in an hour, Geneseo and Colona will have to lay in the Chicago office from 9:00 p. m. until 10:15 a. m., $11\frac{1}{4}$ hours; making in all a delay of $26\frac{3}{4}$ hours between the mailing office and the office of delivery. But supposing the mail train does not arrive at Boston in time for the passengers to make the 5:00 p. m. connection west, say it arrives there at 7:10 p. m., then the passengers will have ample time to make the 9:00 p. m. connection for all points reached by that train and its connections, but all mail brought in by that train for points between Boston and New York, and New York and Washington, and Chicago, including those points, would be delayed in Boston till morning, while the delay, in the case of letters used in this illustration, would remain the same as before, except that the system would not be responsible for the delay at Boston. But how will the writer account for the delay of $11\frac{1}{4}$ hours at Chicago; if, on the other hand, these letters are forwarded to Boston in a through or night pouch by train arriving at Boston at 6:00 a. m., the passengers who came in on that train could make the 8:30 a. m. connection, but the mail could not be taken to the Boston office, distributed, re-pouched and taken to the 8:30 a. m. train in two hours and a half; hence these letters would be subjected to delay from 8:30 a. m. until 5:00 p. m. at Boston—$8\frac{1}{2}$ hours, and would arrive at Chicago at 8:30 a. m., and as this mail could not be taken to the Chicago office, be distributed and taken to the Chicago, Rock Island & Pacific depot in an hour and forty-five minutes, Geneseo and Colona would have to remain in the Chicago office until 10:00 p. m., making a delay of $13\frac{1}{2}$ hours here, and in the aggregate a delay of 22 hours. And as Mokena is only supplied with mail by the regular mail train, the letter for that office would be delayed $12\frac{1}{2}$ hours longer, making in the aggregate a delay of $34\frac{1}{2}$ hours. These delays could not be avoided, under the system advocated in the *Boston Morning Journal,* because it cannot be demonstrated that such a distribution could be made in the Boston office as would do away with them; to accomplish this result every office located on a railway line would have to exchange pouches with every other office similarly located, or, in following out the plan suggested in the article, we would have to discriminate in favor of the few larger offices, and in that case the exchange would have to be direct between office and office. Springfield, Mass., would have to receive and forward as many pouches daily as Boston, or she would not derive the same benefits, and in that event special mail trains would have to be run upon all trunk lines; the messenger service would have to be increased at all such points; the clerical force would have to be doubled, and the post office buildings enlarged, and the compensation of the railway companies instead of being lessened would be augmented beyond computation. The delay shown in the case of Illinois mail, would occur in precisely the same manner with mail matter for all offices in the western states, and reversing the case it would apply with equal force to all mail matter passing from the west to the east.

Geneseo, Colona, and Mokena, Ill., in forwarding mail addressed to offices supplied from the Eastern & Maine Central R. R. would send them to Chicago in charge of a route agent arriving here at 4:00

p. m., the agent would mass them, with all other letters received by him for New England, upon the Chicago office for distribution; and as the first train for Boston departs from Chicago at 5:15 p. m., this mail could not be connected, though the passengers who came in on that train, would have ample time to make the connection. Chicago, in making this distribution, would mass all of Massachusetts, except Berkshire, Franklin, Hampden, Hampshire, and Worcester counties, upon the Boston office for a second distribution. New Hampshire, except Cheshire, Grafton, and Sullivan counties, would be disposed of in like manner, and York county, Maine, would also be massed upon Boston for the same reason. The remainder of Maine would be made up in the Portland Distributing Post Office, and the five counties in Massachusetts, and the three in New Hampshire, named above, would be massed upon the Albany, N. Y., Distributing Post Office, and be there held for this second distribution. The presumption is that this mail would not be forwarded from Chicago until 8:30 a. m., making a delay here of $15\frac{1}{2}$ hours, but supposing the distribution is performed in time to make the 10:00 p. m. connection east, this mail would then arrive at Boston six hours and fifty minutes after the passengers, and as it would arrive there at 4:50 p. m., and would have to be taken from the depot of the A. & B. R. R. to the office, unlocked, distributed, re-locked and taken to the depot of the Eastern & Maine Central R. R., such offices as would be supplied by night pouches from Boston could not make the 8:00 p. m. connection, hence they would have to remain in Boston until 7:30 or 8:30 a. m., making a delay of fourteen hours and forty minutes at Boston, making in all a delay of either $21\frac{1}{2}$, $22\frac{1}{2}$, 30 or 31 hours.

If, on the other hand, these letters should be forwarded to Chicago by night pouch from Geneseo, they would arrive here at 6:30 a. m., and as this mail would have to be taken to the Chicago office, be distributed and taken back to the depot, the 8:30 a. m. connection east could not be made, whereas the passengers could make it without any difficulty; hence the mail would remain here until 5:15 p. m., making a delay of eight hours and forty-five minutes at Chicago, and as this mail would arrive at Boston at 10:00 a. m., and could not be taken to the office, be distributed and taken to the depot in time to make the 12:30 p. m. connection north, such portions of it as would otherwise have been forwarded from Boston in through pouches to the offices of delivery, by the 12:30 p. m. train would have to remain in Boston until the departure of the 3:15 or 8:00 p. m. trains, making a delay of $5\frac{1}{4}$ or $10\frac{1}{4}$ hours at Boston, and an actual delay, to this mail, of $11\frac{1}{2}$ or $16\frac{1}{4}$ hours, in the aggregate.

Under the present, or Railway Post Office system, these letters would be forwarded from the mailing offices to the Boston & Bangor R. P. O. Working upon the same hypothesis in this illustration, as in the former one, we will assume that the train upon which this R. P. O. arrives at Boston arrives in time for the passengers to make the 5:00 p. m. connection west. The clerks in this R. P. O. would place the Geneseo, Colona and Mokena letters in packages with all other letters received by them for the state of Illinois, and on their arrival at Boston would forward them, with all other western mail received by them, to the Buffalo & Chicago R. P. O., by the 5:00 p. m. train. There would be no delay at Boston, providing the trains were run in connection, because the distribution, necessary to prevent such an occurrence, would have been made by the clerks in the Boston & Bangor R. P. O., while in transit between Bangor and Boston. After being pouched by the clerks, this mail would be transferred direct from the depot of the Boston & Bangor line, to the depot of the Boston & Albany R. R., and away it would go, arriving at Buffalo at 12:20 p. m. on the same train as the passengers. At Buffalo it would be transferred from the New York Central train to the Buffalo & Chicago R. P. O., while the trains of both roads were standing in the same depot.

The Buffalo & Chicago R. P. O.'s run from Buffalo to Chicago on the Lake Shore & Michigan Southern R. R. There are two railway post offices passing over this route, each way daily; one departs from Buffalo at 12:25 p. m., and the other at 1:00 a. m., and each of them carry from 60,000 to 70,000 letters and from 12 to 15 tons of papers west, and from 40,000 to 50,000 letters, and from 2 to 3 tons of papers east, daily.

In twenty minutes after the arrival of this mail at Buffalo, it would start on its way toward Chicago, arriving here at 8:30 a. m., and the clerks would commence the distribution of this immense mass of matter—taking up, first Ohio, Michigan, Indiana, Illinois, Missouri, Kansas, Texas, Colorado, &c., because letters and papers for these states must be placed in shape for delivery at way stations, and for forwarding, to points of destination, by diverging lines, between Buffalo and Toledo. Some portions of this Illinois matter, after being distributed, would be sent to the Ohio & Mississippi R. P. O., via Cincinnati, Ohio; some to Indianapolis & St. Louis R. P. O., and other routes, via Indianapolis, Ind.; a large portion to the LaFayette & Quincy R. P. O., via LaFayette, Ind., and the remainder would be forwarded to the railway post office and route agent lines diverging from Chicago, and none of it would see the inside of a distributing post office. In making this distribution they would place the three letters, used in the illustration, in a pouch tagged Chicago & Iowa City R. P. O., (Chicago, Rock Island & Pacific R. R.) and on arrival at Chicago this pouch would be taken direct from the Buffalo & Chicago R. P. O. car to the Chicago & Iowa City R. P. O. car, where it would be opened, the contents distributed, and on arrival of this railway post office at the three offices mentioned—the letters would be pouched, then placed in charge of a messenger, who would deliver them into the hands of the postmasters. No delay would have occurred to the mail from the time it left the mailing office, until it arrived at the office of delivery. But to follow out the illustration we will proceed to consider that the Boston & Bangor R. P. O. does not arrive at Boston in time to make the 5:00 p. m. connection west; say it arrives there at 7:10 p. m.—in that event the passengers and mail, for points west, north and south of Chicago— might as well remain in Boston until 8:30 a. m.; but all matter for the larger or night offices between Boston and New York, including New York, and for all the stations between New York and Hartford, (and the offices supplied by them), on the New York & Boston line, could be supplied before this mail would have left Boston under the arrangement advocated in the *Boston Morning Journal;* because on arrival of this railway post office at Boston, this matter and matter for all connecting lines out of New York, Hartford, New Haven and other junctions, would be transferred direct to the New York & Boston R. P. O., leaving Boston at 9:00 p. m. A distribution of this matter would be made in this railway post office while in transit; mails would be delivered at the principal offices on the line and to the connecting lines, and that portion of the matter addressed to the smaller offices, lying between New York and Hartford, would be carried through to New York, delivered to the day railway post office, leaving New York at 8:05 a. m., and be delivered at all these points before the railway post office, leaving Boston at 8:30 a. m., would arrive at Hartford.

On the other hand, if the letters for Geneseo and Colona were forwarded from the mailing offices, via the Boston & Bangor R. P. O., arriving at Boston at 6:00 a. m., they would be forwarded to the Buffalo & Chicago R. P. O., by the train departing from Boston at 8:30 a. m., and as that is the first through train departing from Boston in the morning, there would be no delay there. They would arrive at Buffalo at 1:00 a. m., and be immediately transferred to the Buffalo & Chicago R. P. O., which railway post office would start for Chicago at once. The clerks in this railway post office, in making a distribution of the 60,000 or 70,000 letters massed upon them, would place the Geneseo letter in a pigeon hole, with a number of other letters for the same place, and on their arrival at Chicago, at 9:00 p. m., they would tie these letters out, and forward them to Geneseo in a night pouch departing from Chicago at 10:00 p. m.; the letters arriving at their destination in time for delivery in the morning. The Colona letter and all other letters received by them for offices, not night offices, between Davenport, Iowa, and Morris, Ill., (121 miles) would be placed in a pigeon hole labelled "Express Mail, Chicago & Iowa City R. P. O., Moline East," and on arrival of these clerks at Chicago, they would tie these letters out, and forward them, in a pouch tagged "Express Mail, Moline East," by the 10:00 p. m. train to Moline, arriving there at 6:12 a. m., and when the railway post office bound east arrives at Moline, at 8:38 a. m., this pouch would be taken in charge by the clerks, be opened, the contents distributed, and the matter delivered at the offices of destination before it would have been, had it been held for the regular railway post office departing from Chicago in the morning. Thus it will be seen, that, under the railway post office system, all classes of mail matter receive the same advantages, as to time in transit, that is enjoyed by first-class passengers, and in some cases better; whereas, under the system advocated in the *Boston Morning Journal,* the mail always arrives at its destination long after the passenger.

What has been demonstrated in the case of mail passing from the east, under this railway post office system, to the west, can be shown equally as well in the case of mail passing from the west to the east.

The difference is this: Under the route agent, mail route messenger, and distributing post office system, the work of distribution would be confined to one or more large offices in each of the larger, or more densely populated states, and mail matter passing over any of the railway lines for points not on that line, would be massed upon the nearest distributing post office, and be there held for distribution in the manner shown above, and after this distribution has been made some portions of the same mail would be massed upon the distributing post office lying nearest the offices to be supplied, and would there be again delayed for a second distribution.

Route agents would make a distribution of such matter as would be supplied direct from their own route; that is, they would perform the local service between the terminal points of their routes only, leaving the distribution for points beyond to be performed in the distributing post offices; whereas, under the railway post office system the clerks not only perform the local service of their routes, but in addition to this, they distribute all that matter that route agents would mass upon D. P. O's. Under this system route agents, mail route messengers, and distributing post offices mass on railway post offices, and thus obviate the delays that would otherwise occur.

As to the statement, "Boston is in a condition to-day of being deprived of mail facilities through the fact that these postal cars are run. If we had no postal cars the mail would be made up in Boston, not only for the 8:30 train for New York, but also at 10 o'clock for New York, the 11:10 Shore Line for New York, both of which last mails are delayed for points beyond New York twenty-four hours. A constant running stream draws off what would otherwise accumulate into an overpowering torrent. The same common sense must be applied to the transmission of our enormous mails upon the lines of railway. With eight express trains in each direction between Boston and New York daily, there is certainly no need of keeping an entire car upon any one train to the exclusion of the others," we have this to say: There are but three through trains from Boston to the west daily, the 8:30 a. m., the 5:00 p. m., and the 9:00 p. m., and the last one is of but little account for through western matter, simply because the 8:30 a. m. train leaving Boston "11½" hours after it, arrives at Chicago 40 minutes before it does, and as the 8:30 a. m. train is a R. P. O., and has a through connection for the west, and runs into New York city, there is no reason why mail for New York should not be dispatched by this train. It will certainly be better protected than it would be if sent in charge of a train baggageman; besides this there is no reason why the Boston office should not, so far as New York, and to it, other western matter is concerned, "dump" itself into this R. P. O. by states. Moreover, if the postmaster at Boston does not forward his New York city, Philadelphia and Washington, D. C., matter to those points by every passenger train departing from Boston for those points, either via the four R. P. O.'s that run through to New York, or have a direct connection through to the same point, or else in through pouches by the trains that are not R. P. O.'s he does not do his duty. He is not expected to forward matter intended for delivery in such a large city by the railway post offices alone, unless all the passenger trains running between his office and those offices are railway post offices; on the contrary it is expected that he will forward such mail by every passenger train running between his office and those points, taking advantage of the railway post offices when he can do so, and when he cannot, pouching direct upon the offices.

Mail dispatched from Boston for all points west of New York by the 5:00 p. m. train will arrive at its destination as soon as if sent by the 10:00 a. m., 11:10, or 3:00 p. m. trains; hence this mail is not delayed at all by not being sent by those trains, and if sent by them it explodes the constant running stream business, because while it may keep the source clear it will flood New York, for as shown above, the stream would be dammed up at that point; in order to prevent an "overpowering torrent," it is necessary that the stream be kept free of obstructions all the way from its source to its mouth. The arrangement advocated would dam it up at all distributing post offices, whereas, the railway post offices assist the flow by keeping the volume in motion from the source to the mouth, and by relieving the main stream at all junctions, and by running these distributing post office blockades wherever they come in contact with them.

"It now costs the Department six hundred dollars per mile per annum for the service on these routes, which indicates partially the enormous expenditure for this service, and even this amount paid is entirely unsatisfactory to the railroad companies, and upon examination probably will prove entirely inadequate to the service rendered," is another statement made in the *Morning Journal,* and in a previous section the statement is made, in speaking of dispatching through mails by every express train departing from New York, that, "This, especially for the through letter mail would secure greater dispatch and would prove no incumbrance whatever to the trains themselves. All the letters that would be required to be sent on each train would not be equal to the Saratoga trunks of a single female passenger in the fashionable season."

The law in reference to compensation paid railroad companies is as follows: *   *   *   *   *   *   *   *   *   *

"Provided: That the Postmaster General be, and he is hereby authorized and directed, to re-adjust the compensation hereafter to be paid for the transportation of mails on railroad routes upon the conditions and at the rates hereinafter mentioned, to wit: That the mail shall be conveyed with due frequency and speed; that sufficient and suitable room, fixtures, and furniture, in a car or apartment properly lighted and warmed, shall be provided for route agents to accompany and distribute the mails; and that the pay per mile per annum shall not exceed the following rates, namely: on routes carrying their whole length an average weight of mails per day of two hundred pounds, fifty dollars; five hundred pounds, seventy-five dollars; one thousand pounds, one hundred dollars; one thousand five hundred pounds, one hundred and twenty-five dollars; two thousand pounds, one hundred and fifty dollars; three thousand five hundred pounds, one hundred and seventy-five dollars; five thousand pounds, two hundred dollars; and twenty-five dollars additional for every additional two thousand pounds, the average weight to be ascertained, in every case, by the actual weight of the mails for such a number of successive working days, not less than thirty, at such times, after June thirtieth, eighteen hundred and seventy-three, and not less frequently than once in every four years, and the result to be stated and verified in such form and manner as the Postmaster General may direct."

There is another section of the law quoted above, however, that applies more directly to the railway post offices, and reads as follows:

"Provided, also: That in case any railroad company now furnishing railway post office cars shall refuse to provide such cars, such company shall not be entitled to any increase of compensation under any provision of this act; Provided, further: That additional pay may be allowed for every line comprising a daily trip each way of railway post office cars, at a rate not exceeding twenty-five dollars per mile per annum for cars forty feet in length; and thirty dollars per mile per annum for forty-five feet cars; and forty dollars per mile per annum for fifty feet cars; and fifty dollars per mile per annum for fifty-five to sixty feet cars; And provided, also: That the length of cars required for such post office railway car service shall be determined by the Post Office Department, all such cars shall be properly fitted up, furnished, warmed, and lighted, for the accommodation of clerks to accompany and distribute the mails."

It will be seen by reading the above extract from the "act making appropriations for the service of the Post Office Department for the year ending June thirtieth, eighteen hundred and seventy-four," first: That all railroad companies receive compensation for carrying the mail according to the weight of the mail they carry; the law fixing the compensation applies with equal force to all railroad companies; it is not limited to those companies providing railway post office cars, but all companies receive, under the law quoted, compensation according to the weight of the mail they carry, whether they carry it in a baggage or a railway post office car; therefore those railroads that are not railway post office lines would receive the same compensation for carrying the mails, if this service were abolished, that they now do, and if the system of direct exchange spoken of above, between office and office on all railway lines, were substituted, they would receive more, because in that event the pouches carried on some of the lines would exceed in weight the weight of the mail contained in them; and without this system of exchange, we have shown that the system advocated in the *Morning Journal* would discriminate in favor of the distributing post offices as against all other offices.

And in the second place: That those companies furnishing railway post office cars of the length and finish required by the Post Office Department are entitled to additional pay of so much per mile, per annum; if these cars were taken off it would not reduce the compensation received by the companies for carrying the mail; on the other hand we have shown that it would increase it, and if this course were adopted, it would plunge us back into a state of semi-barbarism, news would not be received until after it had become stale; business men could not receive bills of goods, bought by them, as soon as they would receive the goods, and they would have to depend upon the telegraph for market reports, etc.;   *   *   *   *   *

and in the third place, any one who can reason at all will see at a glance, that ten tons of mail will weigh as much, if carried in a divided state upon a dozen trains, as it will if carried upon one, two or three trains, and any one who has had any experience in handling mails knows that ten tons of mail, if forwarded a little in this pouch or sack and a little in that pouch or sack, as it would be, if sent on eight or ten trains—will weigh more than it would if sent on one, two or three trains, because in that case you have the additional weight of a number of unnecessary pouches, locks and sacks. Besides this what would be gained by forwarding from Boston and New York, in a divided state, this great bulk of mail matter by every train leaving those points for the west, so long as it must all be concentrated upon two or three trains from Buffalo to Chicago?

None of our western railroads are dissatisfied with their compensation, or at least they are willing to abide by the law governing this matter, and they afford every facility required of them by their contracts, and with one exception these facilities are entirely adequate to "the service required;" and as to the statement said to have been made by the president of one of the leading lines, "that he would carry the mail out of the postal cars without any compensation," we have to say, that we do not believe that he will enter into a contract with the Post Office Department to convey the mail "with due frequency and speed" over his line or lines, and to provide an apartment properly lighted, furnished, warmed, etc., for the accommodation of the route agent who accompanies and distributes the mail, without any compensation, and if he should enter into such a contract the directors of the road would call a meeting at once and vote him out of the presidency. Such talk is put in for effect. Railroads are managed by business men, and business men are not in the habit of cutting off their noses to spite their faces.

Another statement made in the same article is as follows: "Another very important item to the Department would be also a saving of expense in the employment of postal car clerks. These employees are paid nearly double the average paid for the performance of the same service in the office, and they perform about half the amount of work. Postal car clerks between New York and Boston run every alternate week, and make one trip only each day. They work only one-half the time; or, in other words, the actual cost to the Department for doing the same work is four times what it would be if performed in the post offices, and this certainly can only be justified on the ground of great expedition, which we have shown above is not secured by the postal car service," and in another portion of the same article we find, "and were the mails sent directly from railroad station to railroad station in the cities, more time would be saved than all that is now secured upon the postal car trains."

There are employed in the Chicago office, upon the distribution of the letter and paper mail, lodged in the office from all sources, fifty-one clerks, who are paid in the aggregate $51,000 per annum, thus making the average pay, per clerk, $1,000 per annum, and they are not paid any too much either. The average paid the railway post office clerks is $1,245 per annum, being $245 per clerk, per annum, more than is paid to distributing clerks in distributing post offices, and the reason why this distinction is made, is, because the clerks running upon trains are necessarily subjected to greater expense than those employed in offices. They are at home one day and one night, and then out upon the line the same length of time; their family expenses are just as large when they are away from home, as they are when they are at home, and their own expenses, while out upon the line, amount to not less than one dollar per day; in addition to this the strongest of the clerks soon begin to feel the effects of the constant jolting and jarring that they have to endure from the time they enter the car until they get out of it, and it is not long until the most of them are compelled to "go into the shops for repairs;" besides this they are not idle during the time they are not on duty in the cars. They employ this time in arranging their label slips for their next runs; in studying and correcting their schemes of distribution; in posting themselves upon the railway connections, and in passing examinations which determine their fitness for the places held by them. We venture the remark that nothing of this kind occurs in the Boston office, and the further remark that it might benefit the public if this plan were adopted in all distributing post offices. The Chicago office is doing a portion of this, and under its present management it has improved most wonderfully. The distribution is ten times better to-day than it ever was before, and there is the most perfect harmony prevailing between this office and the railway post office service, and the authorities in the office recognize the fact that all that is expended in perfecting, and extending the postal car service is "justified on the ground of great expedition" and the fact that this expedition is secured by this service has been fully demonstrated above.

There are two hundred thousand letters, and from twenty-five to thirty tons of papers, transferred direct from incoming to outgoing trains in this city, daily; none of it is distributed in the Chicago office, and there have been times, when the great mass of mail coming in on the Michigan Southern R. R., has been connected from that road to the other roads departing from the city when the passengers and baggage have been left; no longer ago than January 28, the incoming train (R. P. O.) on the Michigan Southern R. R. arrived at Chicago thirty-seven minutes late (9:07 a. m.) and yet the Galena R. P. O. connection was made in eight minutes, the Chicago & St. Louis R. P. O. in twenty-three minutes, the Chicago, Milwaukee & St. Paul (about two tons of mail) in twenty-three minutes, the Chicago & Green Bay R. P. O. (two tons) in thirty-three minutes, the Chicago & Milwaukee in twenty-three minutes, the Chicago & Cedar Rapids R. P. O. (about six tons) in fifty-three minutes. If this mail had not been made up in the Buffalo & Chicago R. P. O. none of it could have been connected, even had that railway post office arrived on time; and any one acquainted with the work in a distributing post office ought to know that if the distribution were "performed regularly at the offices, and lock bags sent to every principal office, and not opened at any intervening office," it would result in the delay shown in the above illustration, and he also ought to know that the expense of such a system would be much greater than the present one.

It is estimated by the Chicago post office authorities, that, if the railway post office service were abolished, the present post office building would not be large enough to accommodate the distribution alone, and that another building of equal size would have to be occupied in order to perform the work of the office. The same authorities estimate that, whereas, they now employ but fifty-one clerks on the distribution, at an expense of $51,000, that they would then be compelled to employ about 208, at an expense of about $204,000 per annum, and this same state of things would exist in all D. P. O. offices. Besides this other distributing post offices would have to be established; other buildings would have to be erected; additional clerks would have to be employed, and still the delays shown in the illustration would remain the same.

Another statement is this: "Still another difficulty with the postal cars is that the mails being made up on cars running between New York and Washington for postal cars running between New York and Boston, and vice versa, any failure to connect renders the whole distribution of the mail for the day useless, and the mail arriving from Washington in New York in the morning too late for the postal car leaving for Boston, cannot be forwarded on the express train at 10:00 o'clock, as it would be if made up for each city on the line, and for the terminal cities, but it must lie over the entire twelve hours in New York, and go on in the postal car at night."

This statement is certainly a mistake on the part of the author of it, for if there is any one thing connected with the railway post office service, that the clerks pride themselves upon more than another, it is that of understanding their connections; the time of arrival of trains at junctions; and how they can reach a certain line or office by so many different routes, and in so many different ways; each head clerk carries a list of all night offices, and knows just the time each one of them is locked up and forwarded, and they use this knowledge to good advantage whenever they are behind time, often changing their distribution while en route, in order to make it conform to their time of arrival at terminal points; by doing this they prevent the thing of which the *Morning Journal* complains. To illustrate this point, we will state that clerks arriving at Chicago before 3:30 p. m., make the following distribution of mail supplied by the Freeport & Centralia R. P. O.: That portion of the line laying between Decatur and Centralia, Ill., is made up in a package and marked "Main Line, Decatur South," and is forwarded from Chicago by the C. B. & Q. express train to Mendota, where it is transferred to a connecting express train on the Illinois Central R. R. (main line), and by that train carried to Decatur, where it is transferred to the railway post office leaving Decatur, bound south, at 2:17 a. m. Mail for that portion of the same line laying between Bloomington and Amboy, Ill., is made up in packages, by the same clerk, and is marked "Bloomington North," and is forwarded from Chicago by express train on Chicago & Alton R. R., arriving at Bloomington in connection with the Freeport & Centralia R. P. O., bound north; at Bloomington it is transferred to this railway post office, and all offices laying between the two points mentioned are supplied sooner than they could be under any other arrangement. Mail for that portion of the same line laying between Freeport and Amboy, Ill., and that portion between Bloomington and Decatur, Ill., is made up in a package by these same clerks, and is marked "Freeport South," and is forwarded from Chicago by express train on Galena

R. R. to Freeport, Ill., where it is transferred to the Freeport & Centralia R. P. O., bound south.

If, however, these clerks are late and fail to arrive at Chicago before 3:30 p. m., but arrive before 7:30 p. m., they will change this distribution while en route, and will mark the "Decatur South" package "Centralia North" instead, and this package will be forwarded from Chicago in the Centralia pouch, dispatched by the Illinois Central branch express train, and will arrive at Centralia in time to connect with the Freeport & Centralia R. P. O., bound north, thus supplying that portion of the line twelve to twenty-four hours sooner than it could be in any other way. If the clerks are still late, and do not arrive in Chicago until 8:25 p. m., they will mass the "Decatur South," or "Centralia North," with their "Freeport South," mark the package "Freeport South" and forward it by Galena R. R. as before. If they are still late, they will divide the Freeport & Centralia R. P. O. at Mendota, marking one package "Mendota North," and the other "Mendota South," and forward them by the C. B. & Q. R. R. at 7:30 a. m. This train connects with the Freeport & Centralia railway post offices, bound both north and south, at Mendota. A clerk arriving at Chicago in the morning too late to make his regular connections, would go through his mail and make up 233 night offices and 50 express mails that he would not make up if on time.

In conclusion we desire to state that there is no reason why the distributing post offices and the railway post office service should not work together in harmony. They are both engaged in the same cause, that of giving to the public, whose servants they are, the best mail facilities enjoyed by any people in the world. The distributing post offices cannot accomplish this alone, whereas the railway post offices can, so far as the distribution is concerned, (other than that of the letters absolutely mailed in the distributing post offices, and the distribution made of such mail would not be complicated), providing this service is extended to meet the demands made upon it. What is needed to-day is not the abolition of this service, but a proper extension of it, so that mail matter passing from any post office in the land, to any other post office, will make as quick a transit as passengers passing over the same route. This is done now, or can be done, wherever this service has been established, and no other system can be established which will accomplish the same result.

*   *   *   *   *   *   *   *

The service stands open for a full and impartial investigation at all times.

General Superintendent Bangs heard, the day the *Western Postal Record* containing my article was issued, that I was preparing an answer and telegraphed me to send him the proof. As the article was out I could only wire back that I could not, and gave the reason; he then telegraphed to send him 150 copies of the paper, which I did. Afterward he told me that he had distributed these to members of Congress and others to whom he believed they would be useful; he also said that my surmise that the then postmaster at Boston was the author of the *Journal* article was correct, and that he had visited Washington, D. C., since and held a long conference with the Postmaster General and himself, during which he stated that he had read my article and that if the service east was operated upon the plane it evidently was west, there would be no reason for complaint.

The *Boston Morning Journal* article appeared January 16, 1874.

My article appeared in the February, 1874, issue of the *Western Postal Record*.

The Senate passed a resolution January 30, 1874, calling upon the Postmaster General for information relative to the postal service between New York and Washington, New York and Boston, and New York, Albany, Buffalo and Suspension Bridge. He responded to this call in a letter dated March 4, 1874, addressed to Hon. M. H. Carpenter, president pro tempore Senate, as follows:

(Senate Ex. Doc. No. 37, Forty-third Congress first session.)

POSTAL SERVICE.

Letter from the Postmaster General, in answer to resolution of the Senate of January 30, 1874, calling for information relative to the postal service between New York and Washington, New York and Boston, and New York, Albany, Buffalo and Suspension Bridge.

Post Office Department,
Washington, D. C., March 4, 1874.

*   *   *   *   *   *   *   *   *   *   *

The railway post office system is the outgrowth of necessity and the result of years of study and practical experience in this and trans-atlantic countries. Before railroads were introduced, when post offices were few, postage expensive, and transit slow, the mail for all offices upon a route was placed in one pouch, each postmaster assorting the whole contents and taking out such part thereof as belonged to his own office. Between offices of importance, where the mail was sufficient, direct pouches were interchanged, under special lock, not only to avoid the necessity of repeated assortings, but to guard against loss.

With the growth of the country, reduction of postage, increased speed in transit, and consequent increase of mails, it became necessary to establish mail communication by means of direct pouches. The office at the terminus of one or the junction of several railroads would receive, assort, and forward the mail for the offices upon these railroads in a direct pouch to each, and each office would forward to these "head" or "distributing" offices their outgoing mail in the same manner, and, in addition, those distributing offices would exchange with each other. Mail between points where there was no direct exchange was sent to some distant distributing office, there redistributed and forwarded, and reached its destination by a circuitous route and after repeated delays. As offices increased in size and number, these direct pouches correspondingly increased.

It became absolutely necessary to provide some system of mail service that would do away with this multitude of pouches, containing in a majority of cases a small amount of mail, and passing in all directions over the country, under the charge of no particular person, or at least of no person wholly responsible to the Department, meeting on every hand with neglect, and causing great delay, loss and confusion.

To accomplish this the route agent system was adopted.

Under this system these "head" offices would send to the route agent all mail for offices upon this particular route or road. The agent would assort the mail while in transit and exchange with each office and the "head" or "distributing" post office, sending to the latter all mail for points not upon his road. While under this system a perfect mail communication was established between all offices upon the line of any one road, still for points beyond that line the mails remained precisely as before, meeting with repeated delays at the different distributing post offices.

In order that this delay might be overcome, clerks from distributing post offices, familiar with the general distribution of the mails, were detailed to travel upon the cars, making the proper separation and distribution for all connecting roads and routes, thus avoiding the delays in "head" or "distributing" post offices by having the mails ready for dispatch immediately upon arrival at the terminus of a route. The experiment of detailing clerks as here stated was successful, and resulted in the establishment of the railway post office system. By this system all offices throughout the country have an interchange with each other more frequent and effectual than if every office in the land should make up and forward a direct pouch to every other office for which it might have mail. Virtually the railway post office has become a "traveling distributing post office," giving all post offices its benefits, and, most of all, saving and taking advantage of every moment that without it would be lost in transit.

These traveling distributing post offices, in all cases where the Department has the choice, are placed upon trains making the best time and connections. It will be noticed, upon examination of the schedule of any railroad running frequent trains, that all of them cannot be made available for postal service, either for the postal car or direct pouch system. Many of these trains start at hours when there is little or no accumulation of mails, and they arrive at points of destination at unseasonable hours for delivery of mail and too late for connections with points beyond and upon other routes. It will also be observed that trains first leaving important points are frequently the last to arrive at the other end of the line, or else are merged into trains leaving at a late hour. It is, however, the policy of this Department to avail itself of all trains by which mails can be hastened to destination, however frequent the postal car or route agent service may be used upon the same line; and any postmaster failing to make use of all available trains for the dispatch of mails, for points far or near, is deemed to be derelict in duty.

Very respectfully, your obedient servant,

Jno. A. J. Creswell,
Postmaster General.

Hon. M. H. Carpenter, President pro tempore
Senate United States.

The year 1874 witnessed the discontinuance of opposition to the railway post office system, and it moved forward with very much less friction; the number of employees in the whole service then was 2,175, of which 850 were railway post office clerks, whose aggregate annual compensation amounted to $1,058,200. The remaining employees, 1,325, were divided as follows: 936 route agents whose annual compensation aggregated $896,680; 211 mail route messengers, whose annual compensation aggregated $136,540; 124 local agents, whose annual compensation aggregated $94,710; aggregate cost, $2,186,330. To this must be added $165,478.63, the cost of 54 special agents charged to the railway mail service, and $600,000 for car space, making a total of $2,951,808.63.

The cost of the railway post office service during that fiscal year, segregated from the cost of the whole railway mail service for the same period, itemized, was:

850 clerks, average salary, $1,245 per annum $1,058,250
Supervision of the service 34,420
Rent of railway post office cars 600,000

Total $1,692,670

Had the service remained on the same basis as before the railway post office was introduced the cost of maintaining it for the fiscal year would have been about as follows, itemized:

936 route agents, average salary $958 per annum......$ 896,688.00
566 route agents, average salary $958 per annum, in lieu
     of the 850 clerks who were employed at an average
     salary of $1,245 per annum 542,228.00
54 special agents, charged to the railway mail service.... 165,478.63
211 mail route messengers, average annual salary about
     $647 .... 136,540.00
124 local agents, average annual salary about $763.... 94,710.00

Total $1,835,644.63

Subtract this $1,835,644.63 from the cost of the whole railway mail service for that fiscal year, viz., $2,951,808.63, and we find that the improved method of handling mail, first introduced in 1864, had fought its way up and over an antiquated system and its musty advocates within ten years thereafter and demonstrated that it possessed the fundamental principles necessary to a system capable of meeting the needs of an intelligent and progressive business age at an additional cost of $1,116,164—$600,000 of which was expended on car space alone—a sum not twice as large as was subsequently appropriated for special facility purposes for one fiscal year.

The spirit of the armies of the Union pervaded the force employed in developing and solidifying these principles, therefore, it is not strange that no ground was ever lost that was not regained—that the service moved forward with a steady tramp, tramp, until it occupied the vantage ground it has held and been strengthening since early in 1874.

What did this small increased expenditure save to the business public, the bankers, the financiers, the manufacturers, the merchants, the buyers and sellers—big and little—the employers and the employees, and the government? Who can tell? Who can estimate the intrinsic value of time when applied to the earning power of the vast sum of money and its equivalent that was dormant, then, while in transit through the mail all over the country daily? What was the interest on that sum worth per day, two days, or three; what is it worth now per day upon the vaster sum, probably running up close to, and it may be beyond one billion dollars? Ascertain the sum; the time saved can be determined by comparing the old with the new system, as is done in my article of 1874; the remainder of the problem is mathematical.

There were in operation at that time 63 lines of railway post offices, covering 16,414 track miles; 39,199 running miles daily and 14,307,635 running miles annually; number of miles of railroad upon which mail was carried was 67,734, and the annual cost of railroad mail transportation was $8,589,663.

In all the territory embraced in the Fourth Division at that time there was but one railroad route upon which twice daily full railway post office service, each way, had been established, and that was the Lake Shore & Michigan Southern, between Buffalo, N. Y., and Chicago. One of these departed from Buffalo at 12:25 p. m., and the other at 1:00 a. m.

The Wabash Avenue church, which we first occupied about December 20, 1871, was destroyed by fire July 14, 1874. I was not well that day, in fact had been ailing several days, and was lying down in the little room just off from my office, when the fire alarm sounded. I inquired for the location of the fire and was informed that it was raging in the block bounded north by Taylor, south by 12th and west by Clark streets, and east by 4th avenue. It was believed that it would be confined to that block; we, therefore, did not feel concerned, but when it moved out of that block and up the east side of 4th avenue to Harrison, down this street to State, north on State to a point between Van Buren and Jackson streets, we became alarmed, and I arose and with my office force commenced arranging our belongings so that they could be moved, if necessary, without delay whenever the route of the fire could be determined definitely.

When it moved southeast from State street, through Wabash avenue to Michigan avenue, and thence south to Congress street, we knew that our building was doomed, and the post office and our office began sending our effects to the building on the corner of Halsted and West Washington streets in which the West Division station was located.

In making the transfer from one location to the other the post office used the wagons of the mail messenger almost exclusively, which was right, considering the amount and value of the records, equipment, and mail in the office—not mentioning the furniture that had been accumulated during the more than two and a half years of our stay in the church building.

This retarded our exodus, as we found it necessary to attempt to employ outside teams to help us out of our dilemma, but nearly all teamsters declined to assist us because they had other engagements or wished to get out of range of the fire, which by this time was moving west on Congress street, and south down the alley running between Wabash and Michigan avenues, burning all before it. We were alive to the importance of prompt and decisive action in this crisis and I, therefore, decided to take forcible possession of vehicles that came our way unless the drivers accepted employment gracefully.

I remember as vividly as if it occurred but yesterday, though thirty-five years have passed since then, that I was standing in the opening to the dispatching and receiving room, up to which the wagons were backed to load and unload; watching the approach of the fire as it moved on toward us, devouring building after building, driving before it or destroying everything that came within its sweep, and the confusion and turmoil, raging in the streets and alleys, when I saw several carts and drays drawn by frantic horses move into the open space to my right and make a dash for Harrison street. As they passed in front of me I made a jump from where I stood and landed safely on a dray, grabbed the reins that were in the hands of the driver and told him what I wanted, but he refused to assist us and showed fight; had not William C. Walsh, the son of the mail messenger, come to my aid I probably would have been dropped in that maelstrom, and failed to capture the dray, but as it was we "took it into camp," loaded it with our effects and sent it in charge of a clerk to our place of refuge.

Working with the energy that only an unharnessed, irresistible force, moving down upon one can produce, we saved most of our movables and left the church as the fire engulfed it and continued its flight south to Eldridge court, and thence slightly southwest to the place of its origin, spreading over forty-seven acres in all. In the meantime requests were being sent to the railway officials to place the reserve postal cars in positions accessible to the public; the collectors, and the mail messenger, and the clerks who were laying off were instructed to report for extra duty immediately.

The experience of the great fire of 1871 enabled the railway mail service to meet the exigencies of the postal service growing out of this lesser fire without hesitation or friction in any quarter, and the fact that none of the depots, tracks or publishing houses were destroyed simplified the handling of the mail between depot and depot and publishing houses and depots, and between the temporary post office and the postal cars, so that while the character of the work performed in the postal cars stationed in the city, in this emergency, was the same as in the one that preceded it, it was not spasmodic, irregular or uncertain; there was an officer of judgment and experience in charge of the postal service in each depot, and my office kept in touch with them at all hours, so that we might anticipate their needs, the necessities of the service, and provide for them promptly.

The building at the corner of Halsted and West Washington streets was not large enough to accommodate the post office alone, and could not be made so, therefore a larger and more centrally located building was searched for and found in the Honore Block, northwest corner of Dearborn and Adams streets, the site of the present Marquette Building, and the Department leased two floors of the north end of it and provided them with fixtures and furniture suitable for the temporary use of the post office and our office. This selection was influenced by the fact that the large Federal building, then in course of construction, occupied the entire block directly south of it, bounded on the north by Adams street, on the south by Jackson, on the east by Dearborn and on the west by Clark street. We moved into Honore Building August 23, 1874, just a month and nine days after we were excommunicated from the church by fire, and resumed business under more favorable conditions. The splendidly qualified clerks, who had performed extra duty so faithfully and without a murmur, though many were separated from their families, home comforts, the encouraging words and tender smiles of their loved ones, and under additional expense, were soon relieved and they resumed their regular duties, their invaluable and indefatigable labor being acknowledged with gratitude.

The railway post offices centering at Chicago made up the mails they received thoroughly, and pouched upon each other all that would not be delayed thereby, but the packages made up for night offices, express mails, and lateral lines, that could be more expeditiously and economically handled in that way, were sent into the post office to be distributed, as packages, into the boxes which circled that portion of the "round table," fronting the distributer, in the shape of a crescent. The office made up similar packages which were also distributed into these boxes, thus one set of pouches accommodated both services. These boxes could be opened at the back and hooks were so placed that pouches or sacks could be hung back of them, so that when the hour for closing these mails, or any of them, arrived, they were drawn off into their respective pouches, which were then closed and dispatched by the trains indicated by their labels.

This was the most expeditious system possible, when the only twice daily railway post office in that vast division was the one running on the Lake Shore & Michigan Southern railroad between Buffalo, N. Y., and Chicago, Ill.; in fact, it is a system that must exist as long as railway post offices do not run upon all trains by which mails to and from local offices, and those in more distant territory, can be materially advanced in delivery; but its greatest usefulness and most soothing influence depended upon the skill and efficiency of the employee who had charge of the "round table." Unfortunately the one who had charge at that time was not an expert and frequent complaints resulted. Some of these were investigated, the source of irregularities located, and then I requested the postmaster to permit me to place one of my men in charge of this table until the trouble was corrected, and one of his employees drilled in schemes and connections sufficiently to become thoroughly posted and reliable. My request was granted cheerfully, and I detailed to this duty from the Chicago & Burlington R. P. O., Lewis L. Troy, who was destined, later on, to become one of the most capable officers, in many respects, whose names still grace the roll of the railway mail service, though he, and others of them, are at rest in the bosom of the Father. Of him I wish to say a word.

Lewis L. Troy participated in the Civil War; he enlisted in the 9th Regiment, Illinois Infantry, at Belleville, St. Clair County, Ill., and battled for the perpetuity of the oneness of his adopted country during all those dreadful years of blood and sacrifice, with that unyielding courage which has from time immemorial been characteristic of the race from which he sprung, and when he returned to his home at the close of that ever-memorable conflict he was adjutant of his regiment, a fact that attested his fidelity and capacity as a loyal soldier. In 1869 he was appointed a route agent and ran between Galva and Keithsburg, Ill., and in 1871 he was transferred to the Chicago & Quincy R. P. O.; in 1874 was detailed to my office and assigned, as above, to the "round table" in the Chicago post office; later I withdrew him from that assignment and placed him in charge of the desk of the chief examiner and scheme builder; in 1884 he was promoted to the chief clerkship of the division, vice Mr. Campbell promoted; March 2, 1889, he was appointed assistant superintendent railway mail service, and October 5, 1890, became superintendent of the Sixth Division, vice the undersigned promoted to be general superintendent.

On the 17th of November, 1889, he passed out of this life, deeply mourned by a large circle of personal friends, the employees of the division, and his associates and superior officers.

C. G. Weirick had been my chief examiner and scheme builder from 1872 until Mr. Troy succeeded him; the change was a result of the creation of three additional divisions at the close of 1874; in carving these out, the Third and Fourth Divisions were badly disfigured; out of them came the present Fifth, also other divisions and parts of divisions. Indiana and Ohio were taken from my division, and, as Weirick was quite familiar with the service in those states, he went with them as a sort of "appurtenance thereunto belonging." I saw him occasionally afterward; the last time at Grafton, W. Va., as I was on the way to Washington to confer with the general superintendent. While there he became one of the subjects of conversation, and I spoke warmly in his behalf. After my return to Chicago I received a letter from him dated at Washington, in which he stated that he was quite ill; that Mr. Bangs had told him of the warmth of my interest in him, and thanked me earnestly. A few days afterwards I was informed of his death from pneumonia, and that by direction of Mr. Bangs his body had been sent to his relatives in Council Bluffs, Iowa. Those who had been his associates in my office and I, myself, met the body at the Illinois Central depot in Chicago, and they carried the casket in which it rested on their shoulders, through the city to the depot of the Chicago, Rock Island & Pacific Railroad, as a mark of personal regard and esteem.

The creation of the three additional divisions involved the recasting of the territory of the United States into eight, instead of five parts, and changes in the numerical designations of most of the divisions, as follows:

The First Division remained unchanged. Thomas P. Cheney, superintendent, Boston, Mass.

The Second Division comprised New York, New Jersey, Pennsylvania, Delaware and the eastern shore of Maryland. Roswell Hart, superintendent, New York, N. Y.

The Third Division (new) was made up of Maryland (except the eastern shore), Virginia, West Virginia and the District of Columbia. Milo V. Bailey, superintendent and chief clerk to the general superintendent, Washington.

Maryland (except the eastern shore), the eastern shore of Virginia, and West Virginia, were taken from the Second Division, and Virginia, except the eastern shore, was taken from the old Third;

the District of Columbia seems to have been unassigned up to this time, but it undoubtedly was handled by the superintendents of the Second and old Third Divisions, as their lines covered it.

The Fourth Division (new) comprised North Carolina, South Carolina, Georgia, Florida, Alabama, Mississippi and Louisiana. L. M. Terrell, superintendent, Atlanta, Ga. This whole division was taken from the old Third.

The Fifth Division (new) comprised Indiana, Ohio, Kentucky and Tennessee. C. J. French, superintendent, Cincinnati, Ohio. Indiana and Ohio were taken from the old Fourth, Kentucky and Tennessee from the old Third.

The Sixth Division (new) comprised Illinois, Iowa, Michigan, Minnesota, Nebraska, Wisconsin, and the territories of Dakota, then undivided, and Wyoming; the through line of the Union Pacific railway, and the United States mails passing through Canada—all of which were in the old Fourth Division. James E. White, superintendent, Chicago, Ill.

The Seventh Division (new) comprised Missouri, Kansas, Arkansas, Texas, and the territories of Colorado, Indian and New Mexico. Walter L. Hunt, superintendent, St. Louis, Mo. All of these, except Texas, were taken from the old Fourth Division. Texas was taken from the old Third Division.

The Eighth Division (new) comprised California, Nevada, Oregon, and the territories of Alaska, Arizona, Idaho, Montana, Utah, and Washington. I. A. Ammerman, superintendent, San Francisco, California.

This modification of the divisional organization was necessary, not only to insure a continuance of the rate of improvement showing in the distribution and dispatch, but more so to economize the time of the supervisory officers, so that they could visit their lines more frequently, observe their men at work, ascertain their adaptability for the service from all standpoints—moral, physical and mental—note whether they were neat and orderly in person and in the management of their cars; quick of body and mind; and to encourage them with words of cheer, advice and information, inspire higher efficiency, and thus multiply and strengthen the faith which thoughtful men of all classes and pursuits were manifesting in the ability of the service to make good all that had been promised for it.

That this necessity was pressing will be understood when it is known that the area of the states assigned to the Fourth, or Chicago

Hon. Edward J. Ryan
Superintendent First Division R. M. S.
(See Appendix)

Division, aggregated 1,208,532 square miles; that its aggregate population was 15,615,391, three-eighths of the whole population of the United States at that time, and that the railroad mileage was 35,123.

The area of the Third, or Chattanooga Division, was at the same time, 839,435 square miles; the aggregate population 11,459,347, and the railroad mileage 14,902.

The area of the Second, or New York Division, was 129,720 square miles; the population 10,247,629, and the railroad mileage 13,715.

The area of the First, or Boston Division, was 61,973 square miles; the population 3,612,080, and the railroad mileage 5,509.

The area of the Fifth, or San Francisco Division, was 851,870 square miles; the population 1,044,072, and the railroad mileage 2,798.

The First and Fifth Divisions were not disturbed by this reorganization, but for different reasons. The First is a very compact body; it comprises six states of modest area; its most remote boundaries are of quick and easy access from Boston, its headquarters and the general offices of the railroad systems traversing the Division are there also, or close at hand. Its population per square mile was exceeded by the Second Division only, and it has maintained that position steadily; but population, so long as it does not become congested or distempered, offers no insurmountable obstacle to the maintenance of the best class of service; in fact a large population centered in a modest area can be supplied with satisfactory service more economically and with a lower output of mental and nervous energy than it can be if spread over a very much larger territory. The population of the First Division then was 58 per square mile; of Massachusetts alone 189, and Rhode Island 190. At present for the whole Division it is 90; for Massachusetts 349, and Rhode Island 343.

The impression has prevailed quite generally for a long time, I think, that New England in point of population has ceased to grow; this no doubt is due to its very gradual increase, and the large and almost constant migration to the middle and western states of descendants of the grand old Puritan stock which settled that section from 1620 to 1636, the first of whom landed from the Mayflower on a barren rock, where the town of Plymouth, Mass., now stands, December 20, 1620. They are remembered in history, in verse and song and in the hearts of the household of every true American, whether he has or has not running through his veins the blood of those God-fearing and liberty loving heroes, the Pilgrim Fathers; to them countless millions of the sons of man owe a debt of gratitude for planting in that virgin soil, and watering it, the seed from which has grown and is growing, civil, political and religious liberty throughout the world.

> "There is no other land like thee,
> No dearer shore;
> Thou art the shelter of the free;
> The home, the port of Liberty,
> Thou hast been and shall ever be,
> Till time is o'er."

I cannot believe that conditions will ever arise which will make a modification of the limits of that division desirable, but with the old Fifth, now the Eighth, it is different. At the time of the reorganization of 1874, the population per square mile for that division was but $1\frac{1}{2}$; that of California, which was the most densely settled state in the division was $4\frac{1}{5}$; Oregon and Utah were $1\frac{1}{5}$ each. At present the whole division is about 4 per square mile; California about 11; Washington, which has grown faster than any other state in the division, about 8; Oregon about 5, and Utah about 4.

Whether it is desirable, from the standpoint of economy, supervision, and the well-being of the people residing and interested therein, in one way and another, to maintain the integrity of the division, seems to me to be a question in physical geography, rather than one of population. In former days my official duties made me somewhat familiar with the chorography of the division, especially with the northern portion of it, into which two or three of my lines ran; and at a later period, acting in a broader official capacity, I made quite a thorough inspection of it, to familiarize myself with the mail facilities of the division, especially with those of Oregon and Washington, the citizens of which states complained to the Post Office Department that the facilities were inadequate, did not provide properly for the needs of their commerce at home and abroad, which was then in the dawn of a thrifty development, and as a remedy, which appealed to reason and local pride and, under a larger growth, would have had great weight, urged that Oregon, Washington, Idaho and Montana be segregated from the Eighth Division and be formed into an additional division.

My observation and inquiries convinced me that neither the extent of the service, its deficiencies in effectiveness, or the magnitude of the early prospective growth of population, and productiveness, justified such action at that time; it seemed to me that all that was lacking could be provided by establishing some additional service, rearranging some of the existing service and placing at Portland, Ore., an experienced and competent officer of good judgment, who would keep well informed as to the needs of that territory, acting as the direct representative of the Department in such cases as would be sent direct to him from Washington, and in analogous cases, bringing other cases outside of his authorized independent jurisdiction before the division superintendent at San Francisco, and this was the arrangement made finally and is still in force, but I am glad to see that General Superintendent Grant has recommended an additional division that will embrace three of these states at least, and the territory of Alaska, and that it has been approved by the Department. I hope it will be authorized by Congress during the present session.

At the time of my inspection in 1890 the population of the whole Eighth Division, not counting Alaska, which was but 36,500, was not half as large as that of the First Division, whereas, its area in square miles, not including Alaska, which is and was 577,390, was and is more than eleven times greater, and its farm lands in 1900 were only thirteen per cent. of its area, while that of the First Division was 57 per cent. In 1890 the aggregate population of Idaho, Oregon and Washington was 747,542; at the present time it is about 1,403,000, more than 358,928 in excess of that of the entire division in 1874; their aggregate area is 249,500 square miles, of which, according to the last census, 33,869 is farm land, being about $13\frac{1}{2}$ per cent. of the whole area.

A large percentage of the area embraced in the vast domain of the Eighth Division is waste lands—arid and sterile plains, parched with the burning sun, void of moisture and vegetation, the graveyards of extinct volcanoes, and perhaps of lost races of men and lower animals; rugged mountain ranges, mineral-bearing in most cases, covered with forests and topped with towering peaks of volcanic origin, in many instances, are found in every state and territory of the division. Some of these ranges parallel each other, and send out spurs which interlock and pinch out vales and plains at their extremities, so that only narrow passes are found through which traffic by rail and wagon is possible between the different sections. This makes intercommunication, by the usual agencies, slow and tedious, and as the routes of travel are far apart, and sometimes tortuous, that competition which would undoubtedly quicken the pace does not exist, and is not likely to until the Pacific slope rivals Switzerland in tunnel building.

Valleys of fertile lands, through which rivers of clear water flow, producing fruits, flowers, grain and vegetation in great variety and abundance, lie at the base of the foothills of these ranges and between the spurs that are offshoots from them. Some of these valleys are beautiful; those like the Sacramento, San Joaquin, Willamette, Klamath, Umpqua and Rogue River are not only garden spots, but also the delightful homes of a large number of intelligent and prosperous people. Other valleys there are in Idaho, Oregon and Washington, surrounded by the same settings and equally as beautiful and prolific, that have not bloomed because nature has not moistened them with her tears, nor man watered them with labor and skill, but when those states become more densely populated, and men begin to jostle each other, and the more easy and less expensive lands to cultivate are settled to their full capacity, and the supply of their products begins to fail to meet the demand for them, these slumbering places will be awakened to their mission, by the civil engineers and the husbandmen's art and energy, and will bring forth bountiful harvests wherewith to feed and clothe, to shelter and educate their dependents. Who that has studied the census and development of our own land from the Revolution to this time can fail to see in its growth from three to eighty-eight millions, a future in which all these lands will be called upon to maintain additional teeming millions? When that time does come, no nation will outrank our own in transportation facilities or means of rapid transit, be they upon, above, or under the earth; but until then let there be drawn together in a more compact organization, for economy and celerity in the conduct of their postal affairs, upon which celerity in the transaction of other business depends, those states having the same geological formation, similar interests, and bound together and circumscribed in their outside intercourse by the same geographical barriers.

I have said that we moved into the Honore Building August 23, 1874. We remained there until January 4, 1879, when we became homeless once more by fire. I was absent from the office, when the fire was discovered, making a call at the general offices of the Chicago, Rock Island & Pacific railway, and knew nothing of it until I rounded the southeast corner of the Grand Pacific Hotel, where Jackson crosses Clark street, when I saw clouds of smoke ascending from the Honore Building; then I rushed north on Clark street to Adams, thence east to the Adams street entrance to the second floor of the post office, in the northeast corner of which our office was located, facing Dearborn street on the east and an alley on the north. My machinery was working perfectly and I passed up the stairs along the hall, running through the second story from north to south, and entered our rooms under full headway and found Messrs. Campbell, Troy, Montgomery, Skeels, H. B. Armstrong and others lowering the records and furniture through the open windows into wagons stationed in the alley to receive them. I joined in the work, and as soon as possible arranged to have railway post offices placed in position to receive and distribute the mails as was done immediately after each previous fire. The clerks were called in from their layoffs and, as always, responded promptly and efficiently. I quote the following from the Chicago papers to show the action taken by our service:

"THE RAILWAY MAIL SERVICE.

"All the mail matter which was sent to the Rock Island depot for Saturday night has been sent to its destination without loss of time or delay. Captain White, of the United States Railway Mail Service, is responsible for this happy state of affairs, which was hardly to be expected under the circumstances. All of the matter that had accumulated at the post office on Saturday was at once transferred to the postal cars, where it was distributed by the clerks and sent to its destination. All the mail was handled in this manner for several days. A reporter who visited the depot yesterday found nothing but newspaper bags on the floor, with a few clerks and local agent Hubbard in charge. These gentlemen claimed that by distributing the mails on the cars they can be as quickly and advantageously sent to their destination as if it were done in the best post office building in the regular course of work. This method of distribution always worked to a charm. Captain White's behavior during the progress of the fire is highly praised by all who saw him.   *   *   *   *   Gentlemen who came in contact with him during the exciting moments of Saturday speak in the highest terms of his cool and remarkable behavior under the trying circumstances. Yesterday he was busy visiting the different depots, and could not be found."

"THE RAILWAY MAIL SERVICE.

"The value to the country of the Railway Mail Service was never better illustrated than by the fire Saturday. The hesitancy of Congress to make an appropriation to meet the exigencies of the present half year happily terminated in the proper way, and the system was not discontinued January 1, as it necessarily would have been had the appropriation been disallowed. But for this system of distribution in transit, all mails would come into the general office unassorted for division. Had this been the rule, owing to the delays in mails by the snow storms, the Chicago office would have been clogged with hundreds of sacks of mail matter Saturday, most of which would, of necessity, have been destroyed. As it was, not a letter was lost or injured, and it is doubtful if even a paper went astray.

"For the information of the public, Captain White, Superintendent of this service, has issued the following circular:

"RAILWAY MAIL SERVICE.

"OFFICE SUPERINTENDENT, SIXTH DIVISION,

Chicago, January 6, 1879.

"For the purpose of distributing mails during the present embarrassment under which the local post office labors, employees of this service are stationed in Chicago, Milwaukee & St. Paul postal car No. 57, under Madison street bridge, upon which can be mailed until 8 p. m. each day all letters for Wisconsin, Minnesota, Dakota and the upper peninsula of Michigan.

"Upon Illinois Central postal car, No. 38, at foot of Randolph street, can be mailed, until 8 p. m., all letters for offices supplied by the Chicago and St. Louis and Michigan Central lines.

"The public should remember that there is night postal service upon the Chicago, Burlington & Quincy, Illinois Central, Chicago, Rock Island & Pacific, Chicago and Iowa Division, Chicago & Northwestern, Pittsburg, Fort Wayne & Chicago, and Lake Shore & Michigan Southern Railroads, and that all letters for offices supplied by these lines can be mailed at the cars up to the time of leaving. The Pittsburg, Fort Wayne & Chicago postal car leaves at 9 p. m. daily, except Saturday, when it leaves at 5:15 p. m. The other postal cars leave upon the regular night and day trains.

"Respectfully,

"(Signed)   JAMES E. WHITE,

Superintendent."

The post office and our office moved to the basement of the Singer Building, corner State and Washington streets, while the Honore Building was burning. Fortunately the fire department confined the fire practically to the building in which it originated; the streets were not crowded with frantic men, women and children, fleeing Jehus driving furiously, thieves, blacklegs and scoundrels; so our effects were nearly all saved and no one was injured. But the mixture in the basement of the Singer Building was not systematic that night, but it did not take long to arrange it so that some of the work could be resumed in a day or two and shortly the office was in as good working order as it could be placed in such cramped quarters. On the 12th of April the post office moved to the basement of the uncompleted Government Building, and the railway mail service, after remaining in the Singer Building a few days longer, moved into a store fronting Washington street, where Field Annex now stands.

The following year, 1880, we moved into "Economy Block," Dearborn street front, now known as "The Fair" and to the Federal Building in 1881, which occupied the ground upon which the present one stands. That building was the home of the post office as well as of our service until April, 1896; during that month both offices took up their quarters in a temporary post office building erected on the lake front, which was better adapted to the uses made of it, I believe, than any other assigned or provided for the two offices during my connection with the service.

The building now occupied cost $4,000,000, and was completed and taken possession of on October 28, 1905.

APPLICATION OF THE POWERS OF MAN.

In the early days I had many experiences which taught me—though ambitious for territory—that efficient supervision over large spheres of action in a land of "magnificent distances," like the great west, could only be secured through prodigal expenditure of time, and mental, nervous and muscular power and activity. The more unlimited the sphere the greater the expenditure of energy or the lower the efficiency of supervision. The time consumed in journeying from point to point then was more than twice as great as it is now, which, considered from a practical standpoint, was equivalent to enlarging the field of supervision in the same ratio, as the time for actual inspection and investigation was decreased proportionately thereby.

The conservation and application of the powers of man—spiritual and physical—in the different fields of mechanical science is necessary to the discovery of certain principles and truths in the line of civil and mechanical engineering, in mining, and in making waste places productive. It made possible the powerful engines of to-day, and the high speed reached and maintained for long distances, with great loads and up high grades as well as over level plains. These monster machines are one of the products of high mechanical engineering, but they could not have attained their present usefulness without the scientific skill of the civil engineers, who surveyed and directed the construction of the road beds, culverts, trestles, bridges and tunnels, selected rails of suitable weight and applied scientific principles in laying them, especially on sharp curves, so as to prevent the rails spreading and the trains being derailed, or the engines jumping the tracks as they rounded curves at high speed, striking the inside rail at acute angles, and veering over with their great weight and momentum against the outside rail, striking it a terrific blow at another angle.

High speed in such cases, as we all know from experience, endangers the safety of all on board, and if no lives are lost or limbs broken, the railway post office clerks and the employees of the railway and express companies are very liable to be injured by being thrown against their racks and cases, trunks and packages or the walls of their car and to receive grievous bruises and cuts. The best engineers, those who through long experience in handling the same engine upon the same road, have come to know the topography of one and the eccentricities of the other, and having lost that recklessness which seems to be inseparable from the early career of everyone who enters upon a hazardous calling, but which passes from them after they have drunk of the cup of pain and remorse brewed by their own hands for themselves and others, now pilot their trains with such judgment that they move around the curve as gracefully as swans swim among groups of islands.

The mining engineer has become a very important factor in railroad operations, since the country is so largely denuded of forests that what remains must not only be conserved, but be added to by planting and cultivation to meet the demands for other purposes than fuel and car and building construction. Fortunately he finds buried in the earth better materials for all these purposes than grow upon it. Coal (anthracite and bituminous), iron from which steel is made, copper, lead, etc., etc., are found in large beds, or pockets, from Maine to the state of Washington and in Alaska, probably in sufficient quantities to last until some substitute is found—electricity perhaps.

I remember very well that but little coal was used on the old Chicago, Iowa & Nebraska railroad when I ran over it, notwithstanding Iowa had but a small per cent. of timber land. This was because train service was light, and coal largely undiscovered.

The track was built by laying the ties on the rich, black muck and placing light rails on top of them; "fish plates" were not used, consequently the joints were broken and as the era of ballasting had not arrived, in the west at least, when trains moved over low places and through cuts after heavy rains the track would sag, first on one side, then on the other, and travel was not a delight to passengers who were unaccustomed to

"A life on the ocean wave!
A home on the rolling deep."

During my first year on this line our trains were hauled by three of the old style Baldwin or Rogers locomotive engines—the Fox River, Mercury and Titus; they were light weight, but heavy enough for the business assigned them; the Fox River was the lightest, and not as good a steam generator as the other two, both of which made plenty to keep up with the schedule and an excess to blow over the foot path along the side of the track; the Titus, when not dead, was the champion in that line.

There was a bend in the Iowa River between Oxford (now Montour) and Tama City, near which an Indian reservation was located; opposite this bend was a corresponding curve in the track. One day the Fox River, while on her way toward the Mississippi River, holding her umbrella smokestack proudly in the air and the engineer's good right hand resting on the lever, it is supposed that he became absorbed in the splendor of the landscape before him and forgot the danger in front and allowed the crafty creature he was driving to strike the angles of the curve at high speed and she plunged into the placid waters that were flowing below. This demonstrated the danger of moving at high speed around curves.

My opposite, Mr. G. S. Eddy, said to me once that he did not enjoy being derailed; that no matter how soft the ditch in which his car landed he always found it hard, and that if he had anything to do with managing that part of the road over which we ran he would anchor the engine and trains to the track and move the whole thing on skids, but I never thought he was serious—rather that he was jocular—until as I was running east one day, I found him in the ditch just outside of Blairstown, standing in the doorway of his apartment, facing us and trying to keep from sliding down to the other side of the car; he was not hurt—he never was. This was the fifth time he had been in that enchanting position since I had been on the line, while I had escaped entirely, and I could not help crying out that I thought it would be more soul satisfying to stay in the ditch and have his meals and clean clothes brought to him regularly, and his family occasionally, than to live that sort of abnormal life. These few words of consolation and advice seemed to grieve him and he shouted back that he hoped I would be the next one to go off the track. I said I would be glad to share anything with him, but that it would not be right for me to attempt to rob him of any part of the reputation he had acquired as an acrobat under such distressing circumstances.

This accident detained the train I was on about two and a half hours, so when we received orders to move the train got under full headway as soon as possible. Ambitious engineers, in those days, seemed to consider that skill in their vocation, intrepidity and proper interest in the success of their employers demanded that all time lost, no matter how, must be made up before passing the first switch in the direction running, so when the order was received a shrill shriek rent the air, the throttle of the engine was thrown wide open, the piston rods glided backward and forward without friction, the wheels rotated faster and faster and the Fox River opened a hole in the air as she sprinted over the twenty-four miles separating Blairstown and Cedar Rapids, where east-bound passengers ate their supper and west-bound their breakfast. On this occasion the time for supper was limited; the train soon pulled out for Clinton—eighty-one miles away—stopping at Bertram for wood and water as usual, then passing Mount Vernon in dense darkness and on toward Lisbon; as we approached this station the headlight revealed to the engineer a crossing and three cows lying on it; the whistle sounded a quick, sharp warning and the next moment the cows were thrown up against the bank of a cut and rolled back under the trucks of my car, which rose to the occasion, and landed in the ditch, where it rested partly on its roof and partly on one side. I was inside lying in the angle thus created, partly stunned; the letters were thrown from the cases; the papers from the boxes; the fire from the stove and they formed a hot blend around me, but I was on my feet in a moment, trying to stamp out the fire. Soon I heard the conductor calling my name and I answered but was not heard; the calls and answers were repeated with the same result, then the conductor climbed upon the exposed side of the car, opened the door and called again. I explained the situation and requested that water be handed down as fast as possible that I might extinguish the fire; this was done and the fire did but little damage, but we remained where the accident occurred until the next day and then moved on to Clinton; leaving the car, in which the mail apartment was located, behind. I escaped with bruises only, which was gratifying.

That route extended from Clinton to Boone, Iowa; it has long been part of the great Chicago & Nortwestern system, being a portion of the main line extending from Chicago via Clinton, Cedar Rapids, and Boone to Council Bluffs, and Omaha, Nebraska—a system embracing now about ten thousand miles of railroad—which has become under the long and able management of Marvin Hughitt, who entered upon his railway career in a subordinate position early in life, and rose by sheer force of character, intellectual capacity and energy, from one position to another, until long since he became the distinguished head of the whole system, which is one of the best built and equipped railroads, in all respects, in this country. He is an able, unassuming gentleman of positive convictions and determination. While I was stationed in Chicago he did many kind acts, at my request, of which our clerks were beneficiaries.

The rise of the great operatives; the advanced methods of management and construction; the wonderful improvements in every feature of manufacture, commerce and transportation that have occurred all along this and other lines of business, can be traced by the same gradual growth of the human mind in the white flame of practical experience, and persistent delving into specialties, that has marked the growth of our splendidly efficient railway mail service, and moulded it into what it is, for the benefit of mankind, and the end is not yet.

I cannot call to mind, in active service now, any who were prominent in the administration of large railroad properties prior to my entry into the railway mail service; those whose names I can recall are all, or nearly all, I hope and believe, at rest in this life, or in the one beyond, for though some of them were not sugar coated on the outside, I do not remember any whose manhood was not broad, sympathetic, and responsive to the clear ringing notes of distress or who did not extend their uplifting influence in behalf of the worthy, capable, young men struggling for advancement. Those qualities shine brighter in the judgment of the men of gray matter, made in the likeness of the Creator, than the polish of all the drones, fops, and pleasure-seeking do-nothings of the world.

I recall the names of many of these, their faces and forms, and some of their characteristics. Hugh Riddle, Robert Harris, Frank Thompson, P. A. Hall, S. S. Merrell, W. H. Holcomb, Thomas J. Potter, John Newell and many others.

There grew up under these and others, who may properly be called pioneer railway managers, a younger class of men who commenced at the bottom also; some as section bosses, some in the shops, some as station agents, train dispatchers, yard men, some in charge of gravel-trains, and in the offices; they had the benefit of the experiences of these pioneers and were pushed on by the demands and necessities of an ever-increasing population, production, competition, invention, and ambition; the fittest always surviving, and stepping into the vacant high places, until now there is a body of men in middle life, some beyond, who are the stars in the operating firmament of the railroad world to-day—they are familiar with the railway post office service, for they grew as it grew, provided it with improved cars as fast as new methods, material and inventions were discovered, which would strengthen their construction; improved their tracks as fast as increased speed was demanded; augmented the force of their motive power, and have done many helpful things not "nominated in the bond;" have become deeply interested in its success, not wholly for pecuniary remuneration, as most know, but because they have helped nurse it and want their patrons, neighbors, employees, and all, in any respect dependent upon them, to have as good accommodations as any one else has.

These men have always been friends of the railway mail service. Among them may be mentioned Roswell Miller, W. C. Brown, W. H. Newman, E. P. Ripley, George B. Harris, A. J. Earling, F. D. Underwood, William Truesdale, Edward Dickinson, John M. Whiteman, William A. Gardner, &c., &c.

I do not know what improvements will be made in the work of the clerks of the future; no doubt time in transit will be reduced; tracks made more frictionless; retirements on pay at a prescribed age, and under certain conditions earlier; provisions to remunerate them for the additional expense incurred when absent from their homes on official duty; their salaries to be increased until they become fairly remunerative; considering the high grade work they perform; and the increased cost of living; the hazard they are in when on duty; the time allowed for recreation and rest which they must surrender to those studies which keep them fit for first-class service all the time and for emergency duty, resulting from snow blockades, destruction of bridges and tracks, floods, landslides, fires, wrecks and such other contingencies as substitutes may not be available for, and which must therefore be taken care of by the regular force without additional compensation.

It may be asked, Upon what do you base such an optimistic prediction? I answer upon the experiences and successes of the past, and the inherent and everlasting sense of justice that pervades this people, and acts authoritatively whenever the conscience is aroused. I think the past shows that those most directly interested financially; their officers and friends; the record of the achievements, endurance, fidelity and rectitude of the rank and file may be depended upon to arouse the public conscience and to keep it alive and alert until the object sought is accomplished, without trespassing upon the authority of the executive arm of the Government, elective or appointive. This must be supplemented by patience, for patience is needed many times, especially when the excuse is made that all you have estimated for cannot be allowed because a large deficiency in the revenues of the Department exists, and then discover that a comparatively new service, to be exact, twelve years old, that could not perform one satisfactory function, if railroad transportation of mails, and railway post office distribution of the same, were not sufficiently extensive and equipped to insure correct and complete distribution, and prompt and regular delivery at the head office of the rural delivery routes, rarely, if ever, fails to be allowed the full sum of its estimate.

During the brief existence of the rural delivery its expenditures have mounted up from $14,840 per annum in 1897 to $36,950,129 for the fiscal year 1909. If this rate of increase continues for another twelve years, a new schedule of taxation will be in order, the construction of battleships, those safeguards of the nation, be discontinued, and those not independent, do as a St. Paul gentleman, who was recently caught in a snow blockade between stations without food, told a friend he did, "went to bed without anything on his stomach but his hand."

The expenditure for railroad and steamboat mail transportation seems to have been recorded first in the year 1837; for that year it amounted to $307,444. Since 1846 the cost of railroad transportation of mail has been kept separate, and for that year was $587,769; for 1876, the brief season of the first fast mail, it was $9,543,135; for 1886 it was $15,520,191; for 1890 it was $20,869,231; for 1900 it was $33,-424,982; for 1903 it was $36,607,524; for 1908 it was $44,722,985. and for 1909 it was $44,885,395.29.

These figures are of record, therefore historically correct, and show that the principal aid of the Government in supplying its citizens of all classes and conditions with mail, and without which all attempts to provide the semblance of a satisfactory service would be fruitless, because its great auxiliary, the railway mail service, could not exist, had been transporting ton after ton, car after car, and train after train of mail matter over thousands, tens of thousands and millions of miles in the best vehicles that could be constructed, at the highest speed and greatest frequency, sixty-six years before their annual remuneration reached the munificent sum expended in a single year upon a twelve-year-old child of the Department.

The first annual expenditure for all the employees of the railway mail service dates from the fiscal year 1842, and is recorded as $22,987. The expenditures increased gradually from that fiscal year to this; in 1865, the fiscal year the railway post office service was introduced, to $342,071.96; in 1890 it was $5,818,665.00; in 1907 it was $15,248,-601.55, and for the present fiscal year, 1909, it is $18,352,674.70.

Thus it will be seen that a service that has been in operation sixty-six years at least in a crude and dependent way at first, but which began to move into a higher sphere of usefulness twenty-two years later through the introduction of new methods and blood has become the best service of its kind mentioned in the literature and history of the world, and at little more than half the cost per annum of the rural delivery, which is but thirteen years old.

If the service did not exist and the railroad transportation continued, there would be a restoration of the distributing post offices with the attendant delays in the delivery of the mails, augmented by those of rural delivery, or if the first dropped out, the stage coach era would return, and yet the magnificent railway service, the blood of whose employees has been poured out freely while in the discharge of their duties, and who have sealed their devotion to their calling with their lives, maimed bodies and wrecked health, is denied an appropriation for a specific purpose, which many of the most able and experienced men, in and out of Congress, declare to be meritorious in the extreme, on the ground that a deficiency in the revenues of the Department exists, and that, too, in face of the fact that, within twelve years after its birth, the favored service has been allowed an annual appropriation exceeding that granted for the railway mail service employees and officers $16,564,000, and for the employees, officers and car space paid for, combined—by $11,764,000. In view of the above statements, which can be verified by reference to annual reports, I think I may be allowed to say that patience is in order.

THE FAST MAIL

The late George S. Bangs, then superintendent of the railway mail service, is entitled to the credit of introducing the first set of fast mail trains to the public. This occurred in 1875, on the main lines of the New York Central & Hudson River and the Lake Shore & Michigan Southern railroad companies, between New York City, N. Y., and Chicago, Ill.

It is true that when Mr. George B. Armstrong was chief of the service—with headquarters in Washington, April 4, 1869-May 3, 1871 —he presented this subject to, and conferred and corresponded, respecting its establishment on the above mentioned routes, with Mr. William H. Vanderbilt, eldest son of "Commodore" Vanderbilt, who was vice-president of the New York & Hudson River Railroad Company in 1865, and when the New York Central & Hudson River companies were consolidated and created into a corporation in 1869, he was made its first vice-president and "de facto" executive officer, and was also vice-president of the Lake Shore & Michigan Southern Railway Company and of the Michigan Central Railroad.

These advances were well received by Mr. Vanderbilt, and although immediate results did not follow, they enabled the originator

One of the New York and Chicago Fast Mails
New York Central R. R. System

of the railway post office to present his conception and suitable suggestions concerning its establishment clearly to the mind of the executive head of that great chain of railway lines, for consideration and action, when more favorable conditions prevailed. Undoubtedly this, like other problems which he worked out thoroughly in his own mind before attempting to put them into practical operation, he discussed with Mr. Bangs and other confidential friends. At the time the fast mail was receiving his closest attention, Mr. Bangs, upon his pressing request, had become his successor at Chicago, and was recognized there as his chief lieutenant. On May 3, 1871, Mr. Armstrong retired from the service and two days later died, leaving much of the work mapped out in his fertile mind undeveloped, but he had laid the foundation, built some of the superstructure and left behind him a corps of young men who, with others who came in later, have brought it up to its present stage of development.

Mr. Bangs, who very properly' succeeded Mr. Armstrong as superintendent of the whole service, took up the work where his friend and sponsor had laid it down, revived the fast mail project, re-opened negotiations with William H. Vanderbilt and officers of other available lines, which finally culminated in the establishment of that special service on the routes mentioned in the first paragraph of this article.

The first train departed from New York City at 4:15 a. m., September 16, 1875, and ran via Albany, Syracuse, Buffalo, N. Y., Cleveland, Toledo, Ohio, and Elkhart, Ind., and arrived at Chicago at 6:55 a. m. the next day; the first east-bound train departed from Chicago at 8:20 p. m., and running by the same route, arrived at New York City at 3:00 a. m. the second day, thirty hours and forty minutes; it ran thus daily in both directions until July 22, 1876, fifty-five days less than one year, when it was withdrawn by the companies interested, because their reasonable expectation that the extraordinary service they were rendering would be recognized by the Government making provision for a corresponding increase in compensation was not realized. This expectation became hopeless, when Congress on July 12, 1876, passed a bill, which among other commands, directed the Postmaster General to reduce the compensation, fixed by law, for the transportation of the mails by railroads—not land-grant roads—ten per cent.

That the expectations of the companies rested on equity, no one with the capacity to understand the magnitude of the undertaking, could doubt for a moment. The expense involved comprehended the building of a sufficient number of railway post office cars, on plans and specifications drawn to meet the needs of an exacting and hazardous service, to equip five trains drawn by powerful engines for those days, the complement necessary to maintain daily service both ways, and to meet possible emergencies—to provide additional train crews, safety appliances, guards, caretakers, and when all were ready for the start to invest these trains with the "right of way" over all others on the line and to keep them in repair.

When this is known the conviction that the expectation was equitable must grow stronger in the minds of those capable of comparing the extent, quality and cost of the service, and the magnitude of the mail carried by any one line prior to the fiscal year 1875, with that of the fiscal year 1876.

In the latter part of the calendar year, 1875, trains made up wholly or in part of postal cars ran daily between New York and Chicago. One, the fast mail, composed of an engine and four full postal cars, properly equipped with expert railway postal clerks, a chief head clerk, caretaker, etc., departed from New York City at 4:15 p. m., and running by the routes and junctions heretofore mentioned, arrived at Chicago at 6:55 a. m. the next day. The second was a regular passenger train composed of an engine, postal, baggage, express, sleeping cars and passenger coaches, and departing from New York City, made slow running time to Chicago.

The fast mail was well organized and equipped, many competent clerks were detailed to it from lines in the Second, Fifth and Sixth Divisions, the divisions through which the lines composing the route by which the fast mail ran, and which was afterwards known as the New York & Chicago R. P. O. Up to the time the fast mail was introduced, that portion of this route laying between New York and Buffalo was assigned to the Second Division, and that part between Buffalo and Chicago to the Sixth Division, as did all the territory afterwards assigned to the Ninth Division when it was created.

Mr. William B. Thompson, afterwards General Superintendent Railway Mail Service, was placed in charge of the fast mail from its beginning, at which time he was a special agent, assigned as above. Mr. Thompson served within my jurisdiction nearly four years and the compliment was reciprocated by serving under him about six years. It affords me pleasure to testify to his industry, faithfulness, "sticking qualities," and courtesy as a subordinate and superior officer. The original fast mail, as has been stated, was operated but a brief period, but during that time it improved in distribution, and the excellent clerks employed in discipline, esprit de corps and efficiency; nevertheless it was not a fast mail in the sense implied, at any time during its existence. It was held in the yards of the New York Central, in New York City, seven hours, after it should have been scheduled out, for the New York dailies and the News Company packages. I have it on good authority that the average daily weight it carried from New York City was about twenty tons; it is a matter of record that the mail out on the first run consisted of forty-seven pouches of letters, 663 sacks of papers, a very large number of News Company packages, and 182 registered packages, and that the great bulk of the dailies were delivered between New York City and Buffalo. The New York *Times* had 9000 copies of that day's issue on the train and only 1800 were carried west of Buffalo; other dailies sent out large quantities—presumably with the same result.

This train was slowed down several times before arriving at Cleveland, to keep within the schedule; the time made between New York City and Toledo, Ohio, averaged forty-one miles per hour, and between Toledo and Chicago but thirty and one-half miles; thus it is shown that if this train had departed from New York City at 9:15 p. m., the hour that would have benefited the largest number of people, and expedited the most important and best paying mail, and maintained the same speed through to Chicago, that it did to Toledo, it would have arrived at 9:55 p. m., the night before the morning of its actual arrival, and connection would have been assured with the night trains on the trunk lines radiating from Chicago to the west, southwest, north and northwest and south, supplying a very large number of post offices from six to twelve and twenty-four hours earlier than they were with the first fast mail system and none later.

It must be remembered that the system of distribution adapted for the fast mail was especially adapted to the requirements of a p. m. arrival at Chicago, at a time when night railway post offices were the exception, not the rule; when the making of express mails, night offices, and side lines were indicated in order that the mail might be dispatched to destination via express trains in baggage cars, in charge of baggagemen and with the least delay possible.

Making up the mail for night connection in those days, when the schedule by which the train was run provided for a morning connection, was a very extravagant proceeding. As has been said this fast mail was discontinued on July 22, 1876, and the old service was resumed. At the end of that time No. 21, known as the "Western Express," made up of regular passenger train equipment, including postal cars, was scheduled to leave New York City at 6:00 p. m., Cleveland, 3:00 p. m. next day; Toledo, 6:00 p. m., and to arrive at Chicago at 6:00 a. m. the following day, occupying thirty-six hours between termini. Later, a train, called a fast mail train, left New York at 8:50 p.

m. and arrived at Toledo, Ohio, at 4:57 p. m. the next day, the mail for Chicago and the west being dispatched thence by express train arriving at Chicago at either 5:40 or 8:10 a. m. the following day; time en route either thirty-three or thirty-five hours, speed per hour about twenty-eight or thirty miles; if we consider this run as between New York City and Toledo only, the speed was about thirty-seven miles per hour.

In 1882 General Superintendent Thompson, with the hearty co-operation of Postmaster General Howe, devoted his best energies toward securing an extension of this train with a shortening of time to Chicago and the establishment of a connecting fast mail to Omaha, over one of these competing lines, viz., Chicago & Northwestern, Chicago, Rock Island & Pacific, and Chicago, Burlington & Quincy railroads. It was understood that the Michigan Southern railroad had agreed to put the New York and Toledo fast mail through to Chicago by midnight, if a fast mail to Omaha could be secured, but all the above lines declined to accept the most favorable proposals within the power of the Post Office Department. Postmaster General Howe then dispatched Mr. Thompson and myself to Kansas City, Mo., to confer with Messrs. Clark and Kimball of the Union Pacific system, whose headquarters were at Omaha, but who were then at Kansas City attending a meeting of railway lines respecting a reduction of their schedule sufficient to save twelve hours between Omaha and San Francisco. The conference was held and our work was progressing favorably until Mr. Kimball inquired whether the sum offered for the special service, if granted, would be paid in cash or be credited on the company's indebtedness to the Government. Mr. Thompson said that he could not answer that question but would telegraph to the Postmaster General for a decision; the Postmaster General referred it to the Attorney General, who decided that it must be credited on the company's indebtedness to the Government, thereupon the officers of the company declined to accept the proposal of the Government, but later the Union and Central Pacific, of their own motion, reduced their time twelve hours, so that the Department received the accommodation it sought without cost.

The Postmaster General and the General Superintendent, assisted by Mr. John Newall of the Lake Shore & Michigan Southern Railroad, worked persistently and vigorously to secure favorable consideration for the proposition made the three competing lines, from the president and general manager of one of them, but without results, until some time after the death of Postmaster General Howe and the appointment of General Gresham as his successor.

HON. E. L. WEST
Superintendent Sixth Division R. M. S.
(See Appendix)

CHICAGO & COUNCIL BLUFFS AND CHICAGO & ST. PAUL FAST MAILS.

There then came a time when the pool that had existed between these roads was broken temporarily, and those who had continued the negotiations for a fast mail on the part of the Department, found this opening, rushed in vigorously and were conceded a meeting in a room of the Grand Pacific Hotel on March 10, 1884. The Post Office Department was represented in this meeting by General Walter Q. Gresham, Postmaster General; Frank Hatton, First Assistant Postmaster General; William B. Thompson, General Superintendent; and James E. White, Superintendent Sixth Division; the Chicago, Burlington & Quincy railway by Charles E. Perkins, president; Thomas J. Potter, general manager, and others.

The conference continued well into the afternoon, when an agreement was entered into which provided that the company furnish the Government a special fast mail train to start from Chicago at 3:00 a. m., six times per week and run over its lines via Mendota and Galesburg, Ill., Burlington, Mount Pleasant, Ottumwa, Pacific Junction, and Council Bluffs to Union Pacific Transfer, Iowa, where it should arrive at 7:00 p. m. the same day. After the agreement was ready for signature the Postmaster General turned to Mr. Potter and asked him when he would be ready to start the fast mail. Mr. Potter replied, "To-morrow morning, General;" then he turned to me and said, "When can you be ready, Captain?" I answered, "To-morrow morning, Mr. Postmaster General," and we moved out of the Union Depot promptly, March 11, 1884, at 3:00 a. m., and the fast mail arrived at Union Pacific Transfer, Iowa, at 7:00 p. m., the same day, on time.

General Manager Potter's car was attached to the train, and the Postmaster General and party, and Mr. Potter and party visited Burlington, Iowa, the home of Mr. Charles E. Perkins, president of the C. B. & Q. R. R., with whom they breakfasted, and later in the day General Gresham and others of the party who had served as soldiers during the Civil War did themselves the honor to pay their respects to Colonel J. C. Abercrombie of the 11th Iowa Infantry, who lived in Burlington, and had become totally blind on account of his war services. Colonel Abercrombie's regiment was associated with the 13th Regiment, in which I served, and the 15th and 16th Regiments, Iowa Infantry, which formed the 3rd or "Crocker's Iowa Brigade" of the 4th Division of the 17th Corps. General Gresham had command of this division when it was moving into position in front of Atlanta, Ga., the evening of July 20, 1864, and was carried off the field wounded. I was wounded the next day while leading my company from that position in a charge which the 3rd Brigade was ordered to make on the works of the enemy, which crowned a hill from which our front and left was being enfiladed very disastrously.

The Colonel was very much pleased with the call; he had grown gray, was more slender and had that appearance of dignity and refinement, coupled with a sadness of expression, the result, no doubt, of his experience in the army and his misfortune.

In due time the General Manager's car, with the party it brought from Chicago in the morning, started on the return trip, and arrived in that city early in the evening of the same day. En route a stop was made at Galesburg, Ill., where the Postmaster General received a telegram from General Manager Miller of the Chicago, Milwaukee & St. Paul railway, asking when and where he could confer with him respecting the establishment of fast mail service on that line between Chicago and St. Paul. The Postmaster General appointed that evening at the Grand Pacific Hotel. The conference was held and an agreement entered into to run a special mail train daily, except Sunday, for one year from March 13, 1884, leaving Chicago at 3:00 a. m., running via Milwaukee and La Crosse, Wis., arriving at St. Paul at 3:30 p. m., and at Minneapolis, Minn., at 4 p. m., etc. This agreement was subject to the approval of Mr. Alex. Mitchell, president of the company, whose headquarters were in Milwaukee, so on the morning of the 12th, General Manager Miller took the Postmaster General and party in his special car to that city and the negotiations were explained to Mr. Mitchell, who, after asking a few questions, approved and signed the agreement. The Postmaster General, as in the case of the C. B. & Q. R. R., then asked General Manager Miller when he could commence the service; and was told the next day, and he then asked me when we could be ready and I answered, "To-morrow, Mr. Postmaster General," and it was started the morning of the 13th of March, 1884, and has been in successful operation ever since.

The contracts of this company and the Chicago, Burlington & Quincy were renewed twice, making the aggregate period under contract nine years each and as they have continued and improved this special service to this day they have demonstrated that they are steadfast and enterprising servants of the Post Office Department and of the public and their own patrons. At the time these contracts were entered into an agreement was made with the Illinois Central Company whereby it agreed to change the schedule of its main line, Freeport to Centralia, Ill., so that one train would run south and the other north, from Mendota, Ill., at about 5 a. m., on the arrival of the Chicago,

Burlington & Council Bluffs fast mail; this arrangement increased the value of the service through the central portion of the state, and reached more distant sections by trains—mail and express—crossing it to the east and west.

TRANSCONTINENTAL FAST MAIL.

The special service remained very much in this condition in the west until November, 1889, when special fast mail service was established between Omaha, Neb., and San Francisco, Cal., and Portland, Ore. I had talked with the Union Pacific people from time to time about this service after the Chicago, Burlington & Council Bluffs fast mail had been introduced, but could not observe that much impression was being made until 1889. One day in September of that year, I was returning from a western trip and dropped off the train at Omaha, to pay my respects to Mr. W. H. Holcomb, vice-president, and Mr. E. Dickinson, general manager, of the Union Pacific railway and allied lines. I again brought up the fast mail service from Union Pacific Transfer, Iowa, to Ogden, Utah, including in the same conversation the Oregon Short Line, which was under the same management, and the success of which would make a greater success of the main line. The Oregon Short Line breaks from the main stem at Granger, Wyo.; its trains, however, were made up at Green River, Wyo., thirty miles east on the Union Pacific, and moved up to Granger, passed through its gates out over the low land lying between it and Pocatello, Idaho, and on, in a northerly direction, via Nampa, Idaho, Huntington, Baker City, Pendleton, Umatilla and thence due east on the south bank of the beautiful Columbia River, past The Dalles, under the shadow of Mt. Hood, into the active city of Portland, Oregon—945 miles from Granger, Wyoming.

The conversation grew very interesting, and as we proceeded I became aware that Mr. Holcomb was not simply passing the "time o' day" with me, but was in "dead earnest," and wanted to feel well assured that he was doing what would advance the best interests of his company; finally he asked me if I had drawn up an agreement. I said, "No, sir;" then he took me to a room, introduced a stenographer to me and said, I might dictate an agreement, have it typewritten and bring it to him; if it proved satisfactory he would sign it, and I said I would also, subject to the approval of the Postmaster General. We both signed, and I took the train that would deliver me first at Washington, passed my home without stopping, and as soon as I arrived in the Department called upon General Superintendent Bell and explained the object of my visit. In a short time we called at the Postmaster

General's rooms, I paid my respects and the story I had come to tell was repeated. I had not extended my trip west into California and in answer to a question said I had not conferred with the Central Pacific management. The question was asked, why? I answered, the Central Pacific and all the states it traverses are assigned to another division, therefore, I had no right to visit San Francisco and open negotiations without authority, and it seemed best to fasten a spike as far as we had gone, rather than to risk all on the delay such action might involve, where one party was disinclined to consent to a quicker schedule.

I returned to Omaha, closed the arrangement with the Union Pacific and the Oregon Short Line satisfactorily, and said I would go on to San Francisco at once to negotiate with the Central Pacific people for the quickening of the schedule of the train that could connect best with the Union Pacific fast mail at Ogden, thus establishing a fast mail without a break from New York and Boston to San Francisco and Portland, but remarked that I was acquainted with but one of their general officers, and that one fortunately was Mr. Towne. Thereupon Mr. Holcomb said he would tell Mr. Dickinson to take his car and go with me, which he did.

On our arrival at San Francisco I made an appointment with Vice-President Towne for the next day. We called at the office of the Southern Pacific Company rather early and visited Mr. J. W. Fillmore, the manager, first, and found a large, genial looking gentleman, who, during our conversation, expressed a favorable opinion of the "special mail service," and hoped I would be successful in the interview about to take place. Mr. Fillmore escorted us to the rooms of Mr. Towne and introduced us to that gentleman, who welcomed us. Knowing that his time was always occupied, I sketched my mission as rapidly as possible and then gave Mr. Dickinson an opportunity to tell what the Union Pacific Company had bound itself and leased lines to do, and to express his opinion of it as a business transaction. I noticed that Mr. Towne had not thrown up his hands, so I took up the case again to explain a phase of it that I had held in reserve while I was studying the play of his mind, and reminded him that we had perfected an agreement under which the mails would be carried into Portland, Ore., made ready by clerks on the train, for immediate delivery to the carriers on arrival of the train in the depot at 6:40 a. m., and at once by them to the patrons of the Portland office, thus gaining twelve hours in arriving time and twenty-four hours in the actual delivery of the mail over that for San Francisco and on a longer haul. I said, "Please consider this, Mr. Towne, and tell me if you believe the business interests absolutely dependent upon your lines, the traveling public, tourists, sick and well, who are so large a part of your regular and transient population and custom; the financial and commercial houses of San Francisco, will submit quietly to such discrimination long."

Mr. Towne said he had not thought of the subject from that standpoint, but would do so at once, and requested me to call in the morning. I called, and I think it was October 14, 1889, for I have a copy of the original agreement signed that day. It provided for an arrival at San Francisco at 9:45 a. m., instead of 7:30 p. m. of the same day, thus insuring ten and one-quarter hours' earlier arrival and about twenty-two hours' earlier delivery to the addressees.

For the return, or east-bound run, it was provided that the train would leave San Francisco at 6:30 p. m., and arrive at Ogden at 6:30 a. m., second day, and that during the summer months this time would be shortened as much as the company deemed safe. It was also added, "the Southern Pacific Company agrees that the trains which this proposition covers shall be the fastest trains run over their lines between the points named." During this morning call the agreement was signed by Mr. Towne.

When the Ogden & San Francisco fast mail made its first run west, and always afterwards, city distributers for the latter city were employed on it to prepare the mail for immediate delivery by the carriers to the addressees on arrival in the city. The effect of the better schedule and distribution was felt materially by all the towns in the state of California that were supplied directly or indirectly by mail routes that connected with this fast mail train. Towns on the line of the Los Angeles & San Francisco R. P. O., not many miles west of the former city, were supplied with mail from the east via Omaha & Ogden, and Ogden & San Francisco R. P. O.'s, earlier than when dispatched by the more southern route, passing through Kansas City, La Junta, Albuquerque, Ashfork, Flagstaff and Los Angeles. To accomplish this the mail for that line was discharged from the fast mail at Sacramento and forwarded via Stockton, Fresno, Bakersfield, etc.

The negotiations ended, the most important work necessary to place the fast mails in successful operation had to be attended to in Omaha and Chicago. Therefore, we returned to our respective headquarters without delay. New cars and additional clerks were secured, the readjustment of the forces of clerks employed on the Union Pacific, Northern Pacific, and Great Northern was made to conform to the shrinkage of mail on the last two by diversion from and increase on the first by diversion to.

On November 15, 1889, at 7 p. m. (45 minutes late), the first fast mail pulled out of Omaha, with about thirteen tons of mail, a considerable portion of which was destined for the Green River & Huntington, Ore., and the Huntington & Portland R. P. O.'s. Vice-President Holcomb was very considerate of our comfort and enjoyment once more. He placed General Manager Dickinson with his special car at our disposal and never were men blessed with a more agreeable guide, philosopher and friend.

Mr. Edward Dickinson and the writer had as guests on this trip, Mr. Alexander Grant, then chief clerk of the railway mail service, now general superintendent; Mr. John M. Hubbard, assistant postmaster at Chicago; Mr. C. E. Brown, traveling passenger and advertising agent of the Union Pacific; Mr. F. A. Dunneka, correspondent of the New York *World;* Mr. Ernest Lambert, correspondent of the New York *Tribune;* Mr. F. R. Waddell, correspondent of the Chicago *Inter-Ocean;* Mr. M. Fible, correspondent of the Chicago *Tribune;* Mr. C. J. Seymour, correspondent of the Chicago *Herald*; Mr. R. J. Clancy, correspondent of the Omaha *Bee;* Mr. Frank Arkins, correspondent of the Denver *News;* Mr. Robert Gauss, correspondent of the Denver *Republican;* Mr. C. R. Hanna, correspondent of the San Francisco *Examiner,* etc., etc.

The grade of the road from Omaha to Cheyenne seems to me to be up, but some contend that there are long stretches in the Platte River valley of level country; I have noticed, however, in passing over the road many times, that the west-bound trains are always taut; the engine calling on her steam to a greater or less extent, and have been on the train many times when she has swung down from Cheyenne to North Platte at the rate of seventy miles an hour with the engine holding back in the breeching or kicking against the crossbar.

The distance from Omaha to Cheyenne is about 500 miles, mostly up-grade, west-bound as I have said, but whether it is up or down or on the level, we arrived at the latter city on time, changed mail and train crews and moved on to Sherman station, thirty miles west of Cheyenne, and then came to a standstill on the highest point on this transcontinental line between ocean and ocean, 8,247 feet above sea level. A little farther west we came to Dale Creek bridge, made of iron, stretching in a single span of 650 feet from bank to bank of the little stream that flows on and on 127 feet below. From Sherman we moved down grade past Laramie, where "Bill Nye," in early days, published an interesting and humorous newspaper, from which he graduated into the humorous lecture field; it was there also that he learned that the way to avoid buying canned fruits, or buying the fruit and canning it, was to raise it already canned on trees in his country home, and it was here that the populi were wont to decorate the telegraph poles with the badly disorganized "stranger within the gates" with whom they were not "en rapport."

On we rode until we reached Green River, where a stop was made for train orders and to discharge such matter as was to be forwarded by the Oregon Short Line for points and connections between Granger and Portland. During this time the train that had brought us from Omaha was being divided; the cars intended for the Granger & Portland R. P. O. were being switched onto one track, and those that were to constitute our train were being kept together as much as possible on the main line. During this work our special car had been misplaced, and when our train was supposed to be ready to go the signal was given and she pulled out without us, which was not discovered until twelve minutes later; then it took fifteen minutes to correct the blunder. This, with the twenty-three minutes lost before arriving at Green River, gave us an aggregate of fifty minutes to make up before arriving at Ogden; there was a strong head wind blowing down the east slope of the Wasatch mountains and a grade to overcome that in some places was 211 feet per mile, so that it was not possible to make good the loss between Green River and Wasatch. At Evanston, just east of Wasatch, our engine was relieved by a more powerful one, and the engineer by a reckless one, named "Bill" Downing, who understood that it was his business to get into Ogden on time, and he started to do it. The train commenced to climb the east slope of the Wasatch range and with every pound of steam the engine could carry, working with savage energy, she reached Wasatch Station without further loss of time, her speed increasing as the resistance on the up-grade decreased until she reached the summit and the decline began. Downing's hand rested on the controlling lever, but it was motionless; he was using as much power on the level and decline as when breasting old Wasatch with ten cars behind him; and as we approached the opening into Echo Canon the speed continued, where the decline is sometimes 250 feet per mile and the road "as crooked as a ram's horn." Tunnel after tunnel succeeded each other; the speed, considering the chorography, was terrific, and as we looked down into the depth of the canon a feeling of awe came over us like that which takes possession of brave men who look upon death in violent forms from great heights or amidst horrible surroundings.

This ride of seventy-six miles can be shown best by quoting the following from an article written by one of the correspondents who was with us on the trip:

"At Evanston the train was forty minutes late; the distance to Ogden was seventy-six miles, and a freight engineer named 'Bill' Downing was placed in charge of the train. 'Bill' is a typical mountain engineer. He walked to the rear of the car and speaking to one of the reporters said: 'It is seventy-six miles to Ogden and I will not be happy until I make it in seventy-two minutes.' He was told that such a remarkable run was impossible down Weber Canon. When he threw the lever forward and opened her throttle the train made a sudden start that settled everybody's dinner. When the train was finally under way someone remarked that it would be a terrible thing to run off the track, and Captain White thought all the curves on the line were being straightened out by the tremendous speed. The rush of wind outside told of the rapid rate at which the train was traveling. Dust rolled from beneath the coaches in volumes and was caught up by the rush of the wind. Sparks shining like a million of meteors followed in the wake of the rear coach. Faster and faster the train swept down the canon, around curves, across small plateaus, roaring over bridges and tearing through tunnels like a bolt of lightning cast from the sky. Those in the cars could hear the wheels grind on the curves and the continuous striking as they whirled from one rail to another. The train rocked from side to side, the engine traveling as fast as possible on that awful decline."

Another correspondent wrote to his paper: "The run began at Castle Rock. At Devil's Gate, where the track was not so crooked, the pace was awful. 'Three miles in two minutes,' gasped Captain White, reading the speed indicator which had been placed in the special coach. Engineer Downing did not abate his speed a tittle. Down the winding line of Tapioca Gulch the special car in the rear was swinging from side to side. * * * * Still 'Bill' Downing did not slacken his speed. Half of the newspaper correspondents fainted through nervous exhaustion in trying to keep their balance. Nearly all the remaining passengers had already succumbed. Suddenly, in rounding the reverse loop at Antelope Gap the coach was careened until it only hung to the rail by one wheel. As soon as the moment of suspense was over and the coach righted General Manager Dickinson sprang to his feet and called, 'Pull the bell rope, Brown, then run forward and tell Downing to stop this if he wants us to reach Ogden alive.' 'Let the schedule go,' said Mr. Dickinson, to the press agent of the road, then not to run such a risk another second the General Manager sprang to the rear platform of the coach and swung the brake with all his might."

"The seventy-six miles of intricately curved track had been ridden over in one hour and five minutes—65 minutes. It was a hair-

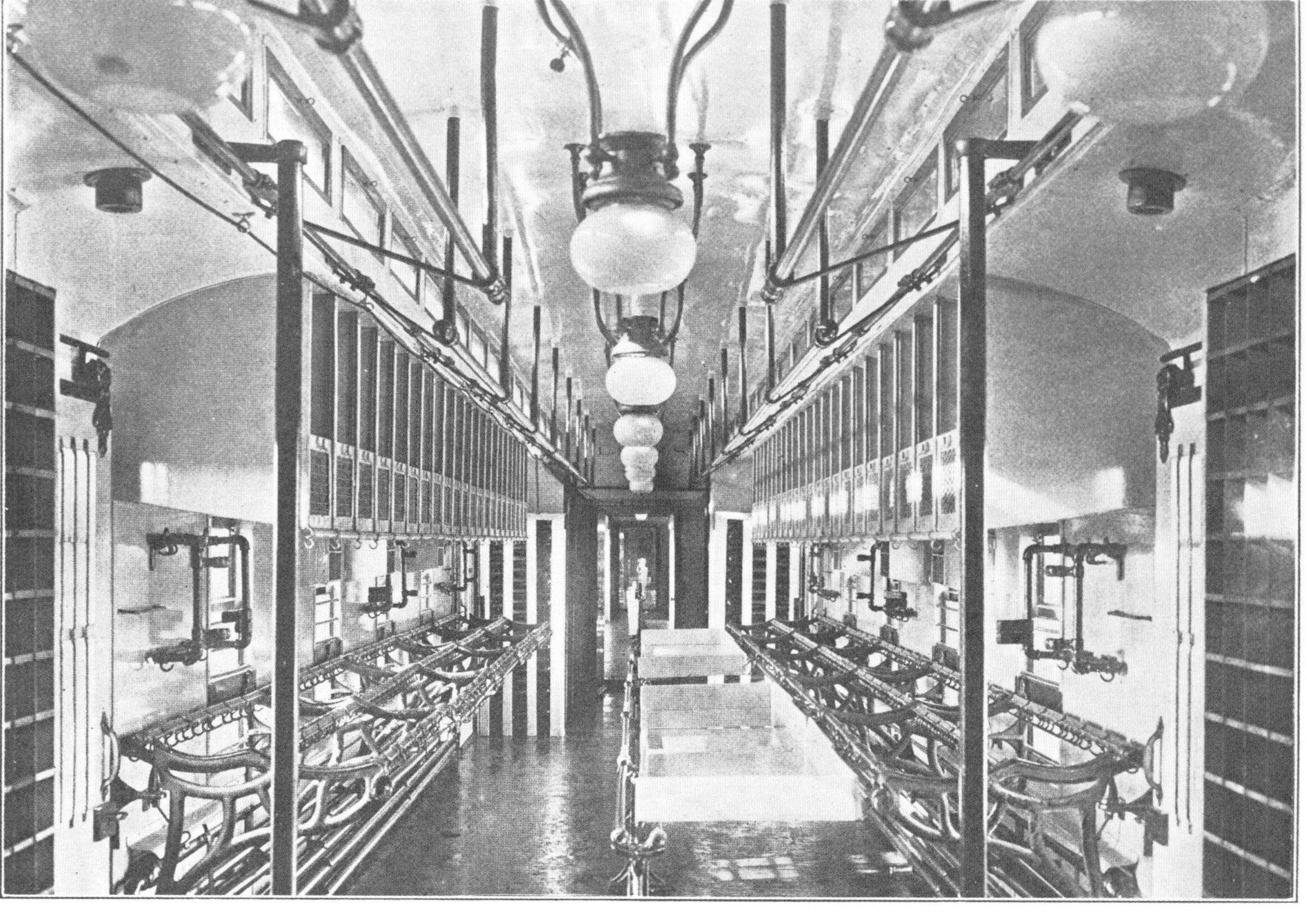

Interior New York and Chicago Fast Mail Car

raising record, and several passengers who went through it have not yet recuperated."

The superintendent of the Eighth or San Francisco Division, Mr. James L. Wilder, joined us at Ogden, fully prepared to insure the distribution of the mail for his territory, and to have the San Francisco letter mail made up to carrier routes so that the carriers could commence the delivery throughout the city without delay. Mr. Wilder was an excellent officer and was for many years one of my chief clerks in the Fourth, Fifth and Sixth Divisions and also served as an assistant superintendent, and superintendent under my jurisdiction. His death was lamented very much.

The run from Ogden to San Francisco was without incident, because not much of the gain in the schedule time between Chicago and San Francisco fell upon that route. The fast mail arrived at Oakland Pier on time, and but for the head wind across the bay the first mail would have been thrown ashore five minutes earlier.

"This experimental trip," Captain White said exultantly, "demonstrates that we can place the people of the two seaboards nearer together for postal purposes by twenty-four hours than they have ever been before and that we can do it every day, as we shall."

"To understand what the new fast mail means," said Alexander Grant, chief clerk of the railway mail service at Washington, "it is only necessary to reflect that the mail we deliver this morning could not otherwise be delivered until a day later. In fact the mail under the new fast schedule was delivered as early as the mail which left Chicago the day before under the old schedule. While there is a gain of but ten hours for passengers accompanying the fast mail, there is a gain of one day in the postal service, as formerly the mail arrived at 7:45 p. m., and could not be delivered until next day."

The party remained in San Francisco until the evening of the second day, visiting places of interest, such as the parks, Chinatown and the Cliff House, from which the sea lions were seen sporting on the rocky island in front; some of them were great powerful fellows with awkward, lumbering bodies. They roared like the "Bulls of Bashan," plunged into the waters, where they were graceful, and had a hale old time.

On the evening of the second day we renewed our long journey, moving northward to Portland, Ore., via the Sacramento, Mount Shasta, the Klamath and Willamette; we stayed in Portland two days, and the party was charmed with it and the generous reception accorded. Two days later we were in Tacoma, Washington, a beautiful, progressive and well-behaved city; it has grown very much since

1889, and is regarded as one of the most important cities in the state; it has a population of more than 100,000. We next visited Seattle of the same state—which has a population of about 250,000 and occupies a commanding position on Puget Sound. In May or June, 1889, it was much smaller than it is now, very much, and was almost destroyed by fire, but its natural advantages had come to be known by men of means and the Government, and those financiers who are always on the lookout for investments, camped in that locality, and if they did not buy city lots and improve them, were willing to loan money to make the improvements and to take mortgages on the improved property as security. Seattle has been booming ever since, and is by far the largest and most aggressive city in the state. As has been said, it is on Puget Sound, and has commerce by water with the outside world via Admiralty Inlet and the strait of Juan Fuca; it is the base of supply for Alaska and is a naval station, and bound to be the great city of the extreme northwest.

The following day we made a trip by the steamer Olympia to Port Townsend and steamed diagonally across the Sound to Victoria, B. C., where we were shown the city, and handsomely entertained in the evening at the Hotel Clarence.

Next day our return trip was commenced. At Seattle we were met by a number of her prominent citizens, driven in carriages about the city and banqueted at the Ranier Hotel. That night we remained sometime in Tacoma and the next day our car was attached to the east-bound fast mail at Portland, at 7 a. m., and moved out up the Columbia River by The Dalles, The Bridal Vale and Mount Hood, over the track of the Oregon Railway and Navigation Company and the Oregon Short Line, and the next morning at 9 o'clock were side-tracked at Shoshone station, Idaho, and were immediately driven in wagons across the country to Shoshone Falls, which is in the Snake River Valley. These falls are higher than Niagara, and the geological formation of the valley, the river's bed, and the country surrounding the crest, and especially above it, is wonderful. It is of volcanic origin and composed of some solid lava, and some disintegrated and decayed substances. It seemed almost impossible for a layman to understand whether he was moving over a new born creation or witnessing the revivification of one that was old when some that are old now were new.

I never saw anything like it but once and that was before the Oregon Short Line was built. I had made a trip over the Butte & Ogden R. P. O. and left the train at Oneida, Idaho, hired a horse, and rode alone, not meeting a human being en route, thirty miles to

Soda Springs, Idaho, and saw valleys that were full of extinct volcanoes down whose sides rivers of molten lava must have flowed, for the craters were scarcely more than a hundred and fifty feet above the level surface which was scarred with crevices more than a foot wide.

We returned in the evening to Shoshone, had Thanksgiving dinner in our car, and then moved down to Soda Springs, which is in the same section of the state, and where there are many springs whose water is strongly impregnated with soda which is forced up some feet above the level of the ground by pressure from below, and bubbles over like water forced upward from a fountain in a park; but this water throws off a sediment which hardens around the circle of the jet until it closes it in; sometimes the mound thus created is fifteen or twenty feet in height and as much in diameter. A hard shell forms on the outside, hard enough to walk upon, but you can break the crust with your pocket knife and the water will ooze through freely. Dead animals are hung at times under improvised shelter, and the water that oozes from the shell is conducted so as to flow over the bodies, which become completely incased and preserved. As soon as the Granger & Portland fast mail arrived at Soda Springs, east-bound, we were coupled onto it and run down to Green River; attached to the Omaha & Ogden fast mail and kept moving until we arrived at our several homes, Omaha, Chicago, New York and Washington.

Fast mail service existed between New York, Boston, Chicago and Omaha at the time of the establishment of this service, from Omaha to San Francisco, and Portland, Nov. 17, 1889, as follows:

MILEAGE.

Boston, Mass., to San Francisco, Cal., 3,293 miles.
New York, N. Y., to San Francisco, Cal., 3,239 miles.
Boston, Mass., to Portland, Ore., 3,306 miles.
New York. N. Y., to Portland, Ore., 3,252 miles.

TIME.

Boston, Mass., to San Francisco, Cal., 109 hours, 45 minutes.
New York, N. Y., to San Francisco, Cal., 108 hours, 45 minutes.
Boston, Mass., to Portland, Ore., 106 hours, 40 minutes.
New York, N. Y., to Portland, Ore., 104 hours, 55 minutes.

RETURN TIME.

San Francisco, Cal., to New York, N. Y., 127 hours, 30 minutes.
San Francisco, Cal., to Boston, Mass., 131 hours, 50 minutes.
Portland, Ore., to Boston, Mass., 120 hours, 50 minutes.
Portland, Ore., to New York, N. Y., 116 hours, 30 minutes.

SCHEDULE WEST.

Left Boston, 7 p. m.; New York, 9 p. m.; arrived Chicago, 12:35 a. m.; left 3 a. m.; arrived Omaha, 5:30 p. m.; left 6:30 p. m.; arrived Granger, Wyo., ———; arrived Ogden, 12:30 a. m.; left at 12:50 a. m.; arrived San Francisco, 9:45 a. m.; arrived at Portland, Oregon, 7 a. m.

SCHEDULE EAST.

Left San Francisco, 8 p. m.; left Portland the following 7 a. m.; arrived Ogden, 8 a. m.; arrived Granger, ———; arrived Omaha, 4 p. m.; arrived Chicago, 7 a. m.; arrived New York, 10:30 a. m., and Boston, 2:50 p. m.

This was considered good time in 1889, and it was a vast improvement over the first fast mail, but a real live fast mail was unknown between New York, Boston and Chicago until the present schedule of No. 35, New York & Chicago Fast Mail, was issued, and all the fast mails that had been running in connection with it quickened their schedules likewise; then a splendid improvement occurred. The best previous time between the cities named and San Francisco and Portland was cut as follows:

Between New York and San Francisco to 87 hours, 53 minutes; between Boston and San Francisco to 89 hours, 38 minutes; between New York and Portland to 95 hours, 35 minutes; between Boston and Portland to 96 hours, 40 minutes.

The effect in expediting the mails all over the west, northwest and southwest by this schedule of No. 35 is most valuable and is so great that man cannot compute it. I, of course, understand that such wonders could not have occurred had not the increase of our mail been phenomenal, indeed it has been so phenomenal that evidently the companies have thought best to encourage it by increased facilities.

This is evidenced by the present schedules of the companies that provided and withdrew the first so-called fast mail:

WEST.

No. 35, leaves New York, 9:30 p. m.; Buffalo, 8:05 a. m.; Cleveland, 11:35 a. m.; Chicago, 8:20 p. m.

No. 43, leaves New York, 3:05 a. m.; Buffalo, 1:15 p. m.; Cleveland, 4:40 p. m.; Chicago, 1:20 a. m.

No. 3, leaves New York, 8:46 a. m.; Buffalo, 7:15 p. m.; Cleveland, 10:45 p. m.; Chicago, 7:30 a. m.

No. 9, leaves New York, 12:51 p. m.; Buffalo, 11:05 p. m.; Cleveland, 2:50 a. m.; Chicago, 11:52 a. m.

No. 21, leaves New York, 5:21 p. m.; Buffalo, 3:40 p. m.; Cleveland, 7:05 a. m.; Chicago, 4:00 p. m.

HON. A. H. STEPHENS
Superintendent Eighth Division R. M. S.
(See Appendix)

EAST.

No. 32, leaves Chicago, 3:00 a. m.; Cleveland, 11:30 a. m.; Buffalo, 5:05 p. m.; New York, 4:04 a. m.

No. 4, leaves Chicago, 8:25 a. m.; Cleveland, 4:20 p. m.; Buffalo, 9:28 p. m.; New York, 7:55 a. m.

No. 30, leaves Chicago, 5:25 p. m.; Cleveland, 1:50 a. m.; Buffalo, 7:30 a. m.; New York, 5:48 p. m.

No. 10, leaves Chicago, 10:30 a. m.; Cleveland, 7:40 a. m.; Buffalo, 1:45 a. m.; New York, 1:49 p. m.

No. 16, leaves Chicago, 1:40 p. m.; Cleveland, 10:25 p. m.; Buffalo, 4:05 a. m.; New York, 3:45 p. m.

If further testimony or figures are needed to convince anyone that the present schedules are made for the expedition of the mail and the benefit of the people as a whole they can be furnished.

HISTORY.

Immediately after my last promotion I made an extended tour of the Pacific coast states to ascertain if the condition of the service in Idaho, Montana, Oregon and Washington was such as to justify compliance with the demand of the citizens of those states that an additional division be created, with headquarters at Portland, Oregon, for their benefit and that of the territory of Alaska, or whether such inefficiencies and insufficiencies as existed might not be remedied in an effectual manner with larger economy.

At the time of this inspection, 1890, the aggregate population of the Eighth division was 2,268,958; less than half that of the First (or New England) division, whereas its area, not including Alaska, which is 577,390 square miles, was more than eleven times greater and its acreage of farm land about four times less, being 13 per cent. of the whole as against 57 per cent. in the First. The aggregate population of Idaho, Oregon and Washington was then 747,542, now it is about 1,457,121, more than 413,049 greater than that of the whole Eighth division in 1874, when it was so designated. Observation and inquiry satisfied me that such deficiencies of service as existed then, and such prospective growth of population and productiveness as were likely to occur in the immediate future, could be provided for by properly placing some additional service and re-arranging some that had been established. In addition to this I held that because of the remoteness of these states from San Francisco, the headquarters of the division, and the physical formation of the country, which was such as to interpose obstacles to free and quick intercommunication between sections, there should be stationed at Portland, Oregon, an experienced officer of our service, known to be of first-class capacity and clear judgment, capable of acting as the direct representative of the Post Office Department in special cases, diplomatically, and without danger of home friction; one who would be in touch with the development of those states at all times, and keep the Department advised of their needs either directly or through the superintendent of the division. This arrangement was perfected and existed until recently. Mr. Frank W. Vaille, the present superintendent of the Thirteenth division, was the first officer so assigned and he demonstrated his fitness in advance.

The tour of inspection was extended south as soon as the railroad and steamboat service in the states named had received critical attention, and some unsatisfactory matters corrected. Some time was given to Mr. Flint in San Francisco, who was acting as superintendent, Mr. Wilder, the superintendent, being very ill and absent. When we left San Francisco we made a short visit to Sacramento, Cal., and proceeded thence to Los Angeles, San Diego, Santa Barbara, Albuquerque, etc., taking Mr. Flint along. My time was fully occupied with correspondence, listening to such suggestions respecting the service as the good people whom I met desired to make, each being encouraged to speak freely, and relief being given when possible; making memoranda of and verifying such statements as seemed in the least doubtful, thus preparing the cases, to which they related, for definite action without further investigation.

It would have been impossible to accomplish all that was done on this tour, if David B. Todd had not accompanied me in the capacity of stenographer, carrying a typewriting machine but little smaller than himself. Our David, however, handled it as easily as David of old did the Philistine warrior, Goliath. David was an unknown quantity to me then, for I had not had time to become acquainted with any one in my office, who were strangers to me, before I was rushed to the Pacific; but before we returned I formed a liking for him and retained him as my secretary until I retired.

While working around Los Angeles I ran out to the suburban town in which Supt. Wilder and his wife were residing temporarily, to see him, and was grieved to find him very ill, so ill that his life was despaired of. He endured his affliction with fortitude; but quickly grew worse, and resigned his office June 1, 1891, being succeeded by Mr. Flint.

James L. Wilder was one of the early appointees of the service. He entered it as a route agent in the state of Wisconsin, and was advanced class by class on merit, becoming in time chief head clerk at

Milwaukee, Wis., special agent of the Post Office Department, assistant superintendent in the Sixth division, and ended his career as superintendent of the Eighth division. He was a rough diamond, true as a man and an officer; competent, faithful, and loyal. His whole service was in the Chicago division, except the time he was superintendent of the San Francisco division. He died at his old home in Oshkosh, Wis., on the 28th day of June, 1892, and is remembered for his many excellent qualities.

More than seven weeks were devoted to this tour and the results were satisfactory to the Department and the people most interested, for the service was very materially improved and the creation of an additional division was deferred eighteen years without detriment to the commercial interests of the extreme northwestern group of states, comprising the major portion of the present Thirteenth division.

The results were:

Thirteen hundred miles of additional railway post office service was established, 613 of it between October 29th and December 31st, 1890; and 17 railway post offices and railroad lines centering at and adjacent to Spokane, Wash., that were under the immediate jurisdiction of the chief clerk at Portland, Oregon, were assigned temporarily to the chief clerk at Helena, Montana, to insure better supervision. Desk room was secured for the latter in the depot at Spokane, and arrangements were made for him to spend a portion of his time in inspecting the lines and examining the clerks. Mr. Barclay was the chief clerk at Helena at that time and I regarded him as a very bright and competent officer.

Many lines were strengthened. Such points on Puget Sound as could be better supplied by rail than by steamboat were withdrawn from the latter and given to the former; the railway post office service, Huntington to Portland, Oregon, was duplicated between Pendleton and Portland; railway post office service was established in lieu of closed pouch service between Blaine and Sedro, Wash., which provided service by rail from the east via Portland, Tacoma and Seattle, with all points north of Anacortes and Sedro on Puget Sound and in British Columbia. The same class of service was extended from Woolley to Anacortes, the clerks running through from Tacoma to Anacortes and connecting at Woolley with the Blaine and Sedro railway post office. Service by clerks was also established between Centralia and Hoquiam, making a line from Tacoma to the latter place, and additional service was placed on the route from Seattle to Portland. Additional railway post office service was established between San Francisco and Pacific Grove, Cal., and between Los Angeles and

National City. Much more was done during the fiscal year 1891, but enough has been mentioned to show that the service in those states was put in first-class condition, and to explain why the people were satisfied.

REHABILITATION.

The clerks of all the divisions had been applying themselves to master the schemes of distribution and to make creditable records on their general work and conduct. They had shown that they comprehended the expectations of the Department, the exalted character of their employment, and the need to excel in it to be counted worthy to rank as members of the corps of clerks composed of the fittest; this, too, independent of the fact that Postmaster General Wanamaker had caused it to be announced that he would present gold medals for the best record in each division, and one at large.

These were splendid medals, not only intrinsically and artistically, but especially because they represented the views of one of the greatest merchant princes of the world, as well as one of the most competent Postmasters General, respecting the importance to success in any business, of thorough knowledge of that business.

The medal contest closed with the calendar year 1890. The awards were made in January, 1891, and the Fifth division held its "Second Annual Reception" at division headquarters on the evening of February 19, 1891.

During this contest a change had occurred in the General Superintendency, the writer succeeding Mr. Bell, who had been appointed Second Assistant Postmaster General. The Postmaster General and the Second Assistant had intended to be present at this reception, but, as the date set for it approached, it was found that it clashed with engagements they could not defer, and so were reluctantly compelled to forego the pleasure. I cannot say that their loss was my gain, because I should have been present in any event, and there was plenty, and more, of everything good and pleasant to insure the enjoyment of all who were expected.

The day preceding the festivities Mr. Grant and I picked up our grips and started for the Mecca of the devout followers of the examination case in the Fifth division. We arrived, were welcomed by a host of friends, and met many other guests, among whom were Superintendents Lewis L. Troy, James P. Lindsay, George W. Pepper and Norman Perkins; Assistant Superintendent Victor J. Bradley; Chief Clerks P. P. Waring, A. J. Miller, F. C. Gore, James McConnell; Postmaster James Brown of Toledo, Ohio, and Assistant Postmasters

Hon. Charles Rager
Superintendent Fifth Division R. M. S.
(See Appendix)

Thompson and Lanning of Indianapolis, Ind., and Columbus, Ohio, respectively.

As on the previous occasion, Mr. Burt was the master of ceremonies, and the toastmaster, and as usual acquitted himself with eclat. Most of the guests responded very pleasantly as they were called out; some addresses were instructive, and all were interesting.

The medal for this division was won by Mr. C. V. McChesney, class 5, Grafton and Cincinnati railway post office, he having distributed 99.98 per cent. of 10,367 post offices correctly into 608 separations in 7 hours and 1 minute—a very excellent record.

Messrs. C. D. Rogers and G. W. Althouse, class 5; E. S. Williams and E. D. Massie, class 4; C. R. Hedrick and J. R. Buck, class 3; C. G. Mendenhall and A. W. Suttles, class 2; L. O. Brookshire and J. E. Bellville, class 1, received honorable mention, and the hearty congratulations of the Postmaster General, through the medium of the General Superintendent, who considered himself highly favored in being instructed to perform this function and in the opportunity to participate in the pleasure of the occasion.

The "Postal Clerks' Lament" by the office quartette, and "Our Wives and Sweethearts" by Harry First—who may be regarded as an expert in that line of oratory—were gems of their class and were enthusiastically applauded. This was a memorable occasion, one that will never be forgotten by the service, I am sure.

The General Superintendent presented one medal for the competition of the whole service for 1891; the officers of the Fifth division offered five for competition in that division.

The following year, 1892, the Postmaster General offered one medal for the best record in each division.

These several manifestations of interest in the service and the evident desire that the clerks excel in their work were fruitful. The receptions at which the medal presentations occurred were rare events. Many members of the division assembled each time they were held at headquarters, escorting wives, mothers, daughters, sisters and sweethearts, and made the banquet room and communicating halls resound with notes of joy and gladness; those of the division were devoted to each other and all to their guests; the addresses were good, full of worthy thoughts, replete with wit, poetry and anecdote; later came music, song, the dance and then the good-nights and good-byes. I believe the receptions produced happiness, harmony, subordination, loyalty, and, combined with the medals, strengthened the determination to excel at a time when the service was not permeated with the *esprit de corps* of to-day. In fact, the habit of making good records became chronic with most of the men and it is so now. With practice the mastery of the schemes has become less of a problem than it was immediately after the dawn of the resurrection.

CIVIL SERVICE EXAMINATION.

The civil service examination has demonstrated that a large majority of those who gain admission into the service are of good intellectual ability and fairly well educated, and the examination case has shown that this majority has the capacity, with proper instruction and encouragement, to memorize the schemes of distribution and schedules of connections at junctions. Nevertheless, it was discovered soon after the present civil service laws and rules became operative that effective provision had not been made to ascertain who were physically unsound, and to bar them from the educational examination as being disqualified for a service demanding perfect physical manhood.

Defective eyesight, heart action, lungs, limbs, muscular and nervous systems are, to a considerable extent, products of the railway mail service, and when they exist they become more active and harmful in than out of the service. If it could be known at the examination that any of these defects were hereditary in the ancestors of an applicant, though apparently absent in him, it would be in the interest of the service, the beneficial associations, and the Government to exclude him from the educational examination. It would also be in the interest of the employees because the nearer the corps approaches the maximum of physical and mental strength, individually and collectively, the greater its capacity for work and the longer its period of usefulness. These demands would be bound to argue for greater consideration of the welfare of the clerks in most respects, larger compensation, retirement on pay when unfitted for work by injuries while on duty, or upon arriving at an advanced age. There are other prohibitory defects, such as impaired hearing, impediment of speech, and the failure to measure up to a fixed height and weight.

This oversight was discussed earnestly in the convention of superintendents of divisions held at Washington, D. C., in 1891. The result was, as expected from experienced and reliable officers, the affirmation of the necessity for a thoroughly reliable physical examination to precede the educational. Upon this, action was taken without delay. The matter was presented to the Civil Service Commission, who assured me they would support any practical measure recommended by the Department. In my report for the fiscal year 1891 I made a recommendation prefacing it substantially with these remarks:

"Unfortunately many of the appointees have been deficient in stamina and therefore could not endure the hardships incident to continuous mental and physical labor under such conditions as surround railway postal clerks, who work upon trains running at a high rate of speed around curves, over crossings and bridges, past other trains moving at the same velocity, and by rattling switches. No one who has not experienced it can understand how great is the exertion required to maintain one's position at the cases and racks so as to distribute mail matter with the utmost freedom of action and accurately, nor can those who have not participated in railway accidents or stood for hours over the trucks of a fast moving car distributing the mail, piece by piece, or spent his lay-off hours in memorizing the distribution and connections of a large number of states, understand the extent of the mental strain and nervous exhaustion that overtakes a clerk at times.

"It is true that Form No. 1, Voucher 4, of application for civil service examination, contains ten questions which are to be answered by the physician who certifies as to the physical condition of the applicant, but these questions are not full enough to determine the candidate's physical adaptability for the service. The physician is not required to make his statements under oath, and as a consequence there are abundant reasons to believe that friendship, personal obligations, family ties, and the desire to accommodate acquaintances sometimes impel him to be more merciful than is consistent with professional responsibility or reputation. If this were not true it would be impossible for the deformed and ruptured or those afflicted with pulmonary diseases to secure appointments. The character of the service and the apparent indulgent and unreliable nature of some of the examinations made by physicians, as indicated in the unsound and effeminate condition of many who are certified and appointed to this service, show the imperative necessity for more stringent rules to govern *physical examinations;* and I therefore recommend that at every place where civil service examinations are held, one or more physicians of acknowledged ability and trustworthiness be designated by the Civil Service Commission or by the Postmaster General to make the physical examination required, and that they shall receive from the applicants whom they examine a reasonable fee for their services.

"I also recommend that the physical examination shall be made on the following lines:

(1)   Minimum height, 5 feet, 4 inches.
(2)   Minimum weight, 128 pounds.
(3)   Condition of sight.

(4)	Is his hearing defective?

(5)	Has he any defects of speech?

(6)	Has he any defects of limb?

(7)	Is he ruptured?

(8)	Has he any defects in the functions of the brain?

(9)	Has he any defects in the functions of the nervous system?

(10) Has he any defects in the functions of the muscular system?

(11) State the measurement of the chest upon full expiration and inspiration.

(12) Is the respiration full, free and unobstructed in both lungs?

(13) State the frequency of the heart's action; are its movements regular, or are there indications of organic, muscular or nervous derangements?

(14) Any indications of derangement of abdominal viscera?

(15) Any indications that the applicant is addicted to the excessive use of intoxicants?

(16) Do you believe him capable of prolonged and severe mental and physical exertion, and equal to the demands of a very exhausting occupation?

(17) Do you believe him to be free from any form of disease or disability which unfits him at present or is likely to unfit him in the future for the performance of the class of work described in question No. 16?

"The minimum height given is as low as should be allowed in view of the fact that the cases, racks and tables used in the postal cars are of a standard and uniform height, and can not be lowered without reducing their capacity or discommoding a majority of the employees of the service.

"By adopting and strictly enforcing the stringent physical examination herein provided for the service will be placed on a better business basis, and the proposed superannuation act would, if it becomes a law, be very materially strengthened and its successful operation insured."

This recommendation was approved by the Post Office Department and also by the Civil Service Commission, and the physical examination was instituted as soon as it could be prepared. In the report for the fiscal year ended June 30, 1892, it was mentioned under the heading, "Civil Service Examinations," as follows:

"It affords this office great pleasure to state that the recommendation made in its last report, that applicants for examination for positions in the railway mail service be subjected to a more stringent physical examination, has been carried into effect. If the examining physician is competent and conscientious it is now impossible for an unhealthy or unsound man to enter the service, and the effect of the change has been very beneficial. The best interests of the service seemed to make a modification of some of the rules desirable, and it is gratifying to record the fact that upon a proper showing the commission invariably co-operated with this office in all its efforts in that direction."

The allusion made to the Civil Service Commission brought out a letter, which I prize very highly. The following is a copy of it:

"UNITED STATES CIVIL SERVICE COMMISSION,

"Washington, D. C., December 29, 1892.

"Hon. James E . White, General Superintendent Railway Mail Service, Washington, D. C.

"MY DEAR SIR: I wish to thank you very heartily for your courteous allusion to the Civil Service Commission in your excellent annual report. The allusion was a matter of peculiar gratification both to myself and to the rest of the commission; particularly coming as it did from a gentleman of your reputation and experience. We have done our best to co-operate in every way with your branch as with all others of the Government service in the effort to obtain the best possible kind of public employees, and we appreciate very heartily so frank and kindly an acknowledgment of our efforts as that you made.

"With assurances of esteem,

"Very truly yours,

"(Signed)   THEODORE ROOSEVELT."

As soon as favorable action was taken upon the recommendation we commenced framing a form of medical certificate to be used wherever examinations were made. Samples of the form followed in the regular army examination of recruits and suggestions from specialists were secured. The division superintendents were very much interested in this innovation and sent to the office all information on the subject they could secure and that they believed would be helpful. The result was the adoption of a form similar to the following:

"MEDICAL CERTIFICATE

"For Railway Mail Applicants Only.

Every applicant for the railway mail service must be examined by a physician, who must execute the following certificate. Applicants who are under 5 feet, 4 inches in height or under 125 pounds in weight are not eligible for this examination. N. B.—The examining physician is requested to read this certificate carefully before beginning the examination.

(All entries upon this certificate must be written in ink.)

---

1. What is the applicant's exact height in his bare feet? (The physician must measure the applicant.) ....feet....inches

2. What is the applicant's exact weight in his ordinary clothing, without overcoat or hat? (The physician must weigh the applicant.) ....pounds

3. Did you yourself weigh and measure the applicant? ....

4. What is the condition of the applicant's sight? (If possible the test should be made with Snellen's cards and expressed in twentieths.) ....
If the applicant has any defect of sight in either eye describe fully. ....

5. What is the condition of the applicant's hearing? (State the distance, in feet, at which he can hear the ticking of a closed watch held in the open hand, testing each ear with the other .....feet, right ear plugged.) .....feet, left ear
If he has any defect of hearing in either ear describe fully. ....

6. What is the condition of the applicant's speech? (If he has any defect describe fully.) ....

7. What is the condition of the applicant's limbs? (If he has any defect in either arm or in either leg describe fully.) ....
(Varicose veins, ulcers, or any deformity should be specially reported.) ....

8. Has the applicant any rupture, either inguinal, ventral, or femoral? ....
(If he has a rupture describe fully, stating extent, whether or not it is kept in place by a truss, and if the retention is satisfactory.) ....

9. Has the applicant varicocele, hydrocele, internal or external piles, fistula in ano or any cutaneous disease? (If so, describe the disease, and state to what extent the applicant is affected.) ....

10. Has the applicant any defect in the functions of the brain or nervous system? . . . .

(If so, describe the defect, and state to what extent the applicant is affected.) . . . .

11. Give the measurements of the applicant's chest:

At rest. . . . . .inches

At full inspiration. . . . . .inches

At full expiration. . . . . .inches

12. Is the applicant's respiration full, free and un-obstructed in both lungs? . . . .

(If not, state to what extent obstructed.) . . . .

13. State the frequency of the action of the applicant's heart:

When sitting. . . . .beats per min.

When standing. . . . .beats per min.

When standing after brief exercise. (The applicant should be required to hop on one foot the distance of about 12 feet.) . . . .beats per min.

14. Are there indications in the heart's action of organic, muscular, or nervous derangement? . . . .

(If so, describe fully.) . . . .

15. Are there indications that the applicant is addicted to excessive use of intoxicating beverages, tobacco, or narcotics in any form? . . . .

(If so, describe fully.) . . . .

16. Is the applicant capable of prolonged, severe, mental and physical exertion, and equal to the demands of a very exhausting occupation? . . . .

17. Is the applicant free from any form of disease or disability which is likely to unfit him for the performance of the work of a railway mail clerk? . . . .

18. Are you a regularly licensed physician, and duly authorized by the laws of your state to practice medicine? . . . .

19. Of what medical institute are you a graduate? . . . .

The person examined will insert in the blank space immediately below, in his own handwriting, in the presence of the examining physician, his full name and post office address.

These spaces to be filled out by the applicant in his own handwriting.

(Full name of applicant.)..............................

....

I certify that I have made a thorough examination of the above named applicant for the railway mail service, divested of all his clothing, and that each and all of the above answers are in my own handwriting and are true.

(Signature of physician.)..............................

(Post office address of physician.)......................

Date,......................"

This certificate has been enlarged and improved somewhat within the last two or three years. The height is now 5 feet, 5 inches, and the weight 130 pounds, etc., etc.

In operating the service it became evident that the controversies that occurred, from time to time, over promotions, and not infrequently with cause, should be avoided in the interest of harmony in the service. To do this it was necessary to satisfy the employees that influence and favoritism had no weight in making promotions; that merit governed as in original appointments to the service. The success that had attended these selections under the operations of the civil service laws and rules suggested the practicability of applying similar methods to promotions. When this point was reached, the General Superintendent called in consultation a number of division superintendents and constituted them a committee to draft a set of regulations to govern promotions, which being submitted to the Civil Service Commission were approved and formulated by it, after consultation with the Postmaster General, who also approved and promulgated them in February, 1897, under this title and caption, viz:

HON. SAMUEL W. GAINES
Superintendent Eleventh Division R. M. S.
(See Appendix)

CIVIL SERVICE REGULATIONS
GOVERNING PROMOTIONS

IN THE

RAILWAY MAIL SERVICE.

APPROVED AND PROMULGATED

BY THE

POSTMASTER GENERAL

FEBRUARY 6, 1897.

In pursuance of the requirements of Section VII of the Civil Service Act, and in conformity with Civil Service Rule XI, promulgated by the President on the sixth day of May, 1896, the following regulations governing promotions in the railway mail service have been formulated by the Civil Service Commission, after consultation with the Postmaster General, and are hereby promulgated:

REGULATION I.

Promotions.

Section 892. Board of Promotions. The General Superintendent, the Assistant General Superintendent, and the Chief Clerk of the railway mail service shall constitute a Board of Promotion, subject to the provisions of Section 3 of Civil Service Rule XI.

REGULATION II.

Classification.

For the purpose of defining the order of promotion under these regulations, the officers and employees shall be classified as follows:

The classification up to and including class 4 shall be as provided in Section 890 of the Postal Laws and Regulations of 1893.

Class 5 shall include clerks receiving salaries of $1,400 and assigned to duty as chief clerks, chief clerks at large, chief clerks in charge of lines, examiners, scheme clerks, and clerks detailed to duty in the office of the General Superintendent.

Class 6 shall include all assistant superintendents.

Class 7 shall include the Assistant General Superintendent, Superintendents of Divisions, and the Chief Clerk in the office of the General Superintendent.

Class 8 shall include the General Superintendent.

Regulation III.

All vacancies above those in the lowest class, not filled by reinstatement, transfer or reduction, shall be filled by promotion: *Provided,* That if there is no person eligible for promotion, or if the vacant position requires the exercise of technical or professional knowledge, it may be filled through certification from the Civil Service Commission.

2. A vacancy in any class, except the lowest, up to and including class 5, shall be filled by the promotion of an eligible from the next lower class of the same railway post office. When a vacancy exists the Board of Promotion shall certify to the Postmaster General the names of the highest three eligibles, and from these names a selection shall be made: *Provided,* That if there shall be in the same railway post office less than three eligibles in the class next below that in which the vacancy exists and if the Postmaster General shall require a full certification, the Board of Promotion shall certify, in addition, as many as necessary of the highest eligibles in the corresponding class of the connecting or adjacent railway post office in the same division, whose clerks, by reason of the character of the mail handled therein, are, in the opinion of the Board, best qualified.

3. A vacancy in any class except the lowest, up to and including class 5, in an office other than a railway post office, shall be filled by the promotion of an eligible from the next lower class of the same office. When such vacancy exists the Board of Promotion shall certify to the Postmaster General the names of the highest three eligibles, and from these names a selection shall be made; *Provided,* That if there shall be in the same office less than three eligibles in the class next below that in which the vacancy exists, and if the Postmaster General shall require a full certification, the Board of Promotion shall certify, in addition, as many as necessary of the highest eligibles in the corresponding class of the railway post offices in the same division.

4. When a vacancy exists in class 6, the Board of Promotion shall certify to the Postmaster General the names of the highest three eligibles in class 5 in the division in which the vacancy exists, and from these names the Postmaster General shall make his selection: *Provided,* That if there shall be in the division less than three eligibles in class 5 the Board of Promotion shall, in order to make a full certification, certify in addition as many as necessary of the highest eligibles in the corresponding class in the other divisions.

5. When a vacancy exists in class 7, the Board of Promotion shall certify to the Postmaster General the names of the highest three

eligible in class 6 in the division in which the vacancy exists, and from these names the Postmaster General shall make his selection: *Provided,* That if there shall be in the division less than three eligibles in class 6 the Board of Promotion shall, in order to make a full certification, certify in addition as many as necessary of the highest eligibles in the corresponding class in the other divisions: *And provided further,* That if the duties to be performed in the vacant position be not confined to any division, the Board of Promotion shall certify the three eligibles in the service who, in the opinion of the Board, are best qualified for the duties to be performed and for the responsibilities of the office. Clerks detailed to the office of the General Superintendent shall be considered for promotion in the divisions from which they are detailed.

6. When a vacancy exists in class 8 the Postmaster General shall promote any person from the next lower class whom he may consider qualified.

REGULATION IV.

Examinations.

1. No clerk below class 5 shall be eligible for promotion who has not passed examination on the states or cities he is required to be examined upon, with a standing of 95 per cent. or better, within three years next preceding the date of vacancy; and to determine his eligibility his last examination on each state shall alone be considered.

2. No person shall be promoted by detail or transfer to a position which may be filled by promotion of an employee who is eligible under these regulations.

REGULATION V.

Case Examination and Car Record.

14. The case examination and car record of a clerk shall constitute the examination for promotion to any position in a railway post office. No re-examination shall be required for promotion to higher positions, eligibility for promotion being determined by the Board of Promotion after considering such qualities as judgment, character, ability, and general qualifications of the person competing. Records of efficiency and case examinations shall be made in such a manner and on such forms as may be prescribed by the Board of Promotion, after consulting with the Postmaster General, and shall embrace the elements which are essential to a fair and accurate determination of relative merit.

15. When in the opinion of the Board of Promotion the qualifications of eligibles are practically equal, they shall be certified in the order of their appointment to the class and line, or office, to which they are assigned.

February 6, 1897.

Since the above regulations were promulgated, changes have been made to accommodate the additional classes and grades that were created, and to eliminate reiterations; intrinsically it remains as in the beginning, which speaks well for the builders.

RECOGNITION OF WORTH.

The fiscal year 1892 was eventful. Among the improvements to be credited to it not the least is the authority granted the Postmaster General to expend not exceeding $20,000 in reimbursing Chief Clerks for the actual expenses incurred, not exceeding $3.00 per diem, when traveling on the business of the Department.

This, and the creation of class 6, salary $1,600 per annum, had been strenuously advocated during the fourteen years immediately preceding this authorization; nine years more of ceaseless effort was necessary to secure the creation of classes 6 and 7, and the restoration of the maximum salaries of classes 4 and 5, viz.: $1,200 and $1,400 per annum, respectively, from which they had been reduced to $1,150 and $1,300 in 1876. This reduction followed a cut down of the force of clerks as much as it could stand without seriously impairing the service, and was made to meet a supposed temporary emergency, but which, unfortunately for those most interested, continued until 1900, twenty-four years. The same Congress, Fifty-sixth, at its second session, raised the salary of division superintendents to $2,700 and of assistant division superintendents to $1,800, with traveling expenses in addition. Provision was also made to pay legal representatives of clerks killed on duty, or who received injuries on duty, resulting in death within a year thereof, $1,000. Section 962, Postal Laws and Regulations of 1893, provided, in substance, that a clerk disabled while in the discharge of his duties, as such, by a railroad or other accident so as to unfit him for the performance of his duties should be given a leave of absence, with pay, and an acting clerk, in periods of not exceeding sixty days each, and not exceeding one year in all, and that a sworn certificate from the attending physician must accompany every application for additional leave. When an acting clerk was employed he was paid at the rate of $800 per annum.

In 1899 provision was made to grant clerks employed on lines daily, or daily except Sunday, an annual leave of fifteen days with pay, the Department also paying the substitute who kept up the work.

The appropriation for the fiscal year beginning July 1, 1902, and ended June 30, 1903, authorized two sub classes, 5b and 4b, salaries $1,300 and $1,100 respectively, which provided for the promotion of clerks of class 4a, $1,200 per annum, running in full railway post offices composed of more than one car to a train, to class 5b, $1,300 per annum; assistant chief clerks of class 4a also, and clerks in charge on the most important apartment lines, in point of work, from class 3, $1,000 per annum, to class 4a and 4b, salaries $1,200 and $1,100 per annum, as indicated by the relative value of the lines. The salaries of clerks in classes 2 and 3 in full railway post office crews, where four or more clerks ran over the whole length of the line, were increased from $900 and $1,000 to $1,000 and $1,100 respectively.

The appropriation act for the fiscal year beginning July 1, 1903, and ended June 30, 1904, provided for an increase of the salaries of the following named officers:

The General Superintendent from $3,500 to $4,000.

The Assistant General Superintendent from $3,000 to $3,500.

Division Superintendents from $2,700 to $3,000, and clerks in charge in full railway post offices composed of two or more cars were placed in class 6, now class 5a, and their salaries increased to $1,500 per annum, in consideration of the increased supervision and responsibility the additional cars and correspondingly enlarged crews and distribution devolved upon them.

In my annual report for 1903 attention was called to so much of section 1409, Postal Laws and Regulations, as reads: "If the average daily distance run is less than 100 and not less than 90 miles, the clerk will be of class 2, at $900 per annum; if the average daily distance run is less than 90 and more than 80 miles, the clerk will be of class 2, and the salary will be at the rate of $10 per annum for each mile of the daily average of miles run. If the average distance run daily is 80 miles or less, the clerk will be of class 1, and the salary will be $10 per annum for each mile of the daily average of miles run," and recommendation was made, in substance, that the class 2, clerks making a daily average of more than 90 and less than 100 miles, be paid on the same basis as the clerks making a daily average of 90 miles or under; that is, $10 per annum for each mile of the daily average of miles run; if he averages 92 miles his salary ought to be $920; if 95 miles, it should be $950; if 98 miles, $980 per annum. This recommendation was renewed in 1904 and 1906.

In my annual reports for 1903, 1904, 1905, and 1906, recommendation was made that the salary of the Chief Clerk in the office of the General Superintendent be advanced to $2,500 from $2,000 per annum; in the two last that the salaries of Assistant Division Superintendents be raised from $1,800 to $2,000 per annum, and in the one for 1906 that Chief Clerks in charge of lines be paid $1,800 per annum in lieu of $1,600.

The fact that all these were persistently recommended, and nearly all won, during my administration, is a most pleasant recollection. The phenomenal growth of all classes of mail; the increase of labor, study, responsibility, and hazard well known to me through observation and participation while engaged in the different classes of the service, and the apparent indifference with which the legislative powers viewed the disparity between the compensation allowed, and the work required, inspired me with the determination to bring about a more just and equitable condition, if possible. Only the highest grade of work was good enough for the people and the officers of the service, and in my opinion only just and equitable compensation, sympathetic and appreciative treatment was good enough for those who performed it. So my best efforts and thoughts were expended during all the years I was in command in trying to bring these conditions about and in this I had the harmonious assistance of all connected with the service.

CASUALTIES.

In the 60's the occupation of railway mail service employees was no more hazardous than that of those engaged in many other callings; indeed, I believe statistics, if obtainable, would show that the lives and limbs of those employed in saw mills, lumber camps, mines, quarries, in the construction of buildings, and on steamboats were in greater peril. Train schedules were then slow and the number of trains limited, two things favoring the minimum of accidents. As the nation grew in population and productiveness, travel increased as did the volume and frequency of shipment of the products of the soil, of live stock of the farm and ranges, of the loom and manufactory; passenger and freight train service was increased and in the early 70's the schedules of some trains were expedited; but the growth of population and the development of the country were not met with a proportionate expansion in trackage facilities, and as year succeeded year, speed continued to increase as did train service. The disparity became more pronounced and accidents, collisions and burning wrecks, the natural sequence, followed, in which the railway post office played an active part. How active and startling I did not know until after my

ACCIDENT AT DANVILLE, VA.
Washington, D. C., and Greensboro, N. C., R. P. O. (See Page 150.)

last promotion, which brought me in touch with the whole country. By that time track improvements were under full headway, double tracks were being laid, some parallel lines had been built, others were in course of construction, and trunk lines were being well ballasted. The country, however, was developing in all respects faster than the transportation service, therefore accidents had not been minimized. The railway post office continued the storm center between the "nether and upper millstone," and it was frequently crushed to splinters and burned to ashes and the brave boys inside were mangled or incinerated, killed or maimed for life. These are evidences of the hazardous nature of the occupation of railway postal clerks.

In the lamentable accident which occurred April 18, 1891, at Kipton, Ohio, on the Lake Shore & Michigan Southern Railway, six postal clerks at work in the New York & Chicago railway post office, were killed, a seventh being injured. Three railway postal cars were running in the train; one was totally demolished, one end of another was crushed in and the third was damaged.

An accident occurred February 15, 1892, near Shreve, Ohio, a station on the Pittsburg, Fort Wayne & Chicago Railroad, in which the railway post office car was crushed and totally destroyed by fire; the bodies of four of the clerks at work in it were incinerated, nothing remaining but ashes.

On July 23, 1893, an accident occurred near Queen City, on the Texas & Pacific Railroad; trains 5 and 6 carrying the Texarkana & Laredo railway post office collided, both cars being telescoped, and three clerks killed and the fourth so seriously injured that he died later.

November 7, 1893, Baltimore & Ohio train 5, to which the Baltimore & Pittsburg railway post office was attached, was wrecked in a head-on collision with a cattle train; two clerks were instantly killed and two seriously injured.

June 9, 1894, Pittsburg & St. Louis railway post office, on Pennsylvania Railroad train 20, was wrecked near Pocahontas, Ill., and was almost destroyed; seven clerks were seriously injured.

September 11, 1895, St. Paul & Minot railway post office, on Great Northern Railroad, trains 2 and 3, met in a head-on collision near Melby, Minn.; both cars were destroyed, and one clerk was killed and three seriously injured.

October 24, 1895, New York & Pittsburg railway post office, train 7, Pennsylvania Railroad, ran into a wrecked freight train near Newport, Pa., and was wrecked, took fire, and four of the postal cars, with about 150,000 letters and 25 to 30 tons of paper mail were entirely destroyed. Six clerks were injured, two of them severely.

November 19, 1895, New York & Chicago railway post office, train 6, New York Central & Hudson River Railroad, was wrecked near Rome, N. Y., and seven clerks injured, two seriously.

January 4, 1896, the Grafton & Cincinnati railway post office, Baltimore & Ohio Railway, collided with a freight train standing on a siding at Schooley, Ohio. The postal car was demolished, three of the clerks were seriously injured, one, Mr. J. C. Edgerton, the medal winner of 1892, Fifth division, died fourteen days later.

June 26, 1897, the St. Louis, Moberly & Kansas City railway post office, Wabash Railroad, train 6, while running at a high rate of speed struck a trestle, which had been undermined by a heavy and continuous flood. The trestle being on a curve moved under the shock of the engine, precipitating the entire train into the raging flood below. All of the clerks, five in number, were killed; there was no way of telling definitely what amount of mail was lost.

September 8, 1897, Kansas City & La Junta railway post office, Santa Fe Railroad, trains 1 and 118, collided near Emporia, Kansas. Postal car on train 1 was demolished and burned, together with the entire mail; mail on 118 saved. Two clerks were killed, three seriously and two slightly injured.

April 15, 1898, St. Louis & Texarkana railway post office, Iron Mountain Railroad, train 54, was wrecked at St. Louis, Mo. The cars turned over, landed on their roofs, but were not seriously damaged. Seven clerks were seriously injured.

August 8, 1898, Boston, Providence & New York railway post office, New York, New Haven & Hartford Railroad, train 70, was wrecked at Canton Junction, Mass.; cause defective switch. Nine clerks were seriously and two slightly injured.

February 6, 1899, Port Huron & Chicago railway post office, Grand Trunk Railroad, train 6, was run into by train 1, at Imlay City, Mich. The car was wrecked; two clerks were killed, one seriously and one slightly injured.

March 5, 1899, New York & Chicago railway post office, New York Central & Hudson River, Lake Shore & Michigan Southern Railroads, train 10, was wrecked at Westfield, N. Y., in a collision and six clerks were seriously injured.

June 5, 1899, Chicago & Minneapolis railway post office, Chicago, Milwaukee & St. Paul Railroad, train 57, was wrecked at West Salem, Wis., in a collision, and five clerks were seriously injured.

August 1, 1899, Chicago, Cedar Rapids & Council Bluffs railway post office, Chicago & Northwestern Railroad, train 9, was derailed near Boone, Iowa. One clerk was killed, four seriously and one slightly injured.

May 9, 1900, Charleston & Jacksonville railway post office, C. & S. & S. F. & W. Railroad, train 36, was wrecked in collision at Hardeeville, S. C. Two clerks were seriously and three slightly injured.

January 4, 1901, Chicago & St. Louis railway post office, Chicago & Alton Railroad, train 46, was derailed at Chicago; cause defective switch. Four clerks were severely injured.

March 23, 1902, Washington & Charlotte railway post office, Southern Railroad, train 38, was wrecked by running into a landslide near Covesville, Va. Two postal cars were thrown across the engine, broken up and entirely destroyed by fire, together with all the mail. Nine clerks were severely injured.

March 27, 1902, New York & Washington railway post office, Pennsylvania Railroad, train 66, was wrecked at Edgemoor, Del., by running into a freight train, damaging one of the cars and severely injuring four clerks.

July 25, 1902, Pittsburg & St. Louis railway post office, Pennsylvania Railroad, train 2, was wrecked by collision with a runaway coal car at Trebenis, Ohio. Two clerks were killed and their bodies were consumed by fire; three others were seriously injured and burned. All the mail was destroyed.

February 23, 1903, Buffalo & Cincinnati railway post office, Lake Shore & Big Four Railroads, train 25, collided with a freight train near Berea, Ohio. The postal car and its contents were destroyed by fire. Four clerks were killed, the bodies of three of them being consumed with the wreck.

April 23, 1903, Washington & Greensboro railway post office, Southern Railroad, train 38, collided with a freight train near Durmid, Va., and was wrecked. Two of the postal cars were destroyed by fire. Three clerks were severely injured.

September 27, 1903, Washington & Greensboro railway post office, Southern Railroad, train 97, was wrecked at Danville, Va. Four clerks were instantly killed, one died later, and five were seriously injured.

March 8, 1904, Chattanooga & Meridian railway post office, A. & G. S. R. R., train 1, was wrecked near Kewanee, Miss. The wreck was consumed by fire; three employees were killed and their bodies incinerated.

March 5, 1905, St. Paul & Spokane railway post office, train 3, Northern Pacific Railroad, was wrecked near Bearmouth, Mont. Chief Clerk Wilcox was killed and Clerk Stuart seriously injured.

May 6, 1905, New York & Washington railway post office, train 52, Pennsylvania Railroad, was wrecked near Plainsboro, N. J. Eleven clerks were injured.

December 7, 1905, Cheyenne & Pocatello railway post office, Union Pacific & Oregon Short Line Railroad, was wrecked near Wilkins Station, Wyo. Three clerks were killed and their bodies were consumed with the wrecked car.

May 4, 1906, New York & Pittsburg railway post office, Pennsylvania Railroad, was wrecked at Springfield Junction, Pa., and four clerks were killed.

The above extracts from my annual reports exhibit the peril confronting employees of the railway mail service when on duty in postal cars, but a more forcible demonstration of the devastation of life and limb, homes and firesides, hopes and ambitions inseparable from this vocation is presented in the following statement.

From 1876 to 1905, both inclusive:

The number of accidents to trains carrying full and apartment
    postal cars was 9,355
Number of clerks killed while on duty 207
Number seriously injured 1,516
Number slightly injured 3,764

Total 5,280

Up to the commencement of my administration there had been 1,796 accidents in which 52 clerks were killed, 482 injured seriously, and 514 slightly. The following year (1891) the Kipton, Ohio, disaster occurred, in which the New York & Chicago railway post office was wrecked, and clerks F. F. Clement, F. J. Nugent, J. J. Bowerfield, James McKinley, Charles Hamell and C. L. McDowell, were killed. A few months later a more horrible disaster occurred at Shreve, Ohio, on the Pennsylvania system, in which a car of the Pittsburg & Chicago railway post office was wrecked and burned, and clerks George C. Mann, J. D. Patterson, D. E. Reese and H. S. Allen were killed, their bodies being incinerated.

I had long felt that some action should be taken by the Government to ameliorate the condition of the clerks injured on duty, and the dependents of those who had lost their lives in accidents while on duty. Those injured had been provided for in a measure, but no provision had been made for the widows and minor children of those killed on duty; therefore I repeated the recommendation, in this behalf, made by my predecessor, in the reports of 1889 and 1890, "That the Postmaster General be authorized to use the funds arising from deductions because of the failure of clerks in the railway mail service to perform duty, and for other causes, in paying to the widow and minor children of each permanent railway postal clerk killed while on duty the sum of $1,000. In the event of there not being a sufficient amount arising from deductions the Postmaster General shall be authorized to make up the deficiency from the regular appropriation for the payment of railway postal clerks." And added this argument: "The policy which obtains of providing for disabled, infirm, and aged clerks by assigning them to duty on routes of minor importance is dictated by philanthropy and is worthy of mankind; but it stands as a barrier to the fullest development of the service. These lines of minor importance are simply feeders for the great railway post offices that span the country, connecting commercial centers with each other and with the intermediate territory tributary to them. Their distribution is rudimentary and local in its nature, just such as may be intrusted to new appointees with the certainty that the minimum instead of the maximum of bad service will result from their lack of knowledge of the work devolving upon them. These lines should be used as kindergartens and common schools, through which the new appointees should pass, and from which they should graduate with honors before being assigned to duty in railway post offices of the first or second-class. But this policy cannot be enforced so long as the present method of providing for the disabled and infirm is continued, nor can the service as a whole approach the maximum of usefulness until all probationers begin their official life in the primary department of the service; but this cannot be done if that department is filled with the worthy class of clerks who have been disabled in accidents, broken down by hard work on important lines, or become incapacitated for further service by reason of old age. It, therefore, becomes necessary to consider what can be done to advance the interests of the service without ignoring the future of these men.   *   *   *   *   In my opinion the best interests of the service, the clerks, and the public can be secured by such legislation as will create a law to be known as

The Railway Mail Service Superannuation Act.

This act shall provide for the retirement of all permanent clerks on one-third or one-half pay who have become incapacitated for further service by reason of age, injuries received while on duty or infirmities not attributable to vicious habits. The fund out of which the clerks so retired shall be paid is to be created by withholding a sum equal to one-half of one per cent. per annum of the salary paid every permanent clerk employed in the service, and one per cent. of the annuity paid those placed upon the superannuated list. This deduction would be slight upon each individual, but would in the aggregate amount to about $31,000 per annum, and as but little of it would be drawn from the fund thus created during the first few years succeeding the passage of the act, it would, by accumulation, reach sufficient proportions to make the act effective as fast as retirements became necessary. That the deduction would not work even temporary hardship to those coming under its operations is shown by the fact that it would amount to but 50 cents on each $100 paid the clerks in active service and $1.00 on each $100 paid those placed upon the superannuated list. The details of the plan can be worked into a bill whenever the proper time to do so arrives."

The above recommendation was renewed in the annual report for the fiscal year 1892, under the caption:

"Provision in Case of Injury."

I remarked in the same report:

"Leaves of absence with pay are granted to railway postal clerks who receive injuries in railway accidents while on duty which incapacitate them temporarily or permanently for service. These leaves cover a period of one year, unless the injured recover and return to duty before the expiration of that period. If the disability extends beyond one year the Department is compelled under existing laws, to retire the clerk from the service. This regulation is a good one, but does not meet the emergency fully and fairly; it does not do full justice to those so badly injured as to be unable to resume duty at the expiration of the year limit or who may never be able to perform the labor necessary to support themselves and families. This office believes that the Department and Congress should not lose sight of the fact that the condition of the family of a clerk so badly injured as to be unable to contribute to its support permanently is, if anything, more deplorable than of one instantly killed, because in the former case the family must not only support itself, but must provide the necessities, such as food, clothes, medicine, and medical attendance, for the disabled head; the positions of the dependents and support are reversed, the load carried by the former is greater than the one that fell upon the latter. Special provision should be made for this class and it is therefore respectfully recommended that there be added to the appropriation bill a specification, as follows:

"For the special employment of clerks who have been permanently disabled in railway accidents, while on actual duty, and who were thereby incapacitated for duty in railway post offices........dollars.

"Doubtless an appropriation of $20,000 per annum would cover all such cases for many years, and this would not be in excess of the sum now paid to acting clerks employed in keeping up the runs of the regular clerks disabled; and as nearly if not quite all incapacitated for duty in cars could be advantageously employed elsewhere the appropriation could not be regarded as a civil pension fund.

"The records of this office show that for the fiscal years 1889, 1890, and 1891, it became necessary to employ acting clerks to keep up the runs of 294 regular clerks who were disabled while on duty. Of these only 12 were unable to resume their regular duties before or at the expiration of the one year limit, and three of these were detailed to positions in the service where the physically perfect man is not an absolute necessity or where the work is not of such a character as to demand strong, active, healthy men, leaving but nine for the three years who could be considered as having been permanently incapacitated for work of any kind, an average of three per year; and it is not known that these nine could not have performed light work had the Department been in position to tender it to them. The presumption is that they could have done so, but the appropriations, as has been remarked elsewhere in this report, have never been large enough to permit the employment of as large a number of clerks as the best interests of the public and the service demanded; therefore, none of it could be expended in the employment of clerks where a pressing necessity for them did not exist.

"If the appropriation bill contained the definite and specific item mentioned the Department could use these disabled clerks as transfer clerks at points of sufficient importance to warrant the employment of such an officer, but not sufficiently so to justify it in encroaching upon a limited regular appropriation and sacrificing more pressing improvements. They could be used in division supply offices, as janitors of dormitories, as watchmen, and where competent for the class of work required, as assistants to chief clerks and as additional help in the offices of the superintendents whenever such additions might become necessary.

"In short, no difficulty would be experienced in providing positions for them which would be advantageous to the service. The cases are full of merit; the men lose their limbs and health in the Government service; there is work which would be very beneficial to the service that they can perform, and the work would keep them from destitution and want."

The following bill was introduced in the annual report for 1893:

"Be it enacted by the Senate and House of Representatives of the United States of America in Congress assembled, That, beginning with the commencement of the first fiscal year after the approval of this act, and regularly thereafter, there shall be withheld from the salary of every person employed in the classified railway mail service by any title or in any capacity whatsoever, except those not paid out of the appropriation for clerk hire, a sum equal to one per cent. per annum of the amount of his salary, as fixed by the Postmaster General in pursuance to law, which shall constitute a fund to be known as

'THE RAILWAY MAIL SERVICE RELIEF FUND,'

and be retained in the Treasury or subtreasuries of the United States of America for the relief of injured and disabled employees of said service. For convenience of disbursement the Secretary of the Treasury may make transfers from said fund to any National Bank designated as a depository of public moneys, or to any post office of the first or second-class.

"Section 2. That the fund provided for in the preceding section shall be applied to the relief of any employee referred to therein who, in the said service and in the line of duty, shall be permanently injured or disabled mentally or physically, not the result of his own vicious habits, so as to incapacitate him for the performance of further duty in said service. If said injury or disability, not apparently permanent when received or incurred shall result in permanency within two years thereafter, the relief extended by this act shall accrue to him from and after the ascertainment of that fact.

"Section 3. That there shall be annually paid from said fund to each of the injured and disabled employees referred to in the last preceding section, the sum named below, to wit: If an employee of the first class, three hundred and sixty dollars; if of the second class, four hundred and ten dollars; if of the the third class, four hundred and sixty dollars; if of the fourth class, five hundred and twenty dollars; if of the fifth class, six hundred and ten dollars; the payment in all cases to be made at such intervals as the Postmaster General may direct, but not less frequently than quarterly, and to continue during the continuance of said disability: *Provided,* That no payment shall be made from said fund until the commencement of the second fiscal year after the approval of this act, nor to any employee for injuries received or disability incurred during his probationary period in said service.

"Section 4. That if additional classes are created by law, the clerks in such classes shall be embraced in this act, and their pay, after retirement, shall be in the same ratio to the salary of the class in which they last served as that of the clerks in the classes named in the third section of this act; *Provided also,* That if the salary of any class embraced in this act is decreased or increased by act of Congress approved, the benefits provided in this act shall be decreased or increased proportionately.

"Section 5. That if any employee entitled to the benefits of this act shall be killed while in said service and in the line of duty, or shall die as a result of any injury received or a disability received or contracted in said service and in the line of duty, within one year from the date of receiving or contracting the same, leaving a widow or minor children under sixteen years of age, there shall be paid to said widow out of the said fund a sum equal to one year's salary of such employee in the class in which he last served; or, if there be no widow, the said sum shall be paid to the legitimate child or children of such employee under the age specified.

"Section 6. That any employee referred to herein who, not having been injured or disabled, as contemplated by the provisions of this act, may after twenty years' service, continuous or otherwise, be retired, if by reason of age, infirmity, mental or physical, he becomes incapacitated to perform further satisfactory service, and shall, upon such retirement, be paid out of said fund during the remainder of his life an annual sum equal to that fixed in the third section of this act for the class in which he last served.

"Section 7. That it is hereby made the duty of the Postmaster General to provide rules and regulations for the enforcement of this act, as well as for the ascertainment of the fact of any alleged injury referred to herein, and the degree of such injury or disability, and to designate any surgeon conveniently located for the purpose, at the expense of the applicant for relief hereunder, to examine the applicant and make report of his condition; and the decision of the Postmaster General as to the fact of such injury or disability, and the degree thereof, shall be final."

This bill, with the most earnest pleas I could make in favor of it, appeared in full, or was referred to, in all the annual reports from 1893 to 1907. The bill and pleas pictured a realization of the dangerous and wearing nature of the calling, and, to some extent, the responsibility for the future of the men and their loved ones, whether it should be brightened with health, happiness, delightful homes and agreeable friends, or be darkened with the anguish of broken hearts. It was shown repeatedly that the calling is extra hazardous; disastrous to the physical man, especially to the nervous and muscular systems; exhaustive to the mind as represented in the intellectual capacity and grasp of memory; that a clerk's maximum usefulness is reached after a long period of diligent study, which is never permitted to wane until that period has been passed and he has entered upon the decline. It was shown that accidents, which strewed wrecks along the tracks, killed comrades, and sent others to hospitals and their homes to be healed; clothed wives and children in mourning, whether the clerk participated in them or not, had a tendency to shorten the span of life; that according to the most comprehensive conception of the relative obligations due from the one to the other, our Government, knowing the character of the business and being one of the highly civilized and enlightened nations, ought to protect the future of men who place their lives in jeopardy if need be every time they enter a railroad train upon its business and who are expected, and justly so, to protect its mails from bandits, thieves, fire and flood, with courage and energy.

Other Governments provide for the future of their postal employees. Many of our best railroad companies and banks, as well as other corporations, long ago organized pension and relief systems for the benefit of all their employees, officers as well as subordinates. This in itself is very good evidence that corporations have souls, notwithstanding the old saying that they have none.

If these other governments and many corporations can carry on successfully this humane work, why cannot we as a nation? The means to do it are contributed under the rules of trade, commerce, and transportation, by the people. It flows into the treasury of each concern in exchange for something each does for them, and is voted out to pay indebtedness of all kinds; some to pay the dividends declared on stock, some to compensate employees, some to meet losses, and last, but not least, some to pension those old and faithful employees who after long service have been found physically disqualified for further duty.

In addition, some corporations join with the employees in maintaining a relief fund out of which benefits are provided members in case of sickness, disability, superannuation and death.

Will any worthy citizen say that our own country, the greatest of all, which should represent, if it does not, the heart and the sense of

Hon. Charles W. Vickery
Superintendent Third Division R. M. S.
(See Appendix)

equity of this people, cannot or will not be as considerate of the well-being of its employees who work in fields of imminent peril, as these so-called "soulless corporations?" Will any one say that such of the servants of the people as are employed on the firing line are not entitled to greater protection against privation and want, even if the line is filled with volunteers, than those who serve in quiet places, exposed to no unusual dangers; who live and die according to nature's formula, without having felt the heart stand still, life's blood forsake its reservoir and felt the shadow of the beyond pause momentarily overhead?

What is it that shortens the allotted life of man in the case of such physically sound men as the railway mail service absorbs? Is it not the natural excitement of the vocation, its encroachments upon the nervous system, the wrenching and straining of the muscles and sinews, the bruising of the body and limbs and the breaking of bones? Look back in these pages and read. Is not the showing appalling? What must be the effect of the sight and recollection of those wrecks upon the brave boys who witnessed them and are exposed to like experiences constantly? Can it be less than shocking?

If all this be as stated, and who can question it, why should our Government, which has faltered in this matter nineteen years or more, hesitate longer? Surely with its matchless resources it need not fear to enter upon a policy so distinctively just, humane and sound.

During all the time that these relief measures were being advocated, equally strenuous, but more successful efforts were being made to strengthen our railway post office cars, to the end that the per cent. of fatalities and injuries per accident might be reduced, or at least kept from growing. Notwithstanding the great and constant increase of speed and train service this has been accomplished, as is shown below.

POSTAL CAR CONSTRUCTION.

Previous to 1867 full railway post office cars were unknown; the limited service had by rail was performed in small apartments partitioned off from full cars, used in most instances almost exclusively to accommodate other business of the companies. Usually cars were divided into three parts, which were assigned to the mail, baggage and express, respectively—the mail being frequently limited to a space not exceeding $6\frac{1}{2}$x7 feet, and in some instances to 3x7 feet.

In the beginning of transportation of mail by railroad, it was made up in distributing and terminal post offices and dispatched in closed pouches and in sacks to other distributing offices, and to local offices in charge of the employee of the railroad designated by the company—as is the case now on lines where service by clerk has not been established, or on trains of important routes where the service by clerk does not furnish all the mail facilities the business transacted along the route and its tributaries require. But when the need of, and demand for more prompt local exchanges became manifest, these same offices made up packages of letters and sacks of papers for the way offices, and dispatched them to the designated route, which was provided with a mail apartment and a route agent, who opened the pouches, assorted the packages and made the exchanges—the packages and papers received in the exchange pouches being treated in like manner.

It has been stated—in substance—that these apartments were not provided with letter cases, and that the unwrapped letters, received from the exchange local offices, were generally thrown into the pouch loose among the packages and papers, and that as the train approached the terminus of the route, the accumulated mass of undelivered packages, newspapers, and loose letters was dumped into a pouch and sent to the post office at that point, or to the nearest distributing post office. It is not doubted that, in the years that intervened between 1834, the year the mail was first dispatched by rail, and 1864, the year the railway post office was introduced, but little distribution, even of a local nature, was required of or made by the route agents, and it is known that the nearer our retrospection approaches 1834 the more evident it becomes that, in those days, it was not necessary that a route agent should be an intellectual giant, with a physique boiling over with energy and endurance, and a memory like that of the daughter of Uranus, in order to discharge his duties to the satisfaction of the people, and his superiors, and I apprehend that this satisfaction was not due to the excellence of the service, but rather to absence of knowledge of anything better, and the prosaic life people lived before the Civil War roused them—stirred all their emotions into action.

As late as 1874 apartment cars without letter cases were in use on the Great Western Railway in Canada, between Toronto, London, and Windsor, and the clerks distributed the letters loosely into boxes such as were used very much earlier, in this country, for packages and papers exclusively. I rode in one of these apartments about that time on the return trip from Toronto, where I had gone to confer with Mr. Sweetman of the Canadian postal service respecting an improvement in the distribution and dispatch of mail passing from one country into the other, and witnessed the work and the interior arrangement of the apartment, but the Canadian service has changed greatly since those days.

It is evident to my mind that the deplorable condition of the service, which obtained in 1834 and later, did not remain unchanged down to 1864; it could not have remained stationary thirty years in any civilized country—the route agents would have died of inertia, and the public brain would have become mildewed and moth-eaten. Moreover, the Civil War came upon us and the country was born again; the immense bodies of men who composed our armies in the field were always anxious about their home folks—longing to hear from them—and the home folks were overwhelmed with greater anxiety about the loved ones at the front, who were in actual or imminent peril at all times, and kept the paths between their dwellings and the post office well trodden, carrying letters to mail and hoping to receive answers to others mailed before. And so an ever increasing correspondence commenced which before the war ended assumed, in connection with the fast growing newspaper and business mails, gigantic proportions for those days, and it is known that as the war progressed the armies increased in numbers and magnitude; the area covered by their operations was extended and they moved farther and still farther from the original lines of hostility—maintaining connection with them only because of the important points they offered for the establishment of depots of supplies. Post offices of long standing were in operation at nearly all these points capable of caring for all the postal business—of whatever character—that came to them during the years the fires of war smouldered, according to the methods and the laws and regulations prescribed by the Post Office Department and Congress, but when the mails passing to and from the armies began to pour into them for treatment preparatory to dispatch either to the north via the distributing post offices, or to the south by military methods and transportation, made up as direct for the different commands or organizations in the field, all the offices that were utilized were quickly filled with mail from cellar to garret; they were completely blockaded—covered up—and calling for help, in which the army and home folks joined.

Every one who can read or hear, knows how sensitive President Lincoln was of the care and comfort of his soldiers; how quickly he responded whenever he was shown that he could lessen their burdens or bring a bit of sunshine into their lives; how his sympathy went out to the wives, fathers, mothers, and sweethearts of these brave men, who had put all these behind them, to follow the flag in its day of peril, and knowing this we know with what matchless energy he caused this obstruction to communication between camp and home to be cleared away; how experts from such offices as New York and Chicago and the force of special agents at the command of the Postmaster General were employed to equip these border offices with the clerks and fixtures necessary to relieve the situation; that they not only did this, but also investigated the entire distributing and dispatching features of the postal service—strengthened some of the distributing post offices in the rear, and worked heroically to systematize and improve the intolerably crude and inefficient character of it so as to meet this most pressing emergency, not only at the front but in the business centers of the east and middle west which were growing rapidly and becoming active in all trade lines. While the Department was thus engaged, the army organized an auxiliary system, which—as is usual with anything it undertakes, in times of war, was well done, and was very effective.

It is evident that the route agent or railway mail service of those days was not passed by unnoticed; letter cases had found a place—a small one to be sure—in the mail apartments, and loose letters for local offices ceased to pass through the hands of the route agents without proper handling—they were assorted into pigeon holes and delivered with the made-up mails as the trains stood at the way stations. These were late letters as a rule, or those that had been overlooked by the postmasters of these way offices when they closed their mails for the train; even when this was broadened out so as to embrace a larger per cent. of the local mail, it did not include the distribution which the railway post office has made famous since 1864, nor was it adequate to the needs of the Government or the people, but, with the means available and the light given those in authority, it was the best possible then; so that it is not strange to us now that the committee of special agents that met in Cleveland, Ohio, on June 24 and 25, 1863—by order of the Postmaster General—to consider and report upon the condition of this feature of the service, should have reported as follows, with respect to the work of the route agents:

"It is believed that to this class of truly useful officers more than to all others, if we except the application of steam in the conveyance of the mail, which of course created the necessity of the system in question, is to be attributed the wonderful improvement in the mail accommodation throughout the whole country, and on the future service of these officers must depend in a great measure the prosperity and efficiency of our postal establishment. The amount of labor they perform and the degree of intelligence exhibited, especially by those running on the most important routes, can hardly be estimated outside of the Department. After their general fidelity to their official trust it may be mentioned as somewhat remarkable that there have been so few cases of delinquency or dishonesty among them up to the present time."

In this connection it is worth remembering that the great innovation which appeared above the postal horizon, a year later, shedding the light of progress over this continent, and destined to dissipate forever the greatest fault of our postal system in the handling of mail—inefficiency—could not be seen by the committee, though it was composed of some of the brightest, most experienced and capable officers then in the postal service, some of whom afterwards became prominent in the Post Office Department, and others were then conspicuous for real ability in the larger post offices. They were of that class of men who would not pass such a glowing eulogy upon these officials if it had not appeared to them merited, in comparison with the conditions they discovered in the distributing post offices, which were noted for lack of system, and the accumulation of mail, which for that reason remained in the offices, frequently waiting distribution longer than was required to transport it to destinations.

My experience and research convince me that on the best lines, in the beginning of the 60's, the service was, and the apartments also, except as to size, about as it was on the route from Cedar Rapids to Boone, Iowa, in the early part of 1866, when my service as a route agent began. At that time our route did not seem to be under the exclusive jurisdiction of Mr. Armstrong, whose headquarters were then in Chicago, for there was direct correspondence between the Department and those employed on it. Special agents visited us occasionally, giving us the benefit of the knowledge they acquired in their intercourse with postal employees on other routes and in post offices, and the terminal postmasters gave us a few words of wisdom whenever they could separate themselves from them.

I am under the impression that Mr. Armstrong's attention was devoted to his grand scheme and to the routes upon which it had been or was about to be introduced, but early that fall, our route was extended east to Clinton, Iowa, its designation changed to Clinton & Boone R. P. O., and we then passed under his exclusive jurisdiction, but during the entire life of that designation we occupied those apartments, notwithstanding the character of our work became national instead of local, and they answered the purpose well, though this series of articles shows that the strength of their construction was tested quite severely for those times.

It should be remembered that collisions were almost unknown then; this was because the traffic was light—so light that one train each way daily, except Sundays, accommodated both the through and way passenger business of most lines—the freight in many cases not justifying an equal. number—none were run at a high rate of speed and though none of the companies had commenced to double-track their lines, employment on railroad trains was not regarded as more hazardous than any other occupation. It was not until the 70's that it began to be so regarded—a change due to the rapid increase of our population, the development of the fertile lands of the west into productive farms, which created business of sufficient magnitude to draw into centers of every large farming community representatives of the professions, mercantile pursuits, and trades, and their concomitants, who built up small towns and commenced to buy and sell; these towns either became larger with the passing of time or languished and died; usually they lived and grew spasmodically; whenever they outgrew the surrounding country, upon which they lived and thrived or failed, they stood still until the country caught up and passed them—then they awoke from their lethargy and made another spurt, but the general trend was upward. When we consider that corn sold for ten cents a bushel, eggs for three cents a dozen and all other products of the soil in proportion, because none but local markets were available, on account of remoteness from railroad and water routes, we can understand how anxious the farmer was to have one of these "darned critters" come to his town, and how anxious the "critter" was to get there, provided, the town, county, state, or general government would lend a helping hand, and one of them usually did. It was a mutual arrangement which was probably the immediate salvation of both parties, and assisted very materially in the upbuilding of the nation.

This increase of population, and development of our resources, started an era of activity and prosperity in which railway building was a prime factor. Travel increased so largely on this account, and the opening of the first trans-continental line, that very early in the 70's the demand for quicker transit from place to place, and especially from one important center to another, was heard in the land, and the companies relegated the old train to the local or accommodation passenger business and put on express trains some times known as "Thunderbolt," "Lightning Express," "Gee Whizz," etc., and then strenuous efforts were made by the officers of the railway mail service to secure a place on these trains for the railway post office car; these were eminently successful in the west, the managers of the roads yielding to our wishes cheerfully.

INTERIOR AND EXTERIOR VIEWS FIRST RAILWAY POST OFFICE CAR

The first full railway post office cars were built by the Chicago & Northwestern Railroad in 1867, on plans provided by Mr. Armstrong, and were placed in service between Chicago, Ill., and Clinton, Iowa, in March, of that year, and between Boone and Council Bluffs, Iowa, in September of the same year. These cars, with the exception of the nails, screws, bolts, rods, brakes, trucks, locks and hinges, used in their construction, were built of lumber. Car building has become an art since, and some of the best specimens are dreams of the mechanical engineer's ideas, of symmetry, strength, and beauty, executed under his eye by his most skilled workmen. Look at a first-class postal car, or a train of them standing on a track, coupled to an engine similar to Pennsylvania engine No. 2999, with a maximum speed of eighty miles an hour, built according to the specifications of Department Plan No. 1, issued May 1, 1904, or Pennsylvania Plan "Mm," which is essentially the same, and weighs 106,000 pounds—48,000 more than the best postal cars constructed prior to 1891, and 28,200 more than those built between that year and 1904, or "M-70,"—Pennsylvania all-steel cars, weighing 130,000 pounds, 24,000 more than those built according to Department Plan No. 1, and 6,000 more than the splendid steel cars of the Erie R. R. Company, built by the Standard Steel Car Company in 1904—and tell me if you ever saw anything—animate or inanimate—that could speed faster, that looked more like it, or more graceful when in motion; if you do not know sit on some grass-covered knoll overlooking a track laid through a level valley and up a mountain side and watch a passenger train approach your position, pass on, ascend the incline and move out of range of your vision, and you will witness the personification of grace, gentleness, submission, power, resolution, energy, destruction.

The first postal cars were well built, but they were not as symmetrical or highly finished, inside or out, strong or convenient as they have since become, but the change has come step by step, just as the development of everything man uses has, as the country has, as the postal business has, as civilization has; it is evolution pure and simple. What is necessary now would have been extravagant then from every standpoint.

These cars were forty feet long and full width; they were without end doors, but had two windows, and upper deck lights, on either side. The case to accommodate paper distribution was built in one end of the car, somewhat semi-circular in form, and consisted of four rows of thirteen boxes each—dimensions 10x12 inches front—rising one above the other from the opening table, upon which the sacks and pouches were emptied, to the rafters of the lower deck; each case was provided with two inferior oil lamps and two or three drawers.

The letter case consisted of three sections, with a capacity of seventy-seven pigeon holes each, put together in angular form; the front of the bottom of these was five or six inches above the table, which began with the left wing of the case and following its contour extended to about two feet beyond the right wing and was about eighteen inches or two feet wide; the pigeon holes sloped back at an angle of about forty-five degrees; the extreme limit of the left wing rested against the inside wall of the car and the end of the right wing against a partition which formed one side of an alley extending from the space allotted to the cases back of the storage end of the car, in which the mail was assorted in bulk and piled as it was loaded into the car, and from which that requiring distribution was taken to the cases, and some of it back after this was made; that for local offices and en route connections was usually delivered from the side doors of the work room. The letter case, like the paper case, was provided with two oil lamps and some drawers; the storage room had one lamp and the car was furnished with a chair, stove, lounge, wood box, ice cooler and other necessities.

Not much change occurred in the structure of postal cars for many years after these were built, nor in the interior arrangement, except that the positions of the letter and paper cases were reversed— the letter case being built in one end of the car and the paper case in the center; this was more convenient for the clerks and economized time and labor, as it brought the storage room next to the paper case, upon the table of which all the pouches and sacks were opened and closed, and from which the great bulk of mail, second, third and fourth class matter, and the made-up packages of first-class was distributed, into the boxes and sacks; it was no longer carried or dragged to and fro across the open space between the two cases.

In 1874 wooden racks were substituted for the circular cases in use in the cars of the Chicago, Burlington & Quincy railway between Chicago and Council Bluffs; the idea originated with the undersigned and was worked out with the assistance of Mr. Troy—then a clerk in my office in Chicago—and the master car builder of the C., B. & Q. R. R., and was a success from the beginning.

The racks occupied the central portion of the cars—just as the "Harrison Bag Rack" does now—and consisted of three or four sections, as the case might be—each six feet long by four and a half feet deep, making, when set up, a continuous rack, running lengthwise of the car, eighteen or twenty-four feet long and four and a half deep, capable of accommodating four tiers of sacks hanging open mouthed on four hooks set a foot apart each way, the capacity of the rack being either seventy-two or ninety-six separations.

The construction of the rack was as follows:—If eighteen feet long, twenty stanchions with slots in upper end, reinforced with steel or iron, were fastened to the floor of the car six feet apart one way and a foot the other; if twenty-four feet long, twenty-five stanchions were required. Fifteen bars of well seasoned wood, each 6 feet long, 7 inches wide, 1 inch thick, were provided, if the rack was to be eighteen feet long; if twenty-four feet, twenty were required; if eighteen feet, twelve bars were furnished with hooks on both sides, those on the side facing the clerk were near the lower edge of the bars —those on the opposite side were near the upper edge.

The first tier of sacks rested on the floor of the car, the first bars being placed just high enough to permit the sacks to hang easily on the hooks when full, each succeeding tier was about four inches higher than the preceding one, and the floor was raised correspondingly. A table upon which the mail was emptied, and the pouches opened and closed, was set into the rack, and some overhead boxes and a row of hooks fastened to the inside wall of the car, back of the clerk standing at the rack, added to the capacity of the car for distribution purposes. German student lamps had been substituted for the old oil lamps, which was a marked improvement, as was the rack, over any previous interior fixtures or furnishings.

In closing out the rack the first tier of sacks was removed first and that row of bars taken down; the succeeding tiers were disposed of in like manner and in regular order; the rack was dressed as the bars were replaced, beginning with the fourth tier and working to the front.

The clerks soon learned the sacks that were filled and tied out most often, and hung them in the first tier and at the end of the rack, so that they could be removed and replaced with the minimum of inconvenience and delay to distribution.

The Seventh Division was cut out of the Sixth in the closing days of 1874, and Mr. Walter L. Hunt, my crew mate of 1869 and 1870 in the Chicago & Iowa City R. P. O., and later chief clerk of the service under Mr. Bangs, was appointed superintendent of it, and filled the office with credit many years.

Some time after our wooden rack had demonstrated its superiority over the circular case, I received a letter from Mr. Hunt, saying he had placed an iron rack made of gas pipe in the St. Louis & Kansas City R. P. O., and invited me to come down and see it. I accepted, and accompanied by Charles R. Harrison of our service—who was becoming very much interested in the subject of bag racks—visited St. Louis, without much delay, and with our host we examined the rack carefully.

It was well put up; the upper surface was level, and I remember it as being stationary—not constructed to close down when not in use. In both these respects it was inferior to the wooden rack; the rise of one tier four or five inches above the next made it easier to locate the position of each sack in the wooden rack in one's mind and prevented mail intended for sacks in one tier, gliding over into those in the next tier, if thrown a little high, thus compelling loss of time in correcting the accidents, also preventing delay to such mail and its being charged as errors against the clerks who distributed it. The two racks suggested the material and form, or general plan, of what was afterwards known as the Harrison bag rack, and that form or principle is still perpetuated, though the whole of the wooden rack was in front of the distributers, whereas the Harrison bag rack has two tiers on either side of the car which are suplemented by portable links that may be used to increase the capacity of the rack whenever the schemes call for a larger number of separations than the regular folding racks and the overhead boxes will accommodate. When in use, one end is hooked onto the rack, the other end clutches the iron rod running lengthwise of the car the full length of the racks. This rack has been improved from time to time and is now in almost universal use.

Two paper cases, thought by some to be improvements, were introduced during this period, but became obsolete long since.

Changes have been made in letter cases, but the angular form has been maintained—though one wing almost always extends along the side of the car for a considerable distance, the greatest change is the reversible sections, which minimize negligence and insure cleanliness. The racks in which are usually hung the pouches to accommodate the made-up letter mail are, in most cases, placed directly opposite the long section and are convenient.

Early in my experience as superintendent of the Fourth—now Sixth division—when the first-class matter distributed in the Chicago & Iowa City R. P. O. was quite heavy, even for those days, the general manager of the Chicago, Rock Island & Pacific R. R., on my request, caused a letter case to be built in each of the cars of that route on the following plan:

The case was built lengthwise of the car down the center of one end of it, and faced both ways; it was composed of three sections, in the angular form, on each side—the center section being much longer than the wing sections—and under it were openings through which letters intended for one clerk but received by the other were transferred; there was also a smaller triangular case in the end of the double case fronting the paper case; in this the center section, while of full height, was very narrow and the wings were also wings of the main case. This case was satisfactory on that particular route at the time it was built, but conditions changed; so large a letter case became unnecessary and was removed and the angular end case restored.

During all this time great interest was manifested, in improving the interior fixtures of the cars, by the officers and clerks of the service, and in locating them to the best advantage. The fact that the angular reversible letter case, the Harrison bag rack, steam heat from the engine, supplemented with the Baker heater and stoves; electricity and compressed gas, supplemented with improved oil lamps for illuminating purposes, all of which have not been displaced, certainly shows that no mistake was made in adopting them, but up to the closing months of 1891, the companies were permitted to set up the frames of postal cars according to the plans and specifications used in building coaches—thus overlooking the fact that because of their assignment in trains they occupied the most hazardous position; that in head-end collisions they were likely to be crushed like egg shells, or to be broken up in derailments, and in rolling down embankments—the other cars piling on top of them.

The awful disaster at Kipton, Ohio, in which six of our clerks were killed, forced the conviction that I could not escape responsibility for such losses thereafter, if I did not utilize all the authority vested in my office to prevent them, and I appointed a committee of three superintendents, Burt, Troy and Pepper, to formulate specifications for framing postal cars, and instructed the committee to confer with the master car builders of some of the most important trunk lines with a view of securing suggestions from these experts as to the best method of strengthening the construction. The committee performed the work assigned them well and made their report under date of September 22, 1891.

The framing specifications submitted with the report provided that:—

"The side sills be composed of two pieces of lumber, each 4x8 inches, with a plate of iron ½x8 inches between, bolted together firmly, the plate bent around, forming an angle against the end sills, which were to be of white oak 8x8 inches, reinforced on bottom with iron plates $\frac{1}{2}$x8 inches; the center sill 5x8 inches, plated with $\frac{1}{2}$x8 inch iron bent around so as to form angle against end sill; it also provided for ten longitudinal sills of long leaf southern yellow pine thoroughly seasoned, instead of six or eight, as had been the practice previously.

End plates, $2\frac{1}{2}$ inches thick, with iron plates $\frac{3}{8}$x6 inches on inner side at bottom; plate turned into angle at end against side plates.

Body bolsters.—Double top and bottom plates 6x1 inch each.

Studding.—$2\frac{1}{4}$x$2\frac{3}{4}$ inches, placed about 18 inches center to center. First and third posts from end of car plated on both sides with $\frac{1}{4}$x$2\frac{3}{4}$ inch iron. All corner and end posts plated with $\frac{3}{4}$ inch iron full height and width, with ends turned into angles against end plate and end sill.

Carlines.—Nine iron carlines $\frac{5}{8}$x2 inches, following the contour of upper and lower deck.

Truss rods.—Two truss rods, $1\frac{1}{2}$ inches in diameter, with $1\frac{3}{4}$ inch ends, and connected in center with turnbuckle.

Platforms.—Whether Miller or Janney, are to be put up in accordance with the established standards, and in addition thereto the platform timbers are to be plated both sides with $\frac{1}{4}$ inch iron the full depth of the timbers, and draft timbers are to be plated in the same manner with $\frac{3}{8}$ inch iron.

Trucks.—Axles should not be smaller than the 1891 M. C. B. standard for thirty ton cars, with bearings and oil boxes in proportion. There should be safety straps under the spring plank and brake beams. Wheel pieces should be plated on both sides with $\frac{3}{8}$ inch iron. There should be six wheels—steel tired preferred—to each truck, with a wheel spread not less than ten feet. Side bearings should be of a section not less than 2x3 inches. Equalizing bars 2x$4\frac{1}{2}$ inches, made of the best hammered scrap.

Brakes.—Air and automatic, latest improved form of application."

The specifications show other items which contributed to the strength of the cars built between 1891 and 1904, but I have not mentioned them, because it is the intention to call attention only to those which were wrought through the application of iron plates to the timbers and angles that were subject to the greatest strain at all times, and to the hardest blows and greatest concussion in derailments and collisions, to the running gear, and brakes.

To these improvements was due almost wholly the fact that cars built as the specifications provided weighed 19,800 pounds more than those previously provided by the companies.

My object in reproducing here so much of the specifications that were first issued by authority of the Government to govern the construction of postal cars is to enable those most interested to see that the first step taken in the effort to afford greater protection to their lives and limbs was a meritorious one, and also to compare that construction with the one provided for, in the specifications of Department Plan No. 1, which was issued May 1, 1904. As will be seen, these specifications were revisions of those issued in 1891, of which I have just written—and were made under the following circumstances:

The dreadful disaster to the Washington & Greensboro R. P. O. at Danville, Va., in which clerks Thompson, Flory, Chambers and Argenbright were instantly killed, and Spies so severely injured that he died soon thereafter, and Reams, Brooks, Maupin, Dunlap and Indermauer seriously injured, occurred September 27, 1903. I read of it in the papers next morning on the way to the Department; it was an awful shock, and by the time the Department was reached I felt that something must be done immediately to still further strengthen the cars, and to provide for a knowledge of the condition of all cars, then in the service. At the Department I passed my own office, proceeding direct to the Second Assistant, and in a brief time we discussed the whole question thoroughly, as we had in part several times previously; the outcome was that I was to send out instructions in line with our conversation; revise the specifications and submit them to him for his approval and that of the Postmaster General. I called Superintendent Vickery—who is well versed in car construction for a layman—in consultation at once, and, after exchanging views, requested him to see if he could not get the Southern Railway people to assist him in drawing up a tracing from which blue prints could be made, showing all the changes decided upon. This he did and was so fortunate as to secure the services of one of their draughtsmen for very reasonable compensation, which I paid out of my own pocket.

Another plan, called Department Plan No. 2, was drawn up by the master car builders of some of the roads with headquarters in Chicago; this plan provided for a lighter construction than No. 1, but for a stronger car than the plan of 1891 called for; however, both plans were adopted, but No. 1 was the preferential plan, and I am pleased to learn that No. 2 is not in use.

The framing specifications of Plan No. 1, as compared with those given above of the 1891 car, were:

"Body Frame.—Composed of ten sills. Side sills each composed of two pieces; outside piece to be 5x8½ inches; inside piece, or sub sill, to be 2½x7¾ inches.

A plate of steel $\frac{1}{2}$x8 inches, to extend back from end sill to center of car, between the sills, and end turned, to form angle against end sill; plates to have cover plate $\frac{3}{8}$x12 inches by 8 inches at break, held in place by eight $\frac{5}{8}$ inch counter-sunk head bolts, main plates counter-sunk for bolt heads on side next main sill; outside sill, sub-sill and plate to be firmly bolted together with $\frac{5}{8}$ inch bolts, staggered and not more than 18 inches apart.

Center Sills.—5x7$\frac{3}{4}$ inches, also plated with $\frac{1}{2}$x7$\frac{3}{4}$ inch steel on outside face, to extend back 18 feet from each end of car and turned over to form angle against end sill. This plate must not be cut to receive tenons on bridging, but a sub-sill, 1$\frac{1}{2}$x7$\frac{3}{4}$ inches by 15 feet 6 inches in length, of yellow pine, bolted to plate and sill, must be mortised for the bridging.

Intermediate Sills.—Two on each side of car, 4x7$\frac{3}{4}$ inches, between center and side sill.

End Sills.—White oak, thoroughly seasoned, composed of two pieces with $\frac{3}{4}$x8 inch steel plate between them. Front piece to be 4$\frac{1}{2}$x8$\frac{1}{2}$ inches; back piece to be 3$\frac{1}{2}$x8$\frac{1}{2}$ inches; back piece rabbeted to receive first floor.

Platform.—To be short standard steel "I" beam construction, to be put up in accordance with the established standard practice. To have 14x7$\frac{1}{2}$ inch white oak buffer beam, plated on top surface with $\frac{3}{4}$ inch steel, to conform with shape of buffer beams; plate to be held in place by countersunk head bolts, fitted with check nuts; wearing surface opposite door, to be machined to a diamond pattern top surface.

Buffer beam to be secured to end sills by at least eight $\frac{3}{4}$ inch bolts, and to rest on, and be secured by bolts, to eye beams.

Two 7 inch 23.46 lbs. bulb beams, installed at each end of car. Bulb and web of beam to be cut away, allowing flange to project down between end sill and serve as a truss rod washer, and also fastened to top of plate covering platform by means of angle iron brace securely bolted to each side of beams; top of beams to be butted to end plate, and flange to rest against stiffening plates on end post.

The poplar strips encasing bulb beams to be formed on the inside to take the shape of beams, and be securely through-bolted by means of round head bolts and nuts. All bolts to be center punched on nut end after tightening up nut in place.

End Plates.—End plates to be three inches thick, with steel plate, $\frac{3}{8}$x6 inch, on inner side and turned into angle at end against side plate.

Studding.—Studding to be not less than 2 inches by 3$\frac{1}{2}$ inches, placed about 18 inches center to center. First and fourth posts from end of car to have 2x2 inch angle iron fitted to inside corner, with one leg turned in to form angle against both sill and plate. All end posts to be reinforced with steel plates, $\frac{3}{4}$x3$\frac{1}{2}$ inches, twisted at right angles at both top and bottom, and securely bolted to both sill and plate. These plates must not be cut to receive tenons of bracing, but an extra piece, 1$\frac{1}{2}$x3$\frac{3}{4}$ inches, extending from end to end over flat surface of plate and mortised to receive tenons of bracing, and all to be securely bolted together.

Safety Bar.—One inch gas pipe suspended at a level of 7 feet 3 inches from top of floor to center of bar and 19 inches from center of car. The bar to extend from the letter case end of car to end of paper distributing racks, located over the aisle, between racks, so as to clear lamps. A ball ornament at both ends of bar for finish. The bars suspended by hangers not more than 8 feet apart, secured to deck ceiling with four No. 18 wood screws. Filing blocks between ceiling and roof at each hanger. The hanger composed of 1 inch gas pipe, screwed into collar at top and a pipe tee at bottom, receiving sections of the bar screwed in same.

One iron brace 1$\frac{1}{2}$ inches by $\frac{3}{8}$ inch at each hanger, extending from bar to deck sill, and secured to same with four No. 16 wood screws. The first hanger at letter case end secured with iron brace $\frac{1}{2}$ inch by $\frac{3}{8}$ inch, 24 inches from center of hanger to end plate. The bar to be gilded. Also short safety bar, to extend from letter case end of car to end of letter case, opposite long bar and secured in the same manner, located 19 inches from center of car.

Carlines.—Ten iron carlines, $\frac{3}{8}$ inch by 2 inches, following the contour of upper and lower deck.

Truss Rods.—Four truss rods, 1$\frac{1}{2}$ inches in diameter, with 1$\frac{3}{4}$ inch ends, and connected in center with turnbuckle.

Vestibules.—Standard short vestibule with diaphragm complete.

Trucks.—Axles should not be smaller than M. C. B. standard for 40-ton cars, with bearings and oil boxes in proportion. There should be safety straps under the spring plank and brake beams. Wheel pieces should be plated on both sides with $\frac{1}{2}$ inch iron. There should be six wheels—steel tired preferred—to each truck, with total wheel base of not less than ten feet. Side bearings should be of a section of not less than 2x3 inches. Equalizing bars, 2$\frac{1}{2}$ inches by 7 inches, made of axle steel.

Brakes.—Automatic high-speed air brakes of the latest design."

These specifications provided for a much stronger car than those built under the specifications of 1891. While those were excellent cars—far better than any previously built—stronger cars had become necessary, and also more thorough inspection and examination of them, by our own officers, while they were in course of construction, and this was provided for. The frequency of train service, both passenger and freight, and the rate of speed, had increased wonderfully; this had increased the hazard to our service. The companies recognized the fact that all their trains were in greater jeopardy and they undertook to minimize the bad results by double tracking their main lines and applying the best safety devices manufactured. They laid down heavier rails, in some instances replacing 67-pound with 100-pound steel rail, ballasted their road-beds with the best material available, took out curves, reduced grades, strengthened bridges, employed track walkers and bridge guards—in short, did everything that suggested itself to the most experienced and skillful managers and operatives, but the accidents did not seem to decrease, so we brought out Plan No. 1 on May 1, 1904.

The specifications given above show how great strength was secured, and it is only necessary to add that the Pennsylvania Company built postal cars after a modification of this plan, which weighed 28,200 pounds more than the cars built after the 1891 plan, and 20,500 more than those cars did after they were vestibuled and mounted on heavier trucks.

I desire, however, to introduce here a communication on this subject, which Superintendent Bradley of the Second division very kindly favored me with, in response to my earnest request for some information.

Mr. Bradley, like all our superintendents, is an officer of great ability, but his headquarters are in the second largest city in the world; in and out of which more railway trains pass daily than any other; where the volume of mail and trade is greater, and the necessities for improved methods of handling and transportation are in proportion. This explains why his services are so largely in demand, and why he has been forced to acquire knowledge not only of the branch of postal service to which he belongs but of other branches as well.

With it all, he finds time to cultivate "his boys" for their good, and the combination helps to make life pleasant for others. It has for the writer.

Mr. Bradley's Letter.

New York, N. Y., May 17, 1909.

Dear Captain: I have gotten together a few facts and dates regarding postal car construction, and send them herewith, hoping that they will be serviceable.

* * * * * * *

HON. VICTOR J. BRADLEY
Superintendent Second Division R. M. S.
(See Appendix)

Postal Car Construction.

In the annual reports of the General Superintendent R. M. S., 1879 to 1886, there is nothing special about car construction except that in 1886 General Superintendent Jamison says: "While many improvements have been made of late in the construction and equipment of railroad lines as a protection to life and limb, the occupation of the postal clerk would seem to be rendered none the less dangerous on this account, as many risks must necessarily be assumed by him in handling the mails which cannot be well avoided, or injury guarded against."

In the reports from 1887 to 1890 there is nothing special.

In the report of 1891 of General Superintendent White, we find the first attempt at framing specifications in the report of a committee (appointed by the General Superintendent R. M. S.) dated September 22, 1891.

In 1903 and 1904 the number of casualties involving fatalities to railway postal clerks was unusually great, there being 18 postal clerks killed during the fiscal year 1903, and the same number during 1904, in addition to 78 seriously injured during the former year, and 90 seriously injured during the latter year.

These deplorable occurrences caused especial study to be given to the subject to ascertain the degree of compliance by railroad companies with the framing specifications of 1891; but better yet, to ascertain whether in view of the increased strength and weight of locomotive engines and other railroad equipment, the framing of postal cars had kept pace with these higher standards of weight and strength. The result was shown in the Department specifications of May 1, 1904, which represented a degree of strength believed to be considerably in excess of any passenger car equipment then existing, and it was particularly specified that division superintendents must inspect every postal car while in course of construction, and verify the dimensions and quality of the framework before it was covered up, and then to make a final inspection of the car before it was allowed to go into service.

The report of 1905 showed that 118 new cars had been built and inspected under these new specifications; and the report of 1906 showed 97 additional new cars, and no doubt similar progress has been made in succeeding years.

On the Pennsylvania Railroad System the Department Plan No. 1 was accepted, and somewhat modified to give what the railroad company believed to be additional strength to the end construction. The first of these cars (No. 6503) went into operation in February, 1905, and was severely tested soon thereafter in a wreck which occurred to New York & Washington R. P. O. train No. 52, at Plainsboro, N. J., at 4:20 a. m. on May 5, 1905. Train No. 52 running at a speed of about 45 miles per hour ran into a freight wreck which occurred a few minutes before train 52 was due. The engine and tender of train 52 was derailed and turned over, falling to the right of the track. This left the new postal car (No. 6503), which deflected to the left, to receive the full brunt of the collision from the wreckage. The postal car crushed through two box cars, breaking them to kindling wood, and finally struck a steel gondola car. The postal car lost its front trucks, and the truss rods were twisted; but outside of this there was substantially no injury to the car. There were twelve postal clerks on duty—seven in the new car and five in the wooden postal car in the rear. The clerks were all of the opinion that the extraordinary strength of the new car had saved their lives. The weight of these postal cars averaged about 104,000 to 108,000 pounds, in contrast with a former weight of about 80,000 to 85,000 pounds.

During the time that the General Superintendent was developing the stronger postal car specifications, Mr. F. D. Underwood, president of the Erie Railroad Company, proposed in a letter to the Department, dated January 28, 1904, to build a steel postal car, and the offer being accepted this car was constructed by the Standard Steel Car Company, and went into service June 7, 1905, on the New York, Salamanca & Chicago line. This was the first modern steel postal car in use on any line in the country. It was number 699, 65 feet in length inside measurement, and weighed 118,300 pounds.

In course of time it was followed up by two other steel postal cars on the same road, these weighing 123,000 and 124,000 pounds respectively, they being 60 feet in length, inside measurement.

Some months later the Pennsylvania Railroad Company prepared specifications for steel postal cars, and the first of these (No. 6546) commenced regular service on the New York & Washington line March 10, 1907. The Pennsylvania Railroad standard is 70 feet in length, inside measurement, and there are at present (May, 1909) 19 of these cars in use on that line. They weigh from 129,000 to 130,-000 pounds.

In these cars a successful effort has been made to construct all of the interior fixtures of steel, so that in one of these cars weighing 130,000 pounds there is less than 400 pounds of wood material.

New York and St. Louis Fast Mail
Pennsylvania Railroad Company. Horse Shoe Curve

The Pennsylvania Railroad now have in service 21 postal cars according to Department Plan No. 1. They also have 19 all steel cars in use.

This year's building program for the Pennsylvania Railroad calls for 47 seventy-foot steel postal cars; 11 seventy-foot steel mail apartment cars and 27 sixty-foot steel mail storage cars. We also hear that the Pennsylvania Company (lines west of Pittsburg) are to build 17 seventy-foot steel postal cars. We understand the outlay for the cars (omitting the last 17 mentioned) will be about one million dollars.

*   *   *   *   *   *   *

With best wishes from all here, I am,

Sincerely yours,
(Signed)   V. J. Bradley.

Mr. E. F. Postlethwaite, assistant to the President of the Pennsylvania Railroad Company, has my thanks for the facts upon which the following statement is based. This statement is given because it shows clearly the improvement in car construction as illustrated by their cost and weight:

Full cars built by that company in 1877, for the exclusive accommodation and distribution of the mail cost $3,565.00, no weight given.

In 1883, a few changes having been made in the construction, these built cars cost $3,880.00 each and weighed 58,000 pounds; they were provided with Baker heaters, and lighted with oil lamps, and had the old style link and pin couplers.

In 1891, the year our first specifications for the framing of postal cars was issued, the cars built cost $5,045.00 and weighed 77,800 pounds. These were lighted with gas and heated by steam.

In 1899, this same class of cars was built with stub vestibules and a heavier truck, which increased its strength and capacity, at a cost of $6,417.00, and weighed 85,500 pounds.

In 1904, our second plan, No. 1, was sent out. The cars built by the Pennsylvania Company by a modification of plan No. 1, though substantially the same, cost $6,926 and weighed 106,000 pounds, which necessitated using stronger trucks with 5x9-inch axles. These cars were lighted with Pintsch gas and heated by steam.

In March, 1907, one month after I retired from the service, this company brought out its first practically all-steel postal car. It was 70 feet long, 10 feet longer than the maximum provided for in the No. 1 car, there being but 400 pounds of wood material in it. This car cost $15,200 and weighed 128,500 pounds.

(This handsome, modern all-steel, electric-lighted postal car was described in detail in the April, 1907, issue of *The Railway Post Office,* with half tones of the interior and of the completed car, and interior plan of the car. This article occupied considerably more than two pages of that number. The description is, of course, too long to be reproduced here, but as the article was written by an expert, with particular reference to the special features of the car, we presume it has been preserved by those interested, and should be referred to by such persons. The plans were introduced during the administration of Capt. White, and with his approval.—Editor.)

What has been accomplished by this evolution in car building is exhibited in the following statement, which is made to cover periods of eight years:

From 1877 to 1884, Inclusive.

Twenty-five clerks were killed and 147 seriously injured; average annual number killed, $3\frac{1}{8}$; seriously injured, $18\frac{3}{8}$; average annual number of clerks, same period, 3,153; killed per thousand 1, plus; seriously injured, about 6.

From 1885 to 1892, Inclusive.

Forty-three clerks were killed and 463 seriously injured; average annual number killed, $5\frac{3}{8}$; seriously injured, $57\frac{7}{8}$; average annual number of clerks, same period, 5,329; killed per thousand, about 1; seriously injured, about 11.

From 1893 to 1900, Inclusive.

Fifty-seven clerks were killed and 385 seriously injured; average annual number killed, $7\frac{1}{8}$; seriously injured, $48\frac{1}{8}$; average annual number clerks in service, same period, 7,576; killed per thousand, 1, plus; seriously injured, 7, minus.

From 1901 to 1908, Inclusive.

Eighty clerks were killed and 750 seriously injured; average annual number killed, 10; seriously injured, 93 6-8; average annual number of clerks in service, same period, 11,803; killed per thousand, about 5-6; seriously injured, 8, minus.

The exhibit is that the improvement made in the construction of postal cars, in double tracking lines and keeping them in good condition, in the handling of trains by men whose moral standing when on duty, at least, is above reproach, etc., has not only overcome the increased hazard inseparable from increased frequency of train service and the very great increase of speed that has occurred during the past twenty years, but has actually reduced the per cent. of violent deaths and serious injuries in accidents to trains upon which railway post offices perform their functions, and this is a matter that should cause us all to rejoice.

SPECIAL SERVICE.

The Gold Train.

The large accumulation of gold coin in the United States sub-treasury at New York City, during one period of President Cleveland's first administration, was gradually reduced by shipments abroad, and by the cashing of gold certificates, until, in July, 1892, it amounted to less than $43,000,000. This sum, the Hon. Charles Foster, Secretary of the Treasury, felt with much anxiety might prove insufficient to meet the demands likely to be made upon it before the drift of business was reversed, and gold, then flowing outward, would commence to flow back to our shores. The margin ran too close to panic conditions; business was becoming more depressed daily; values were declining, and the financial outlook was overcast with clouds that portended misfortunes to many houses doing their utmost to stay the threatened catastrophe.

In this emergency the Secretary deemed it his duty, as a precautionary measure, to order the transfer of $20,000,000 in gold coin to the sub-treasury in New York City from the sub-treasury in San Francisco, in which latter there was then a surplus of $100,000,000. It had been customary for many years to send gold in amounts ranging from $50,000 to $200,000, as registered mail from San Francisco to New York City, enclosed in leather pouches, locked with brass locks, and in rawhide trunks. The secretary first planned to follow this custom but to increase the amount of each shipment to $1,000,000, thus consuming twenty days in the transfer, but his plan became public and was abandoned. After consulting with his assistants he held a conference with the Hon. John Wanamaker, Postmaster General, as to the best and safest method of moving so large a sum in coin, registered as mail, from one city to the other. Mr. J. Lowrie Bell, Second Assistant Postmaster General, and myself discussed the subject thoroughly, and gave our conclusions to our chief. The result of the conference between the Secretary and the Postmaster General was embodied in a letter of which the following is a copy:

"Post Office Department,
"Office Second Assistant Postmaster General.

"Washington, D. C., 20th July, 1892.

"Captain James E. White,

Gen'l Supt. Railway Mail Service.

"Sir: You will consider this as your authority to proceed to San Francisco, California, for the purpose of personally directing the movement by United States Mail, of a number of shipments of registered matter, particulars of which have already been furnished you. You will take such steps en route as may be requisite in the perfecting of arrangements for running the cars through from San Francisco to point of destination, and you will make such details of force from the railway mail service as shall enable you to assign to each car shipment one assistant superintendent and nine trusted clerks to continue in absolute charge until the arrival of the car they accompany at destination.

"Whatever details may occur to you as essential to the successful accomplishment of the service, you are hereby empowered to enforce. This office—by code—must be kept advised of such matters as you may from time to time deem necessary.

"Yours respectfully,

"(Signed)   J. Lowrie Bell,

"Second Assistant Postmaster General."

Complying with the above I departed from Washington, July 21, 1892, and made my first stop at Cleveland, Ohio, where I called upon Mr. W. H. Canniff, general manager of the Lake Shore & Michigan Southern Railway, and had a confidential conversation with him respecting the trip to the Pacific Coast. I closed with the request that he furnish one of the cars that would be needed to transport the gold and guards eastward and deliver it in Chicago, to the Chicago, Burlington & Quincy Railway, in time for that company to deliver it with one of their own to the Union Pacific System at Omaha, Neb., July 26, 1892, also to take care of the treasury cars from the time they were transferred to his company in Chicago until transferred to New York Central & Hudson River Co. at Buffalo, saying that that line would take them through to New York City without delay. Mr. Canniff agreed to perform all this promptly in natural sequence.

I had telegraphed Superintendents Troy, Pepper and Perkins, of the Sixth, Ninth and Tenth divisions, to meet me at the Grand Pacific Hotel, Chicago, Saturday morning, July 23, 1892, for consultation.

They reported promptly and the object of the call was made known to them, the character of the work was explained and they were informed that to transport and safeguard the coin from one coast to the other, five cars would be required, and that meant the detail of five officers and forty-five clerks, and that I would detail the three officers present, Superintendents Flint of the Eighth division and Assistant Superintendent Vaille of Portland, Oregon; that Superintendent Troy would select fifteen clerks, Pepper twelve, Perkins nine, Flint nine, and that Vaille's force would be composed of six from Troy's and three from Pepper's.

I stated that great care must be exercised in making selections, soldiers of the Civil War to be given the preference. The three superintendents with their thirty-six clerks were instructed to center at Omaha, Neb., the morning of Friday, July 29, and Supt. Troy was to have charge until they arrived at San Francisco. I gave him the inspector's commissions for these thirty-six employees to use bound east, without fail, and also west, if tickets could not be secured without cost. It was not deemed best to use commissions bound west, if it could be avoided, because of the suspicion and comments it might cause. Money was provided for living expenses and emergencies, and the superintendents were informed that they must preserve the strictest secrecy as to the object of the hegira to the coast of so many post office inspectors in a body.

They were to tell the clerks that the work of the divisions from which they were detailed had been so exceptionally good for some years that the Post Office Department desired as a measure of encouragement to recognize it in some unusual and attractive way, and believed that an outing across the country to San Francisco, with a few days for sight-seeing in that city, would not only please them, but that in extending to them the courtesies of the Eighth division, the clerks in that far off section would be brought in close contact with them, with the result that they would discuss the service, the methods in vogue in their respective divisions, and these distant comrades would absorb knowledge that would be of assistance to them in their work.

As a matter of fact these men made the trip to San Francisco, arriving there at 9:45 a. m., Monday, August 1, and departing for the east at 7:00 p. m., Thursday, August 4, 1892, without the least knowledge of the real object of the trip, nor were they then aware of it until they were taken down to the cars at the lower transfer the morning of this, the last day in San Francisco, to witness the opening of the army chests containing the Springfield carbines with 2,000 rounds of cartridges, the Colt revolvers, calibre 45, and 1,000 rounds of cartridges, with holsters and cartridge-belts sufficient to equip each member of the guard.

After arranging with the three superintendents at Chicago for the out-bound trip, its secrecy, etc., and providing Supterintendent Troy with sufficient money to pay their expenses west, I called on Mr. W. F. Merrill, general manager of the Chicago, Burlington & Quincy Railway, and conversed with him confidentially regarding the transfer of the gold coin. Mr. Merrill agreed to furnish one of their post office cars, No. 933, as their quota, and to deliver it and the Lake Shore & Michigan Southern post office car, No. 695, to the Union Pacific Company at Omaha, Tuesday, July 26, 1892—mileage not to be charged on No. 695. He also furnished tickets for the clerks, westbound, and agreed to accept the cars in which the gold would be transported either separately, or as a whole, made up as a special train, at Union Pacific Transfer, and to deliver them, as received, to the Lake Shore & Michigan Southern Railway at Chicago.

I then took up the memorandum of Second Assistant Postmaster General Bell, which provided that I fix the code to be used between him and myself, and answered it. It contemplated that there would, very likely, be five shipments of $4,000,000 each, rather than one of $20,000,000, and the one in charge of each shipment was to use the code in keeping us two advised of progress. The draft of the answer I drew off with a lead pencil on yellow paper, and sent a corrected copy in ink to Mr. Bell. It read as follows:

Chicago, July 25, 1892.

Mr. Bell: Thus far the arrangement is all right. The L. S. & M. S. will provide one car, and the C. B. & Q. one. These two will be forwarded to Union Pacific Transfer Tuesday. I will leave here to-night, and see Mr. Dickinson at Omaha to-morrow. Will try to get two cars and a colonist sleeper from him; the sleeper to be used westbound only; if I can get it free, will; if not will get it at reduced rates, but believe I can get it without cost. The men will need sleeping accommodations going west, for they will have to rough it coming east.

I expect to leave Omaha Monday night on Fast Mail, and Troy, Pepper and Perkins, with their men, will center at Omaha Friday morning and leave that afternoon. This will give me time to reach San Francisco and telegraph them before they leave Omaha. Going west, I shall, if possible, provide the men with tickets, if I can secure them without cost, for this will prevent any comment on the large number of commissions.

The C. B. & Q. will provide the tickets over their line free. Coming back we will use the commissions, and if everything works smoothly we will reach Omaha east-bound on the 8th of August, Chicago on the 9th, and New York City on the 10th. (As a matter of fact we arrived at Union Pacific Transfer, Iowa, on Sunday at 7:00 p. m., August 7th, Chicago at 8:15 a. m., August 8th, and New York City at 10:46 a. m., Tuesday, August 9th, 1892.)

I suggest that you arrange personally with the New York Central to carry the train from Buffalo to New York, so that there may be no hitch at Buffalo. Will telegraph you the day we leave San Francisco as follows, if as second section: "Have engaged an old stage coach for the World's Fair." If five shipments must be made, will telegraph the day the first one leaves, "Syracuse and Cleveland division should be extended," which will mean, Pepper in charge. Second shipment, "Portland and San Francisco in good condition," which will mean Flint in charge. Third shipment, "Vaille can be supplied from Los Banos route," which will mean Vaille in charge. Fourth shipment, "Minneapolis and Chicago needs 40 foot additional," which will mean Perkins in charge. Fifth shipment, "White's Bridge should be made a Post Office," which will mean that White and Troy are in charge. I expect, however, to come as a second section and if so will be in charge.

If five shipments, will send Pepper first, so that if a hitch occurs between Chicago and New York City, he can correct it before the second shipment is due.

Keep June schedules of Sixth and Eighth divisions and July of the Ninth before you. If anything happens on the Ogden & San Francisco R. P. O.—such as hot box, broken engine, repairs to track, some other train in ditch, or any other ordinary cause of delay, I will telegraph, "See page 23.—Land slide at 2:05 a. m.," which would mean delayed at Gold Run. Any other time given in the telegram would indicate where the delay occurred. If we are ditched will substitute for land slide "Ruins at 2:05 a. m.," and the number following would indicate how many are unfit to defend.

If attacked will substitute "Strike on again at 2:05 a. m. in Idaho." After that there will be no use in using cipher but will talk out in meeting.

If you find it necessary to call a halt anywhere, you will know what to say. I will understand.

If everything moves right will telegraph from Reno, Ogden, Cheyenne, Union Pacific Transfer and Chicago, "Service in excellent condition."   Respectfully,

WHITE.

Having finished and mailed the above, I took the train for Omaha, where I arrived Monday morning, July 25, and as early in the day as possible saw General Manager Dickinson, who agreed to furnish two of the five cars, viz: baggage car No. 1092, and express car No. 1242. Both were unusually well built cars, and No. 1242 was plated throughout its interior with boiler iron, and its windows were heavily barred. He also agreed to waive mileage on the foreign cars; to issue tickets for the west-bound trip; to furnish a tourists' sleeper to San Francisco, for the minimum charge in one direction, and finally to accept the cars, east-bound, from the Southern Pacific Company, at Ogden, Utah, either separately, with their guards, or made up as a train with all the guards, to push them, or it, through to Union Pacific Transfer and deliver it, or them, to the Chicago, Burlington & Quincy Railway without avoidable delay. This being accomplished, I took passage in the Omaha & Ogden Fast Mail that evening, and changing to the Ogden & San Francisco Fast Mail at Ogden arrived at San Francisco at 9:45 a m., Thursday, July, 28.

I called on Vice-President Towne and Manager Fillmore on my arrival and made satisfactory arrangements for tickets for the clerks from Ogden to San Francisco; for the delivery of the four cars that were to be used to transport the gold, and that were then en route to Ogden, into their own yards in San Francisco, without mileage charge, and on the return trip to deliver them as a second section of their east-bound Fast Mail, running ten minutes behind it, to the Union Pacific Company, at Ogden, Utah. This decided the question whether the $20,000,000 would be dispatched in five separate shipments of $4,000,-000 each, or, as occurred, in one shipment of $20,000,000, by special train. To complete this train, for the best transportation and guard purposes, the Southern Pacific Company furnished as its quota an officers' car with an observation end, and facilities for making coffee. I carried west a letter, addressed to me by instruction of the chief of ordnance, War Department, informing me that the commanding officer of the Benicia Arsenal at Benicia, California, had been directed to issue to me seventy-five rifles or carbines, as I might elect, with not exceeding 3000 rounds of ammunition and such equipment as I might desire. I therefore visited the arsenal and presented the letter to the commanding officer, who accepted it and was ready to comply with the instructions, he having received a letter from the same officer, and to the same effect as mine, but I said I desired a change made in the arms, ammunition, equipment, etc., if permissible. He asked what change I would like, and I said I would prefer sixty Springfield carbines and 2,000 rounds of cartridges, fifty-one Colt's revolvers and 1000 cartridges, fifty-one cartridge belts and the same number of holsters. The commanding officer said he thought that could be arranged, and while I waited he received authority to do so. The invoice of arms, ammunition and equipment turned over to me was made out and I receipted it, requesting that the boxes containing them be delivered to the address I gave. I then telegraphed to Mr. Fillmore, the manager of the Southern Pacific Company, the disposition to be made of the boxes until I could see him; he wired back as follows:

"San Francisco, Cal., August 2, 1892.

"*James E. White,*

"*Army Point, Benicia, Çal.*

"I have given the necessary instructions as per your telegram relative to boxes from Army Point to-morrow morning on Train No. 12.

"(Signed)   J. A. FILLMORE."

I returned to San Francisco at once and called on Hon. J. P. Jackson, the assistant treasurer of the United States in that city, and found his force engaged in packing the coin, $5, $10 and $20 pieces, in substantial boxes, eight sacks, each sack containing $5,000, being packed in each of the 500 boxes. When all were packed the covers were screwed down securely with long screws. On each end of each box was an iron handle. Each box weighed 160 pounds gross and contained 152 pounds of gold, a boxful was worth $40,000. Every box was registered separately and was sealed twice with the official seal in red wax of Col. J. P. Jackson, assistant United States treasurer at San Francisco. The registry numbers ran from 4421 to 4920, inclusive. The entire shipment of gold was 76,000 pounds net, or including the boxes, 80,000 pounds. Col. Jackson's work was progressing finely. I found him very courteous, and was most favorably impressed with him.

I then visited the post office again and had a short conversation with Mr. Backus, the postmaster, about registering the mail in the sub-treasury, thus avoiding one haul and one chance of the transfer becoming known. The next call was on Superintendent Flint, who handed me a telegram from Mr. Fillmore, requesting me to call at his office that afternoon. I called and found that the wife of a member of a gang of train robbers had called at the baggage car of a train standing in the yard of the Southern Pacific, and handed the baggage man a letter addressed to her husband and asked him to mail it. He accepted it, and made a proper delivery, considering the circumstances.

He knew nothing about the proposed shipment of gold east, but he did know the woman, the lawless occupation of her husband, and the losses his employers had sustained at the hands of these marauders, and delivered it properly. It was read with great care, first in the regular way, then between the lines, upside down, down side up, under a magnifying glass, etc., etc., but without finding that this wife was seeking to inform her "lord and master" that the largest "Jack pot" ever heard of in that land once famous for the magnitude and frequency of the game, was in sight and might be had if they could locate it and wipe out of existence as courageous and experienced defenders of anything entrusted to their care as ever lived, and who were well armed and mostly men who had fought on battle fields of the Civil War, and afterward—during their experience in the railway mail service, had come to understand that their civil calling was sacred; that honor, responsibility, fidelity and eternal vigilance were wrapped up in it, that it was fraught with the full culmination of a hazardous occupation—loss of life and limb, wrecked health and sometimes distress and poverty. Does anyone believe that men reared in these schools would flinch if the hour of supreme trial came, when they were equipped to meet it, in part, at least? I did not, nor ever have.

Superintendents Troy, Perkins and Pepper, with their thirty-six men, centered at Omaha on Friday morning, July 29, 1892, as provided in the Chicago conference, and arrived at San Francisco at 9:45 a. m., Monday, August 1, 1892. The whole force remained there sightseeing until the morning of August 4.

The last subjects that threatened trouble were: First, a claim made by one of the companies for mileage on the foreign cars hauled by it, empty, west-bound; that was settled quickly and pleasantly by the company waiving the claim. Second, the presentation for my signature of a paper of which the following is a copy:

"San Francisco, August 3, 1892.

"To the Southern Pacific Company:

"I am directed by the Postmaster General to require your company to furnish transportation for twenty million dollars of gold coin from San Francisco to Ogden by passenger train. It will require four baggage or express cars and it is the desire of the Department that such cars shall be used as may go through to New York without requiring the transfer of the specie en route.

"We shall also require the transportation of fifty men by same train which carries the specie, these men being required as guards.

"I hereby certify that the Southern Pacific Co. has furnished transportation from Ogden to San Francisco by express train for fifty men en route to San Francisco, to return with the specie aforesaid as guards."

This and a similar paper I succeeded in convincing Mr. Towne I could not sign, and he consented to consider a paper which I proposed to draw up, and did as follows:

"San Francisco, August 3, 1892.

"Personal.

"*Mr. A. N. Towne, Sec., Vice-Pres. and Gen. Mgr.*
Southern Pacific Co., City.

"Dear Sir: I hereby certify that the Southern Pacific Company, through you, has provided for the transportation from San Francisco, California, to Ogden, Utah, of large quantities of valuable registered mail, the same to be transported in four express cars, furnished by the Lake Shore & Michigan Southern, Chicago, Burlington & Quincy and Union Pacific Companies. I have post office inspectors' commissions for fifty men, besides myself, who are to accompany and protect said registered mail, all of whom I will provide for when the cars are en route. I will want to leave San Francisco, or Oakland Pier, as may be determined later on, either Thursday night or Friday morning. Will you please make all arrangements in advance, in a quiet way, to effect a safe and expeditious transit over your road.

"Yours truly,

"(Signed) James E. White,
"Gen'l Supt., R. M. S."

The morning of the 4th Superintendent Flint was provided money and instructed to purchase provisions for the trip from San Francisco to Ogden and mattresses, camp stools, chairs and tinware for the whole journey.

Finding that the gold coin had been boxed and registered and that the Southern Pacific Company had made up the train at the Lower Transfer, the observation end of the officers' car coupled to the tender, which was narrower than that car and the engine, enabled the guards who occupied the chairs placed in front of the observation windows to focus their sight in front of the engine and to command the country and the steps on either side of the engine upon which one must mount to gain access to that machine. Then followed C. B. & Q. R. P. O car No. 933, L. S. & M. S. R. P. O. car No. 695, Union Pacific baggage car No. 1092 and express car No. 1242 of the same line, a regular iron clad. The boxes, equally apportioned, were transported in the four cars last mentioned. A "dinky" car was hauled part way to accommodate the train crew.

The chests and boxes containing the ordnance stores were placed in these cars. The guards were shown into their respective cars, then the chests and boxes were opened and the munitions issued to the guards. After this the registered boxes began to be moved from the sub-treasury across the city on heavy truck wagons to the Lower Transfer. As a wagon was loaded a tarpaulin was thrown over the boxes and two guards with arms concealed accompanied it to the train and saw them unloaded. Enough wagons were engaged in the transfer to prevent delay. As each was unloaded it returned to the sub-treasury and proceeded as before. The officers and guard at the Lower Transfer placed the boxes on the floor of each car, one layer deep only, on each side of an imaginary aisle running lengthwise through the center of the car; piled this way each car contained 125 boxes. On top of these were placed the mattresses upon which the guards rested when off duty. There were nine clerks and one officer in each of the four cars carrying gold. In the first, or observation car, sometimes called the danger car, there were nine guards and two officers; five constituted a squad, therefore, there were two squads in each car, and they relieved each other regularly; those who were off duty and lying down either sleeping or resting, were required to keep their carbines by their sides, the barrel resting in the inside curve of the arm and the revolver within reach; those who were on duty were required to occupy chairs and camp stools near the doors and windows, to keep wide awake, their revolvers in holsters belted on their bodies, their carbines in reach and the doors bolted and locked. No one was permitted to enter any of these cars, not even the one to which he was assigned, without first giving the countersign "Grant," a name selected in honor of our old commander.

The provisions, bedding, furniture, etc., that Superintendent Flint was commissioned to purchase in the morning arrived during the day and were placed in the cars. All this was transpiring in the business portion of the city all day and no one except those officially concerned in it seemed to know anything about it. The postmaster of San Francisco had receipted to Colonel Jackson for the registered boxes, and now having checked off the last one in turn I receipted to Postmaster Backus for the whole 500 boxes, containing an aggregate of $20,000,000 in gold coin.

Hon. Norman Perkins
Superintendent Tenth Division R. M. S.
(See Appendix)

We felt that we had done well in placing in proper position on the train everything that had been assigned to our charge, without the knowledge of anyone on the outside.

We left the Lower Transfer secretly as a supposed silk train, and this fable served its purpose well; it was repeated whenever its effectiveness was not likely to be doubted until we arrived at Ogden, Utah. The guards were in their assignments, the doors were locked, all were wide awake as we moved out into the Sacramento Valley on the old Central Pacific track, as a second section of the Trans-Continental Fast Mail, the position we intended to occupy until the last stretch of the run, Chicago to New York, began.

No doubt many are living to-day in that beautiful valley who recall the wonderful "silk train" that moved like an electric flame, bearing re-enforcements of financial strength from the chief port of the Pacific to the chief port of the Atlantic, pausing to repair a drawhead on car No. 695 before commencing the ascent of the mountains towering in the rear of Sacramento City.

A half hour was lost in this operation and then the train moved quietly out into the plains, up the foothills and the climb began; the higher we mounted the more tense the strain upon the couplings became. The monster engine generated and expended force with great urgency—its exhaust represented its vitality just as the action of the human heart presents the condition of the human system of which it is the thermometer, and one skilled in either can tell by the sound to the ear or the touch of the finger whether the limit of the power has been reached or more is generating than is needed to move the load. The strain became greater until in the extreme effort to reach the apex the coupling between the engine and the observation car broke, and the situation became dangerous, but the company had taken the precaution to reinforce the couplings at all points with chains and this was demonstrated to be absolutely necessary when the coupling between the engine and the observation car parted; had the chain been lacking the five cars would have commenced the descent the moment they broke from the power that held them, before air or hand brakes could have been applied—and down they would have started upon a ride to destruction at least—perhaps to death.

The loss in time which occurred at Sacramento, added to the delay in repairing the couplings at Colfax, Cal., put us more than three hours behind the Fast Mail at that point. In a short time it was noticed that our train was being side-tracked in favor of all trains moving west, and I called on the conductor for an explanation; he said he had wired the exact situation to his superintendent but no satisfactory instructions had been received in return. I then requested him to accompany me to the train dispatcher, who occupied a bungalow at one side of the track, and introduce me, which he did.

The dispatcher was told sufficient of the situation to interest him, and he was then requested to place me in direct communication with Mr. Platte who, I believe, was then assistant general manager of the system at San Francisco. This was done, and I telegraphed him that the train had been unavoidably delayed half an hour at Sacramento, repairing a drawhead, twice by couplings breaking while ascending the mountain, and once by the explosion of a torpedo which had been placed upon the track by a flagman who had then taken a position farther east on the track and was waving his flag vigorously to stop the train before it arrived at a point where a gang of track men were making repairs. When the explosion occurred the guards sprang to their feet, arms in hand, ready for the aftermath, but quick inspection showed the character of the alarm and doubtless saved the flagman's life, which was endangered by exposure to the arms in the hands of the guards who had him covered.

Mr. Platte was told that these different delays aggregated more than three hours; that we were ready for a contest with his regular schedule time and were surprised to be side-tracked to let freight and all other west-bound trains pass us, especially in view of the agreement that the train was to run only ten minutes behind the Fast Mail, which was to act as our pilot over the full length of the main line of the Central Pacific Railway. This was impossible then. Therefore, I said I would be pleased if he would "cut us loose" and overtake the Fast Mail as soon as possible. This he promised and commenced to execute immediately. We moved down the east slope of the Sierra Nevada at a spanking rate of speed, passing along the banks of the Truckee River, which flows from Lake Tahoe in an irregular course, northeast, to Wadsworth, Nevada, and thence north into Pyramid Lake, distant about seventy miles. We stopped for water at Wadsworth and then commenced speeding through a valley full of lakes and sink holes, vanishing and reappearing streams, until we passed Humboldt Lake about fourteen miles southwest of Lovelock Station, a lake into which the Humboldt River, the longest in the state, disappears after running a very irregular course, west by southwest, nearly 300 miles. This river rises in Elko County and has many tributaries.

When we commenced lashing the Humboldt's shores our engine was aroused and the tail end of the train cracked like chain lightning;

this alarmed me somewhat because the distance between stations ranged from twelve to thirty-three miles, and the roadbed was as crooked as the river. We were running at sixty-five miles per hour and my alarm was caused by the danger of the whole train or a part of it being swung around some of the many curves with so much force as to derail it and that would have been a very serious matter. The derailed portion of the train would have been broken up, some of the guards would have been killed and it would have been very difficult to secure sound cars to transfer into, the distance between stations being a great obstacle. I therefore sent one of my boys over the tender to the engineer with instruction to tell him that I said he was showing very little judgment in the handling of the train; that my "cut loose" was for New York, not eternity. The engineer came back to the observation car at the next coaling and watering station, I was on the front platform to meet him; we spoke to each other pleasantly, and then he said, "Your opinion of me is about correct. I ought to have known better than to run at such a rate of speed on such a track."

I replied, "Nothing serious has happened, and I am sure you will be more careful after this, but when you strike a good piece of track, reasonably straight, you can let the engine go as fast as steam will carry her, so far as we are concerned." After this we moved along at the highest rate of speed that safety would permit, and caught up with the Fast Mail as she entered the yards of the company at Ogden, Utah. As our train pulled up near the depot we were greeted with the newsboys' call of Salt Lake City morning papers, containing announcements of the shipment of gold coin from San Francisco, Cal., and the sound of the gong announcing to the hungry that breakfast was ready in the restaurant.

As has been said, we departed from San Francisco Thursday evening, August 4, 1892, with enough provisions, cold food, canned meats, fruits, etc., in our cars to supply us comfortably until we arrived at Ogden, and further if necessity arose, and had subsisted upon it exclusively until we pulled up to the Ogden depot. It had been arranged to carry out the relief system with respect to meals after arriving at Ogden as we were doing with respect to the great treasure in our charge. This was the only way to insure warm meals to all and maintain thorough protection over our charge; this was done by requiring five guards in each car to turn over to the remaining five their arms and ammunition and then proceed in a nonchalant manner to the restaurant, eat quickly and resume their posts in their respective cars after giving the countersign; the second relief then proceeded as the first had.

Forty minutes were occupied in this manner, and then we resumed our journey east, but as the first section of the Omaha & Ogden Fast Mail, a position we retained until Green River was reached, where supper was partaken of, as breakfast had been, and we then made the run to Rawlins, Wyo., as the second section, stopped there to change engineers and engines. The relief engineer protested against taking the train out; said he had been "held up" twice down the road near a big tree standing isolated on the plains. It was represented to him that he would be thoroughly protected during every minute of his run; that it would be impossible for a gang of outlaws to interfere with him or his engine, for there was a corps of fifty-one well-armed guards in the cars behind him, who intended to stake everything on it, and that he must make the run and pay no attention to signals, flags or lanterns, but send his engine on under full headway at my risk until that tree was west instead of east of us. This he did, and not long after he left us at Laramie, Wyo. Soon we were climbing the west slope of the Rockies, and when we stopped at Sherman we stood on the summit of this trans-continental line with the muzzles of some of our guns pointing in the faces of tramps who were seeking free rides and repose on the platforms of Uncle Sam's flying treasure houses, unconscious of their close proximity to great wealth. Hearing the low hum of voices, and the shuffling of feet on the outside, we deemed it best to investigate, and some of the guards were marshalled in the space inside of the cars, directly in front of two of the doors, their guns brought to a level, the two doors opened, the muzzles thrust through the openings, the character of the disturbance discovered and those causing it sent flying into the wilderness.

Our next stop was at Cheyenne, Wyo., where the long, gradual descent of the plains commences only to end on the bank of the Missouri River. We expected to make a fast run over the intervening 500 miles of track, and did make sixty-five miles per hour for some time, but after passing into Nebraska the engine slipped an eccentric and we arrived at Omaha, Neb., three hours late.

We left that point as soon as the engine could be exchanged for another, intending to make up our lost time before reaching Chicago, but owing to hot boxes and the number of special trains we met carrying Knights Templar to Denver, Col., we arrived one hour and twenty minutes late, notwithstanding we ran many miles at the rate of seventy miles per hour. For some reason the Lake Shore & Michigan Southern Railway did not make up any time; in fact we arrived at Buffalo one hour and forty minutes late, twenty minutes later than when we left Chicago. We arrived at Buffalo at 1:20 a. m., the 9th, but Vice-President H. Walter Webb, New York Central & Hudson River Company, was determined, we were told, to land the train in New York City on time. Engine No. 880 was selected for the work, and she accomplished it, but it was a lively ride. The train moved without friction, no swinging or rolling, no disturbance of her equilibrium, save at a point east of Rochester, I think, when she came down with a tremendous jolt, and bounded as if she had run against the end of a broken rail, trembled and moved forward as before, smoothly, a mellow, pleasant sound greeting the ear, her equilibrium restored.

There was nothing to disturb the peace of anyone, even as the train swept around the curves that wind in and out of the shore line of the beautiful Hudson. I am sure that all the members of that faithful band drank deep of the majestic and peaceful scenery that greeted us that splendid morning as the sun rose above West Point, the Catskills, the Palisades, and many other gems on the west shore of the river and distributed its fulgency over the waters 500 feet below, flowing gently to the sea, and the other more modest, but soul-inspiring scenes of nature and art on the east shore. As we looked we realized that there is no other country like our own and that we had been in the keeping of Providence from the beginning to the end of our journey.

At 10:46 a. m., August 9, 1892, "The Gold Train" came to a dead stop in the Grand Central Depot in New York City, the run being ended successfully. We found waiting to welcome us Hon. J. Lowrie Bell, Mr. H. Walter Webb, vice-president of the New York Central & Hudson River R. R.; Gen'l Supt. Vorhees of the same line; Mr. J. D. Lang, general manager West Shore road, and Ex-postmaster General Thomas L. James, and many others prominent in public and business life, as well as a vast concourse who had come to witness something unusual and meritorious. Being informed of the facilities provided for the transfer of the registered boxes from the depot to the sub-treasury, I had the carbines, extra ammunition, equipment, camp stools, mattresses, etc., placed in the officers' car under guard, and shortly afterwards in charge of Supt. Pepper temporarily. Then the doors on the discharging side of the cars were unlocked, opened and guards stationed at each. The gates to the yards were opened and five wagons were loaded as quickly as possible, the boxes being checked out of the cars into the wagon, then two armed guards were placed on each wagon, with the driver. I had sent Supt. Troy to the sub-treasury with a book, in which the 500 boxes were entered by number, with instructions to check them out of the wagon and my custody into the custody of Postmaster Van Cott at the sub-treasury.

The New York *Morning Advertiser* said in the next day's issue: "Superintendent White decided that the drive to the sub-treasury in Wall street, where the gold was to be deposited, should be processional. The vans were to be driven in as close proximity as possible. In the event of a breakdown, or accident of any kind, it was understood that every driver should pull his team down, then close up together and stop until orders were received to go on."

The wagons, five in number, left the Grand Central at 11:50 a. m., at 12:40 p. m. the first group of five commenced to pull up at the Pine street entrance of the sub-treasury. In a short time five more followed, and shortly thereafter the last four were en route, all were unloaded, the boxes checked off, placed in the vaults and a receipt given to me for them by Postmaster Van Cott of New York City.

In charge of the train: James E. White, General Superintendent, R. M. S.; in direct charge of guards and cars, Superintendents Lewis L. Troy, Norman Perkins, George W. Pepper, Samuel Flint and Assistant Superintendent Frank W. Vaille; these last five each being in charge of a car, and in each car were nine other faithful, intelligent and reliable men—most of them ex-soldiers of the Civil War. They were:

Armstrong, H. B.	Fry, W. H.	Partridge, Karl
Auld, Royal J.	Geddings, W. D.	Phillips, A. M.
Bradley, A. J.	Grow, E. F.	Potts, John J.
Boyd, Lynn	Grubb, S. A.	Roberts, Homer
Boyle, C. J.	Hamlin, A. J.	Ross, Sidney A.
Buck, E. H.	Heath, Geo. H.	Shaffer, C. L.
Bunn, F. S.	Hobbs, Clarence L.	Shepherd, J. W.
Bittenbender, C. H.	Irvine, E. A.	Shevels, Robert
Crary, L. H.	Lansing, H. J.	Southwick, Frank L.
Cutts, Geo. B.	Le Roy, J. L.	Taylor, J. A.
DeMoe, C. E.	Mahahon, A. C.	Vandervoort, W. C.
Donnelly, R. M.	Meredith, William	Warren, J. A.
Dooley, John E.	Miller, Abraham	Whitney, Frank E.
Eaton, W. C.	Moore, I. R.	Wilson, W. P.
Fishel, John	Morse, John E.	Wright, Abram

For the manly manner in which these splendid boys had borne themselves, their perfect observance of discipline, their intelligent comprehension of duty and responsibility, and their moral and upright

Hon. George W. Pepper
Superintendent Ninth Division R. M. S.
(See Appendix)

conduct and absolute fearlessness the Post Office Department permitted them to remain in New York City and vicinity two days, a courtesy they enjoyed greatly.

The arms, ammunition, equipment and other ordnance stores I had drawn from the Benicia arsenal, I placed in temporary charge of Supt. Pepper, with instructions to meet me in New York whenever I notified him, that we might turn it over to the commanding officer of the New York arsenal, Governor's Island, New York Harbor. This we did on the 19th of August, 1892, and on the 25th of the same month I received a receipt in full signed by Major Clifton Comty.

The disbursements made on account of the Gold Train were $1,640.86.

OBSTRUCTING TRAINS CARRYING THE MAIL.

Mention is made in these pages of mails en route to destinations being delayed in transit through interference with the trains transporting them in pursuance of law and agreement, by employees of the companies, and their sympathizers, who were frequently incited to acts of barbarism by the intemperate language and conduct of their fellows and principals.

Those who participated officially in the obstruction of trains were called "strikers." They struck to enforce recognition of demands made by the association to which they belonged on account of real or fancied grievances; that is, they quit work, "tied up" the roads upon which the demands were made, until they were conceded, or a compromise effected, unless the companies were fortunate enough to secure qualified men to fill the positions vacated voluntarily, and lawful force to protect them and their property. This the "strikers" and their sympathizers used every means at their command, fair and foul, to prevent. Usually as the days were numbered with the past after a strike was declared on, confidence of success wavered from side to side about as frequently as the stock market moved up and down under the influence of the "bulls" and "bears;" until finally a desperate determination to succeed took possession of both parties to the controversy. Then frequently the so-called sympathizers, the natural-born socialist and the anarchist coming into his own, became frantic with excitement which soon passed into the more feverish condition called frenzy. Then came disorder, destruction of life, limbs, and property, as a natural sequence, until the guns opened; then the rabble ran and hid.

The strike of 1888, which was declared against the Chicago, Burlington & Quincy Railroad by the Brotherhood of Engineers and Firemen, Chief Arthur in command, at 4 a. m., February 27th, of that year, continued for about six weeks and spread to other roads, extending over a large area of country. At that time my family resided in Waukegan, Illinois, a suburb of Chicago located on the Milwaukee division of the Chicago & Northwestern Railway, thirty-five miles out. It was my custom, when not traveling, to go home from my headquarters every night and to return every morning; but with the opening of the strike, train service on the Burlington (C. B. & Q.) became very irregular, most trains being dropped temporarily from necessity, and we could depend for mail purposes only upon the east and west-bound Chicago & Union Pacific Transfer fast mail trains. (Union Pacific Transfer, Iowa, is on the east bank of the Missouri River, opposite Omaha, Nebraska, and is the junction of half a score of railroad lines.) These two trains Chief Arthur assured me would not be disturbed by his men; that, instead, they would remain in charge of the engines hauling them, and would handle them skillfully as long as desired.

I knew that "The Burlington" was receiving squads of engineers from the east almost daily, and that sooner or later these men would occupy the vacant cabs. They were members of the organization known as "Knights of Labor," of which Mr. Powderly was Chief. He had just retired from the employ of the Reading Railroad on account of an unsuccessful clash with President Gowen. As they arrived they were sequestered, temporarily, from the wiles and temptations of the offensive hosts, so that in that solemn hour they might reflect, be examined and prepared for the fray unmolested; and take their places quietly and determinedly in the corps that I knew was formed to fight to the finish. As time moved on the passenger and freight trains that had been cut out were restored gradually—as fast as these engineers and firemen became acquainted with the engines and the track, and were properly guarded. It should be remembered, when commenting on this feature of the case, that the Brotherhood firemen vacated the engines with their engineers, thus compelling those who succeeded them to become acquainted with their machines and the course over which they were to run, without coaching, or assistance of any kind—good, bad or indifferent. If this is remembered, and the extent of the different lines of the system involved considered, the time that preceded the restoration of full train service will not seem great; the wonder will be that it was accomplished so quickly; there was no sluggishness, want of energy, or lack of gray matter. The routes involved in the strike extended from Chicago to Omaha, Neb.; Kansas City, Mo.; Denver, Col.; Billings, Mont.; Cheyenne, Wyo., and St. Paul, Minn. Burned-out and broken-down engines and wrecked trains were not unfamiliar objects on these lines; losses which added to the difficulties of the situation and forced the equipment and number of trains to the minimum, notwithstanding that hundreds of thousands of dollars extra were expended in the effort to restore full train service; to furnish their patrons with all customary facilities and supplies while the strikers and their allies pulled the other way with equal vigor and for selfish ends. The company was trying to serve the public; the strikers were trying to make the public serve them.

During the whole time the strike was on, I remained in Chicago night and day, spending much of my time at the headquarters of the Brotherhood, in railway offices, and at the depots, trying to keep posted; the last official act that I performed each night was to digest the information gathered during the day and to telegraph the result and my conclusions to the General Superintendent at Washington, D. C., for his information and that of the Postmaster General. When I slept it was on a cot in my office, but, as a rule, I did not return to the office from telegraphing until after 3 a. m., the hour of the fast mail departure west. One night I retired much earlier, tired and worn; that night, for the first time, Chief Arthur's men failed to take the fast mail out, and officers of the road who had some experience in that line in their younger days, manned the engine and started the train on its westward trip. We were insisting that the companies perform mail service at least six times a week, in both directions, over all their routes, whether they transacted other business or not, and this doubtless influenced these officers to take the course that they did that morning; but they had undertaken to meet the policy of the Department on all their lines and were making good, notwithstanding enormous losses. That policy was not protective enough. The strike was responsible for some serious accidents. One such occurred on the first day it opened, in which five clerks were injured, and nine other accidents which occurred on the system were due to the disarrangement occasioned by the strike.

When Mr. Nash—the General Superintendent—came to Chicago to take observations and to transact some other important business, he insisted upon my taking quarters in a good hotel and eating nutritious food and having as much rest as the emergency would permit as long as it lasted. I complied, and when he returned to Washington he arranged to have me reimbursed for this extraordinary expenditure, for all of which I am thankful to him.

Watching both parties to the controversy as closely as I did all the time, and being received so pleasantly, as I was by both, I could not avoid absorbing information which forced me to form opinions of the situation from day to day, and several days before the strike was declared off I was sure that the end was at hand, and was on the "ground floor" when the "bottom dropped out."

The following is a copy of Postmaster General Dickinson's views respecting the manner in which the Department's interests were attended to during the strike. Of course, they pleased me very much.

*　　*　　*　　*　　*　　*　　*　　*

"Mr. Dickinson being in so genial a mood because of the solution of the complications connected with the postmastership was asked if the current reports that the removals were to continue in the Chicago office were true; especially whether it was a fact that Captain James E. White, the Superintendent of the Railway Mail Service of that division, was to follow in the wake of the railway mail superintendents of New York and Cincinnati, Mr. Dickinson said:

"Whatever they may say of me a good many efficient men have been retained in the service if they are Republicans. Captain White is a very valuable man to the Department and his services will not be dispensed with. I shall never forget the rare good sense, tact and judgment that he displayed during the six weeks when the Post Office Department was insisting that the railroads should carry the mails, notwithstanding the strike. The Department was at that time determined to establish valuable precedents as to post roads over railroads. We were endeavoring to lay down the principle that the railroads must carry the mails if they did no other business. Captain White did not make a mistake all through that crisis. I remained at the Department many a night until late into the night in conference with him as to the situation and he was always clear-headed, firm and accurate in his judgment, and never made a mistake at a time when a mistake might have proved very serious for the Government. No, I have no hesitation in saying that Captain White will not be removed."

The *Inter-Ocean* added:

"It will be seen that the Postmaster General has learned to have the same opinion of the executive and business ability of Captain White as has long been entertained by the general public."

It was hoped that this experience would cause either the executive or legislative branch of the Government to take such action as would leave no doubt as to the meaning of Section 711, Postal Laws and Regulations, (Revised Statutes, Section 4,000), but no action of any kind whatsoever was taken until 1893, when it seemed to me about time for another eruption to break out, involving the transportation of the mail, and I treated the subject in my annual report for the fiscal year, 1893, and again in 1894, the first being before the furious trouble that broke out on the Great Northern Railway in April, 1894, and continued into May of the same year; the second, after the most stupendous strike of the age, which raged with fury over almost the entire west from June 27 to July 24, 1894. The subject received its third treatment in my report for the fiscal year, 1896.

Mr. Bissell became Postmaster General in March, 1893. In my judgment he was one of the strongest men who ever occupied that office; he was governed by sound principles; but I shall have the honor to speak of him further on more fully.

When the fiscal year 1893 was ended, and I commenced to write the recommendations I purposed making in the annual report for that year, this subject knocked hard for admission. No one had said anything to me regarding it, but my own experience in four strikes showed me that we were not prepared to handle interferences; forcible, violent interferences, with a business of which the Government has a monopoly, and which it administers for the people without hope or desire for profit, successfully, with that vigor, positiveness, celerity and justice to all that denotes authority, power and greatness; without which attributes any government must be mediocre and hardly worthy the name.

It seemed to me then, and had for many years, in cases where the mails were being transported regularly by authority of the Postmaster General or his representative, that they should be so continued and protected by the Government through stress and storm of man's making. Any other course I believed would not be just to the companies or to the patrons of the Government, who should not be deprived of any mail facilities, the frequency of supply that they had been enjoying, because of the timidity—political or otherwise—of those having the power and authority to prevent it, and I believed that allowing it would discredit the nation. The decision of the Government that a company fulfilled its obligations sufficiently to entitle it to the full compensation allowed by law, if it maintained service once daily in each direction to destinations over routes upon which the full customary number of trips were prevented by the strikers and their allies, was not righteous or fearless, for it disregarded the interests of its patrons and abandoned the shippers, the merchants, the physicians, and the traveling public dependent on the blocked lines. So, too, the decision that a company in the throes of a strike must perform service once daily each way over its lines if it did no other business, seemed to me unjust, shirking responsibilities, licensing lawlessness as to the other trains, and unworthy of our country.

Believing this, I wrote the following for my 1893 annual report and submitted it to Postmaster General Bissell, who had me stand in front of him and read it, as he had me do sometimes with other matters to which I requested him to give his personal consideration. He listened attentively, approved the bill that I had drawn, the statement and recommendation, and instructed me to put it in my report.

"Obstructing Trains Carrying the Mails.

"To this end a bill was submitted with the report, copy of which, with the remarks preceding it, is given here:

"It will be conceded that the most frequent interchange of mails possible between important commercial and financial centers is necessary to the proper and profitable transaction of business, and that the growth of the nation in civilization, population, wealth, and all that constitutes greatness is in proportion to the general prosperity of its citizens; therefore anything tending to impede the growth of business, to retard the transaction of the same, or to cause a decrease of the general wealth of the country operates to the disadvantage of the Government and should be remedied by law.

"In times of peace and prosperity business flows on as persistently, regularly, and quietly as a stream passing through a level valley; all that is conducive to business interests and to the peace and comfort of the people is responsive. The mails are dispatched by and received from nearly every passenger train passing over railway lines. On some trains they are carried in railway post offices, on others in the baggage cars in charge of train baggagemen; but in every case they go through to their destination without other interruption than such as results from accidents, and in this way cities upon important routes communicate with one another two, three, four, five, or six times daily, and realize by this frequent service much better results than are possible in any other way.

"But local disturbances occasionally occur between an important railway system and its employees, between two railway companies as to the right of way, or between the corporate authority of a city and a railway company, and peace in the vicinity of the trouble gives way to violence, destruction of life and property, and the mail service throughout the whole country is thereby partially or wholly interrupted, failing to meet the needs of business and causing losses of greater or less magnitude to those engaged in it. Moneys due and forwarded in time to meet obligations fail to arrive as expected, notes and drafts are protested, mortgages foreclosed, sales made are not consummated, and the financial standing of individuals and firms is jeopardized, all because some organization or association has determined to put a break upon the business, not only of the company with which it is temporarily at war, but of the whole world, if possible, until it secures its demands. In doing this they say to the agents of the railroad company: 'We will permit the mails to pass, but no baggage, express, or passenger cars will be allowed to do so;' and the railway company says: 'We cannot afford to run a train of one or two cars devoted to the mails exclusively.' Sometimes the company performs service once daily each way over its lines, and thus technically fulfills its obligations to the Government sufficiently to prevent the withholding or reduction of its pay, for the obligation includes the carriage of the mails six times per week each way, or as much oftener as passenger trains may run. The company in such a case is not only willing, but anxious to continue all of its passenger trains and to carry mails upon each; but it is not willing to drop other business usually transacted on these trains and to run a mail car or a baggage car containing only mail in place of every passenger train scheduled, nor should it be expected to. Sometimes strikes occur upon lines that are in financial distress and unable to run a train consisting of one car only, with an apartment from 15 to 25 feet in length devoted to the mails; therefore no service is performed upon that line during the continuance of the strike, the company forfeiting its pay rather than to incur expense exceeding the compensation received.

"In all cases of the nature mentioned the public is deprived of at least one-half of its regular mail accommodations, and in some instances, of all, or nearly all, as is shown in the following statement:

"The two most important mail routes in the United States are the New York Central & Hudson River Railroad (main line, New York to Chicago) and the Pennsylvania Railroad (New York to St. Louis).

"Two exclusive mail trains are run daily each way over the former, and in addition twenty-five passenger trains carry mail westward and thirty-one eastward. All of this service is provided because it is demanded by the business interests of the country and is recognized as desirable by the Department. It is not to be understood that the lines and offices tributary to this route receive and dispatch mails by all of these trains, but that all carry mails to and from some offices and lines. What mails shall be dispatched by certain trains depends upon the advantages derived thereby. If a certain number of trains arrive at a given office in the night it is not necessary to dispatch mails for that office by all of them. It is sufficient to dispatch it by the last train leaving the initial point in time to permit of its being delivered as soon as that office is opened in the morning, thus economizing labor and equipment and minimizing exposure to depredation or loss in transit. The same principle applies to dependent lines; therefore it will be seen that if the operating of train service is not protected by law the condition of the mail service in periods of disturbance will be in the future, as in the past, very detrimental to private and public interests; for should a strike occur upon a line like the New York Central & Hudson River Railroad fifty-six of the sixty trains carrying the mail would be abandoned, simply because the strikers would not permit them to proceed if carrying anything besides mail.

"How disastrous this would be no one can understand until he realizes that the New York Central & Hudson River Railroad, as a mail route, derives its importance from the fact that it starts from the great seaport and financial center of the country; that the mails to and from Europe, and from and to the New England states, for and from a great part of the states of New York, Ohio, Michigan, and Illinois, the Dominion of Canada, and the northwestern and western states, Asia, and the islands of the Pacific ocean, pass over this route, and therefore those states and countries are involuntary participants in the evil effects resulting from interruptions to train service on that system.

"The Pennsylvania system is of equal importance, for it commands the south, southwest, portions of the west, the countries referred to, and some of the South American countries. At present it carries mails westward and southward on forty passenger trains, and eastward and northward on fifty. If the conditions spoken of arose in New Jersey or Pennsylvania the company would probably be permitted to run from four to eight of these trains, consequently the patrons of the Department would be deprived of the benefits that they now derive from either eighty-two or eighty-six trains, and this deprivation would be seriously embarrassing at times and should not be permitted.

"As the Government has a monoply of the mails it would seem to be its duty to protect its customers, particularly as it can easily do so by passing a law making it an offense, punishable with fine and imprisonment, for an unauthorized person or a member of any organization or association to interrupt the passage of a train carrying United States mail. To this end I respectfully recommend the passage of the following bill, or a better one if possible, as early as may be practicable:

'A Bill to prevent unauthorized persons from interfering with railroad trains carrying the United States mails by authority of the Postmaster General or officers of the Post Office Department.

'Be it enacted by the Senate and House of Representatives of the United States of America in Congress assembled, That if any person or persons, acting in his own or their own behalf, or as the agent or agents, or as a member or members, officer or officers, or as the representative or representatives of any organization or association, shall delay, obstruct, or prevent the passage of any train on any railroad in the United States by which mails are being transported by order of the Post Office Department, the same having been designated by the Postmaster General or his authorized agent or agents to carry the mails, for the purpose of aiding, encouraging, or contributing in any way to the success of a strike against any railroad company whose trains are designated as above, or for any unlawful or malicious purpose, shall be deemed guilty of an offense against the laws of the United States of America as represented in this act, and, on conviction thereof, shall be punished by a fine of not less than fifty dollars nor more than five hundred dollars, and be imprisoned for not less than six months nor more than two years for each offense.' "

In my report for 1894 I said on the subject:

"This subject received considerable attention in the report of this office for the fiscal year ending June 30, 1893.

"The treatment it received then was suggested by the difficulties experienced in operating the railway mail service during the existence of labor troubles that had occurred in previous years. The stupendous disturbances of April, June and July of the present year were not anticipated, but having faith in the maxims, 'History repeats itself,' and 'In times of peace prepare for war,' and, knowing from actual experience that the provisions relied upon to prevent the mails being obstructed while in transit or to successfully grapple with an emergency of that character had proved inadequate and unsuccessful in the past, it was deemed highly important to the dignity and revenues of the Department and to the tranquillity, comfort, and social and business relations of its citizens that a law be enacted making it an offense punishable with fine and imprisonment for any person to knowingly and willfully obstruct or retard the passage of a train carrying the mails. This law should be so free from ambiguity, so prohibitory and repressive in its character, that all men may understand it if they will."

(Then follows the draft of the proposed bill.)

"Had this or a similar bill become a law previous to April 1, 1894, it is believed that all the trains carrying mail would have been excepted from the embargo placed upon the train service of the Great Northern Railway when the strike, which practically tied up that system from April 13th until May 1st, was ordered. Such a law would have lessened if not averted the destruction of property, the loss of life, the paralysis of business, the hardships and pecuniary losses to which all classes and conditions of men were subjected, and as well prevented the decrease in the revenues of the Department and the increase in expenses of the Government which resulted from the unparalleled strikes which raged with barbaric fierceness over one-half of the Republic from June 27th to July 24th of the present year.

"During that period trains ran with great irregularity and many of the lines centering at Chicago from the east, north and south were operated intermittently, while all of the trans-continental lines, except the Great Northern, which was seriously impaired by washouts, were effectually blockaded. The mails for the Pacific coast states, Asia, the islands of the Pacific, and some of the British provinces accumulated in Chicago, St. Paul, and elsewhere, waiting to be dispatched by the first line opened. During the continuance of the strike the Department was thoroughly informed of the condition of the train service on all the lines affected, of the practicability of other avenues of supply, of the location of delayed mails, and availed itself of every desirable opportunity presented to forward the mails to their destination; but the territory covered by the obstructed lines was so extensive and in some instances so difficult to reach that it could not afford as much relief as it desired.

"With relation to the mails for the Pacific coast and for foreign countries, supplied thence by water routes, they were sometimes forwarded by the Great Northern, sometimes by the Santa Fe, and at other times via the Union Pacific and Northern Pacific, and if not delayed by washouts or mob violence, reached their destinations ultimately; but always long after due. Those dispatched by the two first named lines were forwarded to destination by steamers sailing from Portland, Oregon; Tacoma and Seattle, Washington; San Francisco, Los Angeles and San Diego, California, as the route by which dispatched from the east indicated. No other avenues of supply were available to the Department, for the Southern Pacific lines centering at San Francisco from Portland, Oregon; Ogden, Utah, and Los Angeles, California, were almost as useless as before they were surveyed. They were in the vice-like grasp of a mob which defied state authority and resisted the militia sent to quell the disturbance.

HON. JOHN W. HOLLYDAY
Ex-Chief Clerk to the General Superintendent R. M. S.

"It cannot be doubted that the strike would have extended over a much greater territory than it did, and that more serious obstructions to the mails would have occurred, had not the Government interposed and employed the judicial and military force to protect its interests and those of its citizens. But it is not unreasonable to assume that the necessity for the heroic and admirable action taken would not have arisen, with respect to the transportation of the mails, had such a law as has been referred to existed.

"If, then, there are reasons to believe that obstructing trains carrying the mails can be prevented by enacting a law prohibiting it and prescribing suitable penalties for violating it, why should it not be done rather than permit a condition to exist which has, and will as long as it continues, place the business interests of the country, the prosperity and happiness of the people, the life and limbs of the servants of the Government, and the revenues of the Department at the mercy of such howling mobs as disgraced this country and civilization in Chicago, St. Paul, Sacramento, Battle Creek, Hammond, Blue Island and elsewhere in April, June and July of the present year (1894)?"

When the strike against the Great Northern Railroad was declared, Mr. Charles Neilson, then Assistant General Superintendent of the Railway Mail Service, was in St. Paul, Minn., and immediately advised our office of the situation. It was clear that the same old nauseating "bluff" the strikers had played before was being played again. They were practically "killing" passenger trains carrying mails in pursuance of law, telling the company that they could proceed with the mail unmolested, and the representatives of the Post Office Department that they would not think of obstructing the transit of the mails; this, too, in face of the fact that the companies' obligation was to carry the mails over their mail routes as often as trains ran thereon, or in the language of Revised Statutes 4000, "Every railway company carrying the mail *shall* carry on any train which may run over its road, and without extra charge therefor, all mailable matter directed to be carried thereon, with the person in charge of the same."

On my own responsibility I had met this fabrication squarely July 27, 1877, I believed, in the notice given, "To Strikers, Rioters, and Other Parties Whomsoever," when a strike was in progress on the Chicago, Burlington & Quincy Railway, see page 17, and was anxious that in this crisis some more competent and learned official of the Government should meet it under practically the same conditions and see if he would not reach substantially the same opinion. I was then, and am now, convinced that it is the only correct and logical opinion possible, and that a policy based upon it and executed fearlessly will win every time.

When this strike was declared, Postmaster General Bissell was at his home in Buffalo, N. Y. After examining, with the assistance of Mr. Todd, some books borrowed from the office of the Assistant Attorney General for the Post Office Department, and finding decisions I believed applicable to the case, I wrote and telegraphed to him, citing these, and asking him to write or telegraph the Attorney General to give an opinion as to the meaning and scope of the law. He wired me to call on him myself and to lay the case before him. I called at his office, but was told that Mr. Olney was at his home in Massachusetts, and was referred to Mr. Lawrence Maxwell, Jr., who was acting. I called upon him, presented the telegram received from Mr. Bissell and some papers relating to the case submitted; was asked some questions, the answers to which were taken down, and a corrected statement in duplicate prepared. Then Judge Maxwell astonished me by saying, "If you will wait a few minutes you can take the opinion to the Department." I never waited for anything so cheerfully in my life. When the opinion was handed to me I read it, thanked Judge Maxwell, and moved as fast as I could towards my office. In my judgment, the opinion was all wool and much more than a yard wide—wide enough to win the Great Northern and Chicago battles, and all the others that occurred during that calendar year, 1894.

The opinion read:

"DEPARTMENT OF JUSTICE,

Washington, D. C., April 21, 1894.

"*The Postmaster General.*

"SIR: I have the honor to acknowledge the receipt of your communication of to-day relating to the stoppage of passenger trains carrying mails on the Great Northern Railway. The statutes of the United States provide that 'every railroad company carrying the mail shall carry on any train which may run over its route, all mailable matter directed to be carried thereon, with the person in charge of the same.' The statutes also make it an offense for any person to 'knowingly and willfully obstruct or retard the passage of a train carrying the mail,' and that it is no excuse that such person is willing that the mail car may be detached and run separately. He is bound to permit the mail to be carried in the usual and ordinary way, such as is contemplated by the Act of Congress and directed by the Postmaster General. It would seem from your statement that the persons who have entered into the combination to which you refer have brought themselves within the further provisions of the statutes of the United States, which declare that 'If two or more persons conspire to commit an offense against the United States and one or more of such parties do an act to effect the object of the conspiracy, all the parties to the conspiracy shall be liable to a penalty of not less than one thousand dollars and not more than ten thousand dollars, and to imprisonment for not more than two years.'

"Respectfully,

"(Signed) LAWRENCE MAXWELL, JR.,

"Acting Attorney General."

During the continuance of this strike, I received a telegraphic statement of the condition of the service and the pulse of the strikers every forenoon from Supt. Troy, and showed it to the Postmaster General; he became very much interested in it, and if the usual time of receiving this particular telegram arrived, and it was not taken to him, he would call for it. Of course it could not be taken to him until it arrived, but he was restless until he had seen it. This telegram was not sent from Chicago until Mr. Troy had seen the representatives of the railway companies, visited the stockyards, seen the town authorities, some of the officials of the strikers, and collected all the news; it was an important telegram. One day it failed to arrive when due. I called on Mr. Bissell a little while after, and told him so, but I said "Mr. Troy will send it without fail as soon as he collects the news, and he is doing that faithfully and as quickly as he can." Hour after hour passed, but the telegram was not delivered. The Postmaster General was vexed and growing more so; finally I wired Troy substantially: "No telegram since last night; hot; if you regard your own interests wire at once." Back came the answer: "Don't understand. Sent telegram at usual hour." Mr. Troy took the matter up with the Chicago telegraph office; it wired Washington; Washington found it had been harboring it for some hours, and rushed it up to our office with explanations and apologies. These were related to Mr. Bissell and he asked that the manager call on him next morning, which he did. The interview may have been soulful, but it was not a symphony of peace, rest, and brotherly love, but a quickstep in promptness and a march in system. During the interview the Postmaster General said that the error in handling the telegram in that office came near causing him to remove Mr. Troy, one of the best officers of the Department, etc. To prevent more errors of that character a special wire was run into the Department building to give me direct connection with Chicago until the end of the strike; that was a great convenience, avoided delays and unnecessary expenditure of time.

Mr. Bissell said to me that whenever I received important news after office hours—news that I thought he should know without delay, to come with it to his home, and if he had retired to route him out; if he was out his people would know where he could be found and would tell me, and I must find him. Once I found him at the White House, and sent in my card; he came to a small room in the north front of the building to meet me; twice I found him in bed. Once, on a Sunday morning, when I was supplied with newsy telegrams, I called and was conducted to his bed chamber by his orders, and found him in bed, wide awake, ready for business and kindly as usual; after a few preliminary remarks I showed the telegrams and he said: "Stand up and read them, Captain." So I stood at the foot of his bed and read.

When he became Postmaster General, the "Civil Service Regulations Governing Promotions in the Railway Mail Service" had not been introduced, and transfer clerks, where not more than two were assigned to the same station, were outside the classified civil service breastworks. The former was introduced during his term of office, and the latter also; the last gave him more trouble than the first, because in these smaller places an inexperienced man could, in a very brief time, perform the duties very well. One day he said: "Captain, the demand for these small excepted places is something awful. You know there are very few places that can be given to those who think they deserve recognition, and I am afraid that I will have to make changes in those places, but I don't like to. I am a civil service man; am the head of the Civil Service Club in Buffalo, and believe in it fully; but what am I to do in these excepted places, that evidently were excepted because they were not important enough to require protection?" I replied, in substance, that the changes could be effected by assigning the clerks then occupying the excepted places to road duty as fast as vacancies occurred on lines not too large for them, and filling the vacated positions with those demanding recognition, if they were of good character; this would satisfy his people undoubtedly, because the aspirants could not be appointed to railway post offices, except as provided in the civil service laws, regulations and rules; whereas those holding the excepted places were eligible for assignment to them. He said, "That is the solution; we will do it that way."

Speaking for the railway mail service, I am glad to say that we never were blessed with more consideration and just treatment than we received from Mr. Bissell and Mr. Wilson; the former was very much pleased with the record made by it during his administration.

But to return to the subject, obstruction of trains carrying the mails. The opinion rendered by the Acting Attorney General provided a substantial foundation for the position that the Government took respecting interference with its business, and on which it fought a splendid fight and won, I believe, for all time. Sixteen years have passed since that victory. If a strike has occurred anywhere in this country in the interim, involving interference with mails in transit on railroads, I do not know of it; I know none occurred before I retired from the service. The honor is due two men, who were fearless in the discharge of duty; President Cleveland and Postmaster General Bissell.

I remember one demand that nearly resulted in a strike of a different character, a strike on the part of the highest officer of a short line of road, now part of the Chicago, Milwaukee & St. Paul system. It connected with the Illinois Central main line at Warren, Ill., and extended north to Mineral Point, Wis., supplying several fair sized offices. The accommodations furnished for the mail service were good, larger, in fact, than the service required, but I do not remember that any one in our service, or connected with the Post Office Department, ever complained of too much space so long as it was furnished without charge. In this case the officer had come to the conclusion that his company was not being paid sufficiently for the service it performed, and so stated in a letter to my office. I replied to the effect that he was receiving the maximum pay of his line; that it was not possible to pay him more until he carried a greater weight of mail, etc.; but my friend, who was a very agreeable gentleman, frank and fair as a rule, was not convinced and came back two or three times insisting on an increase of compensation, saying at last that if his contention was not allowed by a certain date named he would cease carrying our agent. During this correspondence I had made a full statement of the case to the General Superintendent, and suggested a way to overcome the trouble. He agreed, and telegraphed me to handle it as I thought best. So I visited the general office of the Illinois Central in Chicago, and requested that I be given a half dozen trip passes, in an assumed name, good between Freeport, Ill., and Dubuque, Iowa. This was done, and I took the first train destined for Dubuque, passed Warren, and got off at Scales Mound, Ill., went to the hotel, engaged a room and had a talk with the landlord; found him a very modest and pleasant gentleman in middle life; took him into my confidence; told him of the difficulty with the Mineral Point and Warren Railroad, and requested him to send some reliable person to me who was familiar with the country between Scales Mound and Mineral Point and who was able to carry the mails between those points once daily, except Sundays, in both directions. He sent the man. I told him my plan, which was to start a wagon from Scales Mound and one from Mineral Point at the same hour each morning, providing sufficient relays, paralleling the railroad between Mineral Point and Darlington, Wis., and running from Darlington via Shullsburg to Scales Mound; arriving there as early in the afternoon as possible, and taking away from the railroad all the passenger business we could. This was all arranged to take effect, if need be, on a certain date named. The gentleman who was to furnish the service was to start from Scales Mound with the first train and go through to Mineral Point. I was to start from Mineral Point at the same hour of the same morning with a team and driver, and go through to Scales Mound. After the arrangements were all perfected I said to the gentleman who was to equip and handle the route, "I do not believe that it will be necessary to put it in operation, but be ready. I will go down to Warren on the next train, and give away our plans, and what has been done, in the station house, where the agent will hear it, and know who I am; and then I will go to Mineral Point, the headquarters of the company, and see what will develop. You can talk all you want to now, the more the better." This program was adhered to. I arrived in Mineral Point that evening and went to the hotel immediately, where I found the officer on the lookout for me; an interview was requested, which I granted, and in a half hour I telegraphed to the mail contractor in embryo, at Scales Mound, "The stage route will not be needed," and he, good man, understood.

RECORD OF MAIL IN TRANSIT.

For many years after the railway post office was instituted no record was made of pouch mail in transit from offices of origin to offices addressed. Looking back to those days now, it does not seem strange that mails were lost frequently then without any one seeming to know or care. Was this not due in a large measure to postal officials who derived but little of their earnings from the offices they occupied; who enjoyed hunting and fishing more than office work; made the conduct of the post offices intrusted to them secondary to the private business that they were engaged in; used it to draw custom to the latter, and failed to realize the responsibility that the offices placed them under to the Government and its patrons? What of the people? Were they not too much attached to the quiet, uneventful life of the town and country? Did not that life tend to dwarf the development of alertness, energy, drive and push, that rouses the mind to observe inaction, sluggishness, lack of system, and irregularities; to make inquiry, investigation and urge reforms?

Supposing the people and postmasters had been wide-awake to their privileges, trusts, obligations and interests, could such an occurrence have happened as I am about to relate?

I had been in my assignment as Chief Clerk at Omaha about six months when one day the clerk in charge of the railway post office that was to depart for Ogden that day made a requisition for a supply of pouches and locks, his car being short of the number required to maintain its exchange with offices in Colorado, Wyoming, Utah, Idaho, Montana, Washington and Oregon, and the Ogden & San Francisco railway post office, which was the base for Nevada, Arizona and California.

On a route 1,032 miles long, constituting the base of supply for the post office in such an empire of rugged mountains, low-lying valleys, deep gorges, and torrential streams; dependent upon star routes after the mails were dispatched from the railroad, it was inevitable that shortages and excesses of equipment should occur occasionally; that these might be equalized quickly, Omaha had been constituted a pouch and lock depository, and into this the clerks in charge of the Omaha and Ogden railway post office had been instructed to turn the excess at the end of each run, and if a shortage instead of an excess existed, to ask for what they needed. The Omaha office was to check in and out of the depository.

In filling the requisition for pouches and locks spoken of, it developed that one year, to a day, previously, excess pouches and locks had been brought in from the west by this railway post office, and taken with Omaha mail to the post office; there was some excess mail also, part of which was enclosed in a large leather pouch, known in the inner circles of the postal service in the "wild and wooly west" as "bull hides;" its capacity was about 10,000 letters. This pouch was mixed with the excess empties, was thrown with them into the cellar, and notwithstanding its great weight and frequent handling was piled away with them. When it was brought up as a pouch of pouches, a glance satisfied me that it was full of mail. I felt of it and knew that I was correct, opened it with my key, and found it full of letters addressed to Omaha, Neb. I turned it over to the postmaster, who caused it to be distributed into private boxes, the general delivery, some to banks, railway offices, and other important business concerns; a printed slip of explanation accompanied each delivery. The most remarkable feature of this most remarkable blunder was that I found on making inquiry that no one remembered that more than the usual number of complaints of losses and delays had been received during the year.

Another case I remember was small in the value of the mail matter involved, but otherwise the blunder, the lack of system, the sacrifice of official business in behalf of personal, was, at least, as great. This, too, occurred in my early days as chief head clerk at Omaha, Neb. Colonel Armstrong was General Superintendent at Washington, D. C. Special agents were about as scarce in the west as "hen's teeth," which will account for the Colonel sending me a complaint received at the Department from a gentleman living in a small town supplied with mail by a star route heading from Fort Kearney, which was a military post in Kearney County, Nebraska, south of the Platte River, a stream with a very treacherous bed in those days. I have not heard of its being macadamized or covered with asphaltum since, but many bridges have been thrown across it. He requested me to investigate the non-receipt of a registered package at the office to which it was addressed in Nebraska; this was equivalent to a command, and I started on the investigation at once, taking a Union Pacific train at Omaha and alighting at Kearney Station, which is in Buffalo County, north of the Platte River. There I hired a man with an ox team to take me across the river to the fort, where I arrived somewhat in adavance of the fly season, and called on the postmaster, whom I found in the midst of a most wonderful medley of discordant elements. In addition to being postmaster he was the sutler of the post, and editor and publisher of a newspaper called "The Centoria," I believe; its mission being to convince the natives and denizens of this great and growing country that our beautiful capital city on the Potomac, where it was located by the Father of his country, and where the nation's most magnificent public buildings have been erected with the people's money, should be given up to the owls and bats and the tramps and wanderers because it was not in the exact geographical center of the Republic, and a new one built on the spot where Fort Kearney stood. Fort Kearney has disappeared; it has no place on the map of the United States, or in the Postal Guide, although it has in history, but Washington, D. C., has grown more grand and beautiful each year.

I am sure that the postmaster had other engagements, but only He that knoweth all things could reveal what they were; but they were enough to cause me to approach him with the business of my journey into that strange land as gently as I could. I did not wish to add a feather's weight to the mighty burden he was staggering under and which made the surrounding universe tremble as it had, not many years before, under the ponderous tread, the mighty weight, and rush of vast herds of buffaloes, that roamed the alkali plains, fed upon the short succulent grass, and furnished sport and food for the Indian. I showed the letter that I had received to the postmaster; he examined his records of registered matter in transit, searched his books in which he entered those received and dispatched, and finally said that the package had not been in his office, otherwise he would have a record of it. While he was searching his records, I kept running my hand through the mass of newspaper exchanges, second-class matter, merchandise, letters, etc., piled upon a table back of his press and type; shortly, to our mutual astonishment, the package appeared on the summit of the pile. The crimson tide that swept over his face and neck told of his humiliation and confusion.

The postmaster's name was Sydenham; he was a Christian gentleman, and for many years after he retired from official and business pursuits at Fort Kearney he was a faithful clerk in the Omaha and Ogden railway post office.

The losses and delays that occurred to closed pouch mail became a source of anxiety, annoyance and embarrassment to the limited number of field officers in the service, especially to those in charge of divisions, with lines stretching out for hundreds of miles through sparsely settled sections and supplying carelessly-managed offices, that sometimes failed to receive their mails and made no effort to discover whether they had been delivered when the train passed, and were afterwards found by chance under station platforms, in the grass and weeds by the roadside, and sometimes in out-of-the-way places, such as vaults, piles of rotting lumber, fence posts and all sorts of out buildings, abandoned wells, etc.

LIST OF EXCHANGE POUCHES AND SHORTAGE SLIPS.

After I had been located in Chicago some time the clerks were required to provide themselves with lists of exchange pouches due to and from them at terminals, and to check them in and out of their railway post offices on these lists. This uncovered the irregularities of handling, and insured immediate report to their superintendent, either direct, or through the chief clerk, if one intervened. This started an inquiry immediately, and was a move in the right direction, but later it was found to be insufficient to meet all phases of the trouble; it did not provide for the discovery of the same class of irregularities at way stations and junctions, or of pouches made up in one large post office for another and not intended to be opened in transit, but which were, inadvertently, in an intervening railway post office, the contents distributed with other mail and the pouch thrown on the pile of empties, thus losing its individuality, and the mail enclosed in it its distinctiveness. In such cases the pouch would not be missed until the day it was due at the office of destination; then its failure to arrive would be reported.

This was further improved, in truth, it may be said, perfected, between 1894 and 1900. Up to 1894 the pouch list and checking off system applied to terminals only; then it was extended to way offices and junctions, and later the "shortage slip," originated by Supt. Troy, was introduced.

With the pouch list, which gives an excellent record of the exchanges and the "shortage slip," which is dispatched in lieu of every missing exchange, and the instructions governing the use of them by railway post offices, post offices, transfer clerks, mail messengers, train and station baggagemen and others who handle pouch mail, losses and delays are located promptly. Ultimate and absolute loss is often prevented by locating the place of disappearance, and the news of the delay is carried to the post office to which the pouch is addressed, at the exact hour it was due, if the train by which it should have been delivered, arrives on time. In all cases a record can be made of a pouch from the time it is dispatched to a train by the initial post office until it arrives at the office addressed; if lost, missent or delayed in any way the explanation of when and how will arrive at that office by first train and will be referred to the superintendent of the division at once. If it is due to be dispatched over any part of the route it travels in charge of a train baggageman, and if he does not receive it, but does receive a "shortage slip," he must send that to his superintendent, who will send it to the Superintendent of the Railway Mail Service for that division. This will insure prompt action..

To throw additional light on the subject and system, a quotation from my annual report for 1900 is here given.

"Every railway postal clerk in charge, transfer clerk, mail messenger, train or station baggageman, or other person handling pouch mail, is furnished with a list of the pouches he should receive and dispatch, arranged under the following headings:

How label of pouch reads.	Where received.	Train No.	Day dispatched.	No. of pouches.

"The headings are self explanatory.

"When a pouch is received or dispatched by any of the employees mentioned above it is checked off on the pouch list. Whenever it is necessary for a railway post office or a post office to make two or more pouches for the same address the clerk making them is required to prepare the pouch slide label as follows: Mark with pen or pencil upon the pouch slide label the figures of the number of pouches made up to one address, marking the first pouch '1,' the second pouch '2,' and so on, until the final or last pouch is made up, the latter to be marked with its proper number in regular order, and, in addition, with a cross, thus (X), which cross will indicate the last of the series of pouches made up and labeled to same address. Thus a permanent record of all first-class mail in transit is made. But this record was defective in that it did not give the cause of the failure to receive, or locate the place where or route upon which the pouch disappeared, or was turned from its regular course, and therefore did not afford as much information to the officers tracing the pouch as was desirable or possible.

"This defect has been overcome by the introduction of the 'shortage slip,' which the late Supt. Troy originated and tested successfully. This slip is filled out and forwarded by the first person who should have but did not receive a pouch due him, and describes the same, giving the address on the pouch slide label, cause of failure, etc., which he hands to the next to whom the pouch is due, and in this way it passes from hand to hand, just as the pouch would have done had it not been lost or missent. The fact that a 'shortage slip' is received in lieu of the pouch should be shown on the pouch list by the letters 'S. S.' ('shortage slip.')

"To illustrate the matter a sample 'shortage slip' is given below:

Date........................

    SIR: I am short pouch due by this train as per address on the other side of this slip, at...............................

from..........................   Train No.......

| Cause
of
Shortage | Train late and failed to connect.
Pouch not brought from post office.
Messenger failed to make train.
Unknown; proper official notified by wire. |

    (Erase all but one line above.)

    (Signature)...........................

    (Title) ....

To..................................

(The other side.)

<table>
<tr><td>

MAIL SHORTAGE NOTICE.

This notice must be addressed exactly as the pouch it represents, and is to be forwarded to destination in lieu of every pouch of mail short.

Insert here address of pouch short. }

For ....

Via ....

From ....

</td></tr>
</table>

"The 'shortage slip' contemplates that when any one whose duty it is to receive a pouch fails to receive it, he shall score out all of the causes on the 'shortage slip,' except the real cause; if the cause is not printed on the 'shortage slip' they should all be crossed out and the real reason given, if known, and it should then be forwarded in regular order to the destination of the pouch which it represents, proper record being made by each clerk or other employee on the pouch list to show that it was a 'shortage slip' and not the pouch itself. The person in charge of the delayed pouch will handle the same as if it were a regular pouch and on time, except that each one handling it will note upon his pouch list and also upon his trip report the fact that he has received a delayed pouch. The railway post office or post office to whom the delayed pouch is addressed will, on receiving a 'shortage slip' in lieu of it, forward the slip to the Division Superintendent who has jurisdiction in the premises (the postal clerk with his daily trip report; the postmaster in a penalty envelope) with a statement as to when and from what source the missing pouch was afterwards received. If not received, that fact is reported, and proper steps taken in the case."

This valuable innovation was tested very thoroughly during the two subsequent years, at the end of which time our opinion of it was expressed in the annual report for the fiscal year 1902 as follows:

"The 'shortage slip' has now become one of the essential features of the service, and its advantages are becoming more and more apparent, now that its introduction has become general throughout the entire service. If a pouch fails to make its regular connection a 'shortage slip' is made out, and dispatched in lieu of it. The cause of the failure of the pouch to connect is thus disclosed and reported at once to the proper officer of the service by the railway postal clerk, or to the proper official of the railroad by the employee of that railroad, and long and vexatious investigations thereby avoided. Taken in connection with the requirement to check all pouches in and out of mail cars and mail wagons, it furnishes a complete trace from office of dispatch to office of destination."

RESIDENCE.

The employees of the railway mail service were not restricted in the selection of their place of residence until 1894. Previous to that year many lived miles from the route to which assigned and when trains were "snowed in," or the track over which they passed to reach their own route was blocked with wrecks, washed out bridges, or floods, they were unable to report at the head of their route in time to take out the first run of their regular tour of duty; the result was that the clerks who were on duty were compelled to continue on the run until the delayed clerk reported, or a qualified substitute could be obtained, otherwise the run went out alone and continued down the line until a regular clerk or substitute, who had been notified to do so, reported at the train and took charge of the mail. This was detrimental to public interests and imposed hardships on the clerks.

In 1894 a committee of superintendents was appointed to pass upon the blanks then on our list, and to recommend the discontinuance of such as had become, in its opinion, obsolete or unsatisfactory, and to submit to the General Superintendent such additional blanks as in its judgment had become necessary. Other matters pertaining to improved and uniform methods of handling the service were considered and recommended by the committee. After it had completed this work it discussed the importance and advisability of recommending that an order be issued requiring "the clerks in the railway mail service to take up their residence at some point on the route to which they are assigned, satisfactory to their division superintendent," and recommended it.

When the work of the committee was received it was examined carefully, and most of it approved and made effective. The recommendation respecting the residence of clerks I approved, and submitted to the Postmaster General through the Second Assistant Postmaster General, Hon. J. Lowrie Bell, who approved it and directed me to issue the necessary order to carry it into effect. This I did June 2, 1894, in the following language:

Washington, D. C., June 2, 1894.

General Order No. 378.

Residence, Place of.—Ordered: That all clerks in the railway mail service performing duty in railway post offices take up their residence at some point on the route to which they are assigned satisfactory to their division superintendent on or before May 1, 1895.

Those who can do so, without considerable pecuniary loss or sacrifice of home property, will be expected to comply with this order at once; the others at the earliest moment possible; none later than the date named.

By order of the Postmaster General.

JAMES E. WHITE, Gen'l Supt.

The order aroused some indignation and was brought to the attention of the Senate of the United States by Senator Hoar of Massachusetts, and in February, 1895, Congress passed an amendment to H. R. Bill 8,272, providing "that all clerks hereafter appointed to the railway mail service and to perform duty in railway post offices shall reside at some point on the route to which they are assigned, but clerks heretofore appointed and now performing such duty shall not be required to change their residence."

This bill having become a law by direction of the Postmaster General I issued General Order No. 383, which after reciting the above amendment, stated, that it "having become a law, General Order 378 is hereby revoked. Clerks now living upon the lines to which assigned will retain their present residences."

This action had become necessary by the growth of the service, the importance of the mail to the business public, and the absolute necessity for a thoroughly regular and reliable mail service, and it has helped to bring this condition about.

PROTECTION OF CLERKS WHILE IN THE DISCHARGE OF THEIR DUTIES.

In 1894 several railway postal clerks were assaulted and injured by vicious and drunken men while discharging their duties in their cars. The assailants belonged to that class in whom brutal instincts predominate, but which they mistake for a superior creation absolving them from the restraints and obligations imposed upon the "common herd" of mankind. Being no respecters of laws and regulations, they cannot comprehend how the free-born American citizen, realizing the distinction and liberty thus acquired, can hold sacred those things that they despise, and if need be will voluntarily place his life in jeopardy to enforce and defend them. The assaults usually resulted from efforts made by conscientious clerks to enforce the laws and regulations relating to entry into railway post offices by unauthorized persons. The trouble continuing, notice was taken of it in my annual report for 1896, as follows:

"During the past two years several railway postal clerks, in the discharge of their duty, have been assaulted by persons not connected with the Post Office Department, and in two instances at least were so badly hurt that they could not finish their runs, and consequently the mails were thereby delayed in reaching the addressees.

"These two clerks were, in fact, so seriously injured that they were obliged to go to the hospital for treatment. These assaults generally grow out of the fact that the clerk is instructed to allow no unauthorized person to enter his car or apartment, and in attempting to enforce the regulation is maliciously and unwarrantably assaulted.

"Unfortunately, it has been found that there is no warrant of law to enable the legal representatives of the Government to prosecute the guilty parties, and it is with the view of correcting this that I earnestly urge the passage of a measure by Congress whereby such assaults will be classed as offenses against the United States.

"There is on page 755, section 3869, of the Revised Statutes of the United States, a law making it a felony to assault a letter carrier while in the discharge of his duty, and it is no more than just and proper to protect our clerks in the same manner. A statute reading as follows would meet the case:

"Every person who, by violence, enters a railway post office car or apartment assigned to the use of the railway mail service, or who willfully and maliciously assaults a railway postal clerk while in the discharge of his duties as such; and every person who willfully aids or assists therein, shall for every such offense, be punishable by a fine of not less than $100, and not more than $1,000, or imprisonment for not less than one year and not more than three years.

"Such a measure is of especial importance to the patrons of the Department and likewise to the Department, for when a clerk is so badly injured as to be unable to distribute and deliver the mails received by him, both private and public interests are more or less embarrassed, and in many instances those who transact their business almost exclusively by mail suffer serious losses.   *   *   *   *
Where the clerk is seriously injured the mail in his custody cannot be guarded properly and consequently is at the mercy of the assaulting party or parties. Besides this the Department rightfully allows the salary of the clerk injured to run during the time he is unable to per-

form his duties, and consequently it is put to the additional expense of employing an acting clerk to keep up the run of the injured clerk until he returns to duty."

Shortly after the Department's recommendations were received by Congress—the 54th, I think—a bill was introduced by Mr. Livingston of Georgia, reading exactly like the draft we suggested. He ventured the opinion that it would meet the case. It did not become a law then, however. In the next annual report and in each that followed it until 1903, it appeared in connection with an earnest recommendation that Congress legislate for the protection of the clerks. It seems very strange that in a matter so simple of understanding, so manifestly in the interest of the Government and its people, so humane in its object, so thoroughly in the line of self-preservation, for it was to protect the representatives of the Government employed in a business of which it has a monoply, that it should have been permitted to linger before Congress seven years without action, when it is not unreasonable to assume that if its importance had been realized fully, it would have become a law in less than a month after the date of its introduction; nevertheless I am thankful that it passed finally.

RAILWAY POST OFFICES ON ELECTRIC AND CABLE CAR LINES.

In my annual reports for 1895 and 1896 glowing comments were made on this service and a splendid future predicted for it, all of which has been justified since. It was placed in charge of the General Superintendent of the Railway Mail Service during the last half of the calendar year, 1895; before June 30th of that year it had been introduced in Boston, Brooklyn, Philadelphia, New York and St. Louis.

During the fiscal years 1896 and 1897 my office and those of the division superintendents worked heroically to develop and extend it, and we were successful. It was inaugurated in Chicago, Cincinnati, San Francisco, Rochester, N. Y.; Northampton, Mass., during the fiscal year 1896.

STATEMENT.

On October 26, 1895, the annual miles of service was 73,356. The number of separate lines in the four cities, Boston, Mass.; Brooklyn, N. Y.; Philadelphia, Pa., and St. Louis, Mo., was 10; the number of clerks employed on such lines was 17; the number of cars was 12; the number of pieces of mail handled daily was 78,932; average number of crews 19; miles of routes, 112.71.

On June 30, 1896, the annual miles of service was 907,863. The number of separate lines was 21; the number of clerks employed, 75;

Hon. Still. P. Taft
Superintendent Seventh Division R. M. S.
(See Appendix)

the number of cars and apartments was 45; the number of pieces of mail handled daily was 505,481; the average number of closed pouches handled daily was 398; number of round trips with clerks per day, 196; number of crews, 60; average number of miles run daily by crews, 279.45; miles of routes, 198.58.

Whenever it was possible to do so, special letter boxes, painted white, the color adopted for these cars, were located at important street intersections, several squares apart, from which collections were made by the clerks on each trip; collectors in districts outside, or beyond the postal car routes, were instructed to deposit their mail in these boxes wherever their routes touched them; this provided additional facilities to many districts not traversed by street railway post offices.

Arrangements were perfected, whereby twelve of the principal branch offices and all the railroad stations in Boston were brought in touch with the General Post Office through the postal cars in operation on the "West End Street Railway;" 45,000 letters were made up to carrier routes daily in the cars on this one route, and a saving in the handling of 328 pouches daily was effected. A cross-town service between Dorchester and Back Bay was established, which made a gain of two hours in the transit of the mail passing over that route from one section to the other. These cars also ran to the railroad stations and exchanged mails with the steam railway post offices, making an earlier delivery by two hours of mail arriving at the different stations for many of the branch offices, and in some instances effecting a delivery the day of its arrival, of mail that previously remained undelivered until the following day.

Very great improvements were made in New York, Brooklyn, Philadelphia, Washington, Cincinnati, Rochester, N. Y., and Northampton, Mass.

In Chicago eight cars, equipped with crews of two clerks each, running on four lines reached direct eleven of the largest branch offices, and, by connecting lines, four others. A good feature of the service in this city was the arrangement whereby each car as it passed around the "loop" in the downtown district—the great wholesale and retail center—exchanged mails with the cars on the other lines, keeping much of it in motion from the time it was mailed until it was delivered. Twelve round trips were made daily, except Sundays; on that day but three were made.

Excellent arrangements prevailed in St. Louis. Two lines equipped with three cars were in operation, one line made twelve round trips daily, the other five; the aggregate daily mileage was 254.73; these cars exchanged mails with four branch offices, eleven sub-stations and four fourth-class post offices. One feature of the St. Louis service, which was an improvement upon that of any other city, and that realized my dream, was the delivery from the cars to 63 carriers of mails for their routes where they intersected, thus giving an additional delivery practically to these routes. At that time about 1,000 pounds of mail was collected daily from the 288 letter boxes visited by the clerks on these cars. The interior of the cars were so fitted up that the carriers could arrange their mail, in regular order, for early delivery while riding from the main office to the point nearest their routes.

The growth of the service during the fiscal year 1897 was healthy. At its close this showing was presented:

No. of separate lines	33	Increase	12
" clerks employed	102	Increase	27
" crews	87	Increase	27
" cars	65	Increase	20
" round trips per day	343	Increase	147
" miles of routes	303.68	Increase	105.10
Annual miles of service with clerks	1,619,829	Increase	711,966
Pieces of mail handled daily	593,860	Increase	88,379
Average No. of closed pouches handled daily	568	Increase	170

The annual report for 1898 showed:

No. of separate lines	40	Increase	7
" clerks employed	112	Increase	10
" crews	98	Increase	11
" cars	71	Increase	6
" round trips per day	388	Increase	45
" miles of routes	379.47	Increase	75.79
Annual miles of service with clerks	1,744,694	Increase	124,865
Pieces of mail handled daily	1,889,092	Increase	1,295,232
Avg. No. of closed pouches handled daily	971	Increase	403

Those who read this and compare the statements for the four years, 1895, 1896, 1897, and 1898, will understand that the service was managed by officers who believed in it; believed that when developed and extended every section of all our greatest business centers, and all the states in the Union, would share alike in the benefits of the increased expedition afforded the mails by this service. But while success was crowning our efforts the unwelcome truth was forcing its way into my mind that the full possibilities of the railway mail service could not be wrought out economically unless it could control the boundaries of the collectors' routes penetrated by the railway post offices, their schedules and those adjoining, and have at its command a sufficient number of clerks to overcome the shortness of the routes. This I found was too much to hope for, and being desirous that it be utilized to its full capacity I made the following statement in the report for the fiscal year 1897:

"The distribution of mails on electric and cable lines in cities has been continued and extended during the past year with considerable success. It is a question in my mind, however, whether this class of service ever can be made to accomplish what was hoped when the system was inaugurated. The runs are too short as a rule to admit of the distribution of any great quantity of mail either way. It was hoped that on outward trips from the main office or depots we would be able to distribute the mail for carriers so that upon arrival at the several branch offices the mail would be arranged in such shape that the carriers might start immediately on their routes, and that on inward trips the mail taken from the branch offices or collectors might be distributed and pouched to outgoing trains, and thus avoid delay in the main office. We do indeed accomplish a great deal in that direction, but lack of time as already mentioned and lack of facilities on account of the limited space obtainable has prevented us from accomplishing all that we hoped to. I am still of the opinion, however, that the service is worth all it costs, and that it would be a step backward to abandon it.

"By arranging matters so that collectors can connect with the postal cars on street car lines, considerable time can be saved by having the mail properly sorted, canceled and distributed in part before arrival at the main office or railroad station. More to this end could be accomplished probably if what might be strictly called the city service were placed in charge of the postmaster or superintendent of mails than if retained, as at present, under the jurisdiction of the railway mail service. It is all performed within the territory covered by the delivery of the post office, and does a class of work for the proper performance of which the people have always been accustomed to look to the postmaster. It is so closely in touch with the collection and carrier service, and its successful operation depends so much upon its relations with these branches, that in my judgment it could accomplish the greatest good if placed under the same control.

"There are a number of electric lines throughout the country which perform the same service practically as a regular railroad line, running, as they do, beyond the limits of any one city, and supplying a number of independent offices. Such service should be controlled by the railway mail service, but the lines running entirely within the limits of a city can be handled more harmoniously and more satisfactorily, I think, through the local office.

"If this change is made, these cars should be manned by clerks from the post office and not by railway postal clerks, as is the case to a great extent at present; and such clerks should be taken upon the post office rolls, as an offset for the post office clerks on railroad lines working city mails, who can be taken up on the railway mail service rolls, as suggested in a preceding section of this report.

"I merely suggest these changes for your consideration. If in your judgment this service should be controlled from this office I assure you that it will be my constant effort to promote its efficiency and to extend its usefulness."

The proposition was approved by the First and Second Assistant Postmasters General and in December of the fiscal year 1898 we commenced carrying the suggestions into effect. It was understood that the railway mail service would carry on its roster the clerks employed in the street railway post offices until the year ended. We did this and in addition took upon our rolls many of the clerks who were assigned from some of the principal post offices to city distribution in our cars; it being our policy to assume such distribution as rapidly as we could secure sufficient additional force to do so. Our observations had convinced us that it could be done more generally and more economically in this way than in any other way, and time has shown that we were correct.

CITY DISTRIBUTION IN RAILWAY POST OFFICES.

The late Supt. R. C. Jackson, of the Second division, placed on record the fact that about the first work done in the New York & Washington railway post office "was the distribution of the letters for delivery in New York City; separations being made for the delivery boxes, for the several stations, etc., so that a gain of four hours was claimed in the receipt by the public of the great south mail arriving in the morning."

This railway post office was introduced in October, 1864, I think. It was the second inaugurated, and, as is indicated in the statement just quoted, the Civil War was being waged with unparalleled energy, drawing thousands of men into the field almost daily from the north; but for these armies the mail from the south at that time would not have been large. Mr. Jackson said in his "Sketch of the Railway Mail Service," published in 1884, in writing of this line, that "At the termination of the war, in consequence of the return of soldiers to their homes, the work fell off to almost nothing for a few months. It was gradually built up again by the reopening of mail communication throughout the south."

After this, and until 1899, the principal part of this distribution was performed by city distributers sent out each evening from such important post offices as Boston, Mass.; Chicago, Ill.; New York, N. Y.; Philadelphia, Pa.; Portland, Oregon; St. Louis, Mo.; St. Paul, Minn., and San Francisco, Cal., on outward-bound trains to the meeting point of a railway post office—usually a fast mail—to which they transferred and commenced distributing the mail to carrier routes, the same as if they had remained in their home office, but the result was radically different, the mail was delivered to the persons addressed from two to four hours earlier, and more than that in some cases.

In 1883 the New York and Chicago fast mail, which required a stronger force of clerks on west than east-bound trips, to distribute the general mail, began to utilize the surplus strength east-bound in making up the New York City mail for branch offices, stations, and large business concerns; the following year it handled 14,000,000 pieces in this way. The growth of this class of work was slow for reasons given in the following extract from my annual report of 1894:

"There were prepared for immediate delivery to stations and carriers, by railway postal clerks during the fiscal year ending June 30, 1894, 483,667,275 letters. This work was in addition to the regular distribution to offices and routes, of which 10,339,973,790 pieces were handled by them. The number of letters treated for immediate delivery to stations and carriers as above was but a small part of the aggregate number prepared for immediate delivery during that period, and the aggregate was but an infinitesimal portion of the number addressed to offices of the first importance. Those prepared in excess of the number handled by railway postal clerks were separated by city distributers, sent out from certain post offices to meet incoming trains, and no record of the number distributed by them appears in this report, because the work was not done by the railway mail service. That which was handled by postal clerks represents the time that they would otherwise have been unemployed while on duty; in some instances, such as the lines operating between Boston, Mass., and New York City, New York, the force used would not have been employed but for this class of distribution. The paramount duty of a railway postal clerk is to complete the distribution of the regular mail received by him; whatever time may remain to him after this has been accomplished can be employed upon the separation of city mail; consequently the extent of this class of work possible to railway postal clerks, under existing conditions, depends upon the quantity of ordinary mail they receive. The east-bound mails are always lighter than the west-bound, and as the lines must be provided with sufficient force to distribute the largest mail received, there is usually a reserve force on east-bound trips that can be utilized to separate the mails for stations or carrier routes, thus avoiding the delay in delivery involved in dispatching it to the main offices for the same treatment; but the east-bound mails fluctuate in quantity, and no one knows at the commencement of a trip whether it will be above or below the usual amount received on that day of the week. Sometimes some of the regular connections are lost, then more time can be given to city distribution; sometimes double connections are received; a publishing house sends out an unusual quantity of matter, or a business concern floods the mails with circulars or letters soliciting trade, then little or no time can be given to the preparation of city mails, for it would not be satisfactory to the Department or the public to delay the mails for one or more states a day in order to expedite the delivery of those addressed to a single great city.

"There can be no doubt as to the desirability of disposing of the mails for commercial cities in the manner outlined, because such treatment would be of great advantage to the public, in that it would advance business transactions of all kinds materially —some of them a day at least and almost all, several hours. It is not necessary that all the mails addressed to these large cities and dispatched by railway post offices should be separated in transit; those brought in after the carriers have departed on their last tour for the day and a reasonable time before they start on their first tour of the following day should be thrown into the main office for separation, but those received at other hours would be greatly expedited in delivery if so separated. Considering the fact that our clerks can devote some portion of their time to this work on east-bound trips it is the opinion of this office that the work can be performed more economically by the railway mail service than by post offices, after it is systematized and the clerks become familiar with it. I would suggest as a beginning that a list of the offices that would receive the greatest benefits from such advanced separation be prepared, that there be transferred from these post offices to the railway mail service a sufficient number of city distributers to insure the proper preparation of the mails for immediate delivery and that there be added to the appropriation for clerk hire whatever sum may be necessary to cover the salaries of those so transferred. This arrangement ought not to increase the expense of city distribution at any time, and after the railway postal clerks have acquired the knowledge necessary to work the mails the cost would not be as great as if the whole separation fell upon the post offices, for it is assumed that the decrease in the number of city distributers employed in the offices affected would correspond to the increase of this class of work performed in railway post offices."

The following year this separation passed more largely to the railway mail service. Some of the city distributers of the offices named, who dead-headed on outward-bound trains to the point of meeting inward-bound railway post offices, and while returning to the starting point, separated the mail to carrier routes, stations, etc., were returned to their respective offices; others were transferred to the railway mail service and were utilized with the crews upon the distribution of the city and general mail in both directions, unless the lines to which such clerks were transferred ran between two large cities, and the trains to which their cars were assigned, arrived at both in the morning; in that event it was the ultimate intention to make the distribution of the mail for these terminal cities their paramount duty; their studies and examinations were to be upon the schemes of those cities, and they were to have understudies who could in a little while assist by making up direct for large concerns, banks, hotels, manufactories, general offices of railway lines, mailing houses, etc., leaving the finer work for the more expert distributer, and later be able to assume the duties wholly in emergencies, and to perform the special work in the event of the promotion, death or removal of the clerks so assigned.

Improvement was very noticeable at the close of 1895; more so at the end of the fiscal years 1896, 1897, and 1898, due largely to the methods employed by the late Supt. Lewis L. Troy to secure the co-operation of postmasters, business concerns, and the public after he was instructed to take up the city distribution for Chicago in railway post offices. These methods were emphatically approved by the General Superintendent, who instructed other superintendents to put them in force in their divisions as far as possible, and urged the Department to send copies of the circulars issued by Supt. Troy and the postmaster at Chicago, Ill., to the postmaster at each of the principal cities throughout the country, with instructions to have a supply of them printed and distributed by carriers of their respective offices.

The circulars read as follows:

"To the Public:

"The distribution of letter mail to stations and carriers of the Chicago post office will hereafter be performed, as far as possible, in the railway post office cars.

"To enable postal clerks to do this work it is imperatively necessary that all letters for persons residing within the district tributary to the Chicago post office should be addressed not only to street and number, but also to the carrier route, if within the limit of the main office, and to the station where the party addressed is served by carrier from a station of the Chicago post office. For example:

<blockquote>
"Rowell, Hitt & Co.,
   "141 Clark St.,
"Carrier 65.   "Chicago, Ill.

"Mrs. J. Russell Brown,
   "151 W. Sixty-third street,
"Station O.   "Chicago, Ill.

"Loomis Bread Co.,
   "151 W. Madison street,
"Station D.   "Chicago, Ill.

"Wood, Coal & Co.,
   "1402 Wabash avenue,
"Carrier 230.   "Chicago, Ill.
</blockquote>

"The public is earnestly requested to co-operate with the railway mail service in securing the prompt delivery of matter on arrival at Chicago by making the address of letters full and complete, as above indicated.

"Letters should not be addressed to street corners, as the four corners may be served by four different carriers, and postal clerks can not determine which of the four would be the proper one to make the delivery.

"Carrier numbers and letters of stations can readily be obtained from your correspondents in the city.

"All letters not addressed to street and number are sent to the main office at Chicago for distribution, and this necessarily results in delay in delivery.

"(Signed) Lewis L. Troy,
"Supt. R. M. S."

This circular was issued on the 1st of July, 1895, and on the 15th of the same month the postmaster at Chicago issued a notice to the business public which read as follows:

"To expedite the business of the post office all incoming mail, with unimportant exceptions, will hereafter be distributed on the railway post offices by clerks of the railway mail service. Distribution of mail

Hon. Lewis L. Troy
Late Superintendent Sixth Division R. M. S.

on the railway post offices directly to carriers enables this office to promptly deliver all incoming mail. This end, however, can be attained only by the hearty co-operation of the business public. If mail is not addressed to street and number it cannot be distributed to carriers by the railway postal clerks. Hence, as a natural consequence, distribution to carriers is delayed, and the work left undone until the mail reaches the Chicago post office. Loss of time occasioned by neglect to use street and number usually makes a difference of one delivery at least in placing the mail in the hands of the letter carriers. Business men are interested in securing the immediate delivery of mail on its arrival in the city, and their interests suffer materially by the nonobservance of the rule which enjoins the addition of street and number to an address. Merchants distribute thousands of addressed envelopes yearly for the use of out-of-town customers. Very often such envelopes contain stamps, so desirous are the senders to promote business. Such expense is incurred because it is thought to be a good investment. Many of these envelopes bear addresses like the following: 'Chas. Smith & Co., Chicago, Ill.'

"As a means of expediting the distribution of mails in the railway post offices such an address is of comparatively little value. The postal clerk at Minneapolis, Indianapolis, or Omaha handling such a letter probably never heard of Smith & Co. Even if its reputation as a leading house had reached the postal clerks they would have no idea what part of Chicago its business was located in. Postal clerks do not learn distribution to firms by name. They learn it by street and number only. It is impossible for a clerk to memorize the street and number address of every business house and building in Chicago. Neither can he carry in his head the names of the large buildings in Chicago. He must have street and number on each envelope if his work is to have any good results and a saving of time is to be effected. Therefore, when a letter addressed to 'Chas. Smith & Co., Chicago, Ill.,' is picked up by a postal clerk it is thrown to the pouch labeled 'Chicago' to await local distribution in this office. On the other hand, take the letter properly addressed, thus, 'Chas. Smith & Co., 104 Dearborn street, Chicago, Ill.' The postal clerk probably does not know where Dearborn street is, and may never have been in Chicago in his life, but he knows his 'scheme,' and throws the letter thus addressed to carrier's district No. 36, section 1, post office. The letter goes at once to carrier 36 when it arrives in Chicago, and is delivered without delay. The other letter addressed merely 'Chicago' comes in the general mail and takes its turn for distribution, remaining in the office an hour or more after the properly addressed letter has been placed in the hands of the person for whom it was intended.

"The delivery of mail fits into the arrival of incoming mail. The mail distributed on the road goes out at once by carrier. The mail merely separated on the road is held for distribution, and has to await the next trip of the carrier before it can be delivered.

"These facts ought to convince business men of the absolute necessity of insisting upon the use of street and number as part of the address on mail of every sort and character. Envelopes printed in any other way are practically of no value, and do not expedite the delivery of mail in the least. It results, too, in giving the outside public the impression that the mere use of the word 'Chicago' is sufficient, an error responsible for most of the confusion and delay in the delivery of mail.

"It is estimated that more than 50 per cent. of the business mail for Chicago is addressed without street and number. Under the old system, by the employment of special clerks who were compelled to memorize thousands of addresses a great deal of the unaddressed mail was given partial train distribution. The volume of business, together with the change in the service, render the continuance of this practice impossible. The new service, by reason of its wider ramifications, will give the business world greatly increased facilities in the delivery of mail from out-of-town points if the business world will only co-operate to the extent of addressing its mail properly. Where mail is not addressed by street and number, this office will not undertake to deliver it as promptly as that which is properly addressed."

The circular letter of the postmaster of Chicago was delivered at the business places and homes of all the residents of that city by the carriers, and the one issued by Supt. Troy was sent to all the postmasters in the Sixth division. The results of the two were remarkable. In a brief space of time thousands of letters were received by the addressees from business and social correspondents several hours earlier than usual, because they had added to the address that they had previously placed upon the envelopes, the street and number, and, if within the limit of the general post office, the carrier route also; or if supplied by carrier from a station, the designation of the station, as shown in Mr. Troy's circular. The harmony of action that characterized the postal authorities in Chicago; in fact, throughout the whole section within the influence of that city, soon worked a revolution in the comprehensibility of addresses, which is responsible for the wonderful decrease in the number of letters sent into the Chicago post office for separation to station and carrier routes because the addresses were not full enough to enable the city distributers in railway post offices to dispose of them in that way.

It will be remembered by the reader, that in the suggestions made to the Second Assistant Postmaster General in my annual report for the fiscal year 1897, respecting the transfer of the street railway post office service to the supervision of the postmasters, I said, if this is done the clerks employed in them, who are charged to the railway mail service, should be withdrawn therefrom, and be assigned to the regular railway post offices, and that the post office clerks, performing city distribution in the regular railway post offices, should be returned to their respective offices, or be transferred to the railway mail service.

After the suggestions were approved, the transfers to the railway mail service were made gradually, but were not completed until the fiscal year 1899. But during the intervening years, 1890 to 1899, the number of pieces of mail distributed for city delivery by railway postal clerks in railway post offices had increased from 226,429,575 to 519,870,465.

From that time on, every effort possible has been made to systematize that feature of the service and in doing it many unsatisfactory conditions and unreasonable demands had to be met and adjusted. It always had been the practice to confine this class of distribution to those trains arriving at these great cities too late to permit of the work being done in the offices in time for the first carrier delivery in the morning; as time wore on and important railway post offices arrived later in the day in some of these centers, but early enough to insure a substantial gain in the delivery of the mail, if made up to a limited number of carrier routes, to the branch offices, stations, banks, commercial houses, hotels, etc., it was extended to cover them, because it enabled those who desired to gain one day on their business correspondence to do so, thus, for all practical purposes, bringing the producer and consumer, the buyer and seller, one day nearer each other, a consideration too important financially to be overlooked by the dealer, or to be ignored by a Government interested in the welfare of its citizens.

A few postmasters made themselves very disagreeable by insisting upon a wide distribution at unseasonable and unprofitable hours, apparently to give their own men more leisure for athletic exercises, etc., and demanded that intricate and impractical separations be made regardless of whether there were compensating benefits; changed the boundaries and mixed the territory of carrier routes without substantial reason in some cases, thus forcing a new scheme, the re-memorizing of the distribution; destroying the stability of knowledge once acquired; imposing absolutely unnecessary hardships upon men already burdened, and in this way retarding the development planned, until the officers of the service were compelled to take the stand that before the railway mail service accepted a scheme from an office inquiry would be made to determine whether all the routes provided for were of such importance as to justify their being made up in the railway post office. In other words, if there were reasons to believe that unnecessary work and study were demanded we would participate in providing the specifications for the scheme sufficiently to act as a check upon the scope of its construction, and, if this failed to keep it within justifiable limits, we would make the schemes used in this distribution in railway post offices the same as we made those governing all other distribution made therein, or, if we used those made in post offices, we would mass on the main office the mail supplied by carrier routes, which would not be advanced in delivery because of being so made up, and also whatever was supplied by routes not of sufficient importance to justify the increase of labor and money that it might involve. This question was finally set at rest, but that we might continue to "hang on the jagged edge" there arose another live question, but the dispute preceding its settlement was a family one, and a harmonious one at that, and was, Should this work be assigned to clerks of the same class in all crews? If so, what class? And should they be eligible like all other clerks of that class on their respective lines for promotion to the next higher class, subject to the civil service promotion regulations, and if promoted carry the assignment to city distribution with them? Or should a special corps be created from class 3 clerks to perform this special distribution, and if they had leisure afterwards, do whatever the clerk in charge directed, and not be eligible to promotion, on the ground that stability of employment on the special work was essential to efficiency, and this could not be secured if the assignment changed every time one of these class 3 men was promoted?

My office held that these clerks would be entitled to promotion if, in addition to keeping up their studies, work and examinations on city distribution, they passed the examinations required of clerks of the same class assigned to general distribution, and made such records as would entitle them to advancement under the civil service promotion regulations. In my judgment any other course would be pre-eminently unjust; to illustrate: Three men were appointed to the service as probationers on the same line the same day; one of them had more days to his credit as a substitute, and in consequence received a permanent appointment first; three months later a vacancy occurred in the special corps and this clerk was promoted to it; this ended his eligibility for further promotion. A month later both the others entered class 3, but as no vacancy existed in the special corps, neither was assigned to it, both continued on the general distribution; a month later one vacancy occurred in class 4, and two months later another; as both these clerks had the best records in their class they received these promotions; passed the danger point of life assignment to class 3. Being clerks of fine capacity they were advanced on merit alone from one class to another, and in a series of years became chief clerks, assistant superintendents, division superintendents, and general superintendent; Why not? Five of those who have been General Superintendent; all of those who are Division Superintendents, Assistant Superintendents and Chief Clerks moved up in that way. The facts are that a corps so constituted, so far as advancement of individual members of it is concerned, would be isolated from a progressive future, as much so as a leper is from mankind. That is why the above decision was made. The Superintendent of one division assigned the city distribution to his clerks in charge and thus overcame the question of isolation from promotion; but there were resulting disadvantages to such an assignment, the principal one being that it would in time unfit the schoolmaster of the crew for that position; from being an encyclopedia of general information respecting distribution he would become a specialist, and that would be very undesirable. During all this time improvement—extension and system—was advancing and in 1904 the number of pieces distributed was 673,918,710 and in 1906 it had increased to 828,446,795; in 1907 to 944,449,105, and in 1909 to 1,132,338,710, which shows that the clerks were mastering this distribution as they had that undertaken for the first time in 1864.

Thus far city distribution has not been confined to any special class uniformly; more clerks of class 3 and under are engaged in it than of other classes, but whoever is so assigned performs other distribution also, and studies and passes examinations upon it. The question of promotion is not an open one longer; it is assured to those best qualified for it. As the service grows modifications in assignments, in methods of handling it, will become necessary, and those in the saddle now, as well as those who will follow, will know by experience what to do.

PRIMARY SEPARATION OF SECOND-CLASS MATTER.

Away back in 1872 the New York City post office occupied cramped quarters, even for those days. I do not know whether that was their first experience in that line, but I do know it was not the last; for I have observed that each time they have vacated a building they have moved into one large enough to accommodate all the federal offices located in the city. But ages before the building began to show signs of wear the other offices would be forced to other shelter by the monster that waxed fat and fatter on the ever increasing torrent of food forced into its maw, by the great business concerns of that city, and especially by the endless chain of publishing houses of all kinds, sending matter printed in all forms and languages, seasoned with all kinds of morals, religious and political, to be digested.

New York did not enjoy the unenviable distinction of being the "onlyest" in this respect; "there were others." But in 1872 the New York post office became sadly crowded, notwithstanding that it had obtained some relief the preceding year by discontinuing the practice of making a more or less complicated distribution of all mail, and substituting for it, by authority of the General Superintendent of the Railway Mail Service, the separation of the mail by states, except in those cases where because of the nearness of the states to that office, and the number of routes by which they were supplied, some portion of them would be delayed thereby. In the greater emergency that arose in 1872, wherein the daily newspaper mail accumulated in that office so largely that it interfered with the proper treatment and prompt dispatch of other mail of a higher class, and usually considered of a greater intrinsic value, Mr. Bangs, after making a personal investigation into the conditions confronting the Department, during which he visited the mailing rooms of the largest publication concerns, and held conferences with the publishers, returned to Washington, D. C., and after consulting with the Postmaster General addressed a letter to them, which bore date December 11, 1872. In this letter he explained the difficulties of the situation and presented a remedy which he had formulated, and asked them to co-operate in putting it into effect. This letter he sent to them by Captain M. J. McGrath, an expert in the treatment of mails, saying: "He will fully explain the details, which are few and simple, to all to whom he may come, and is fully authorized to carry them into effect so far as the Department is concerned. He will be assisted by the postmaster at New York and his subordinates, and also the Assistant Superintendent of Railway Mail Service in that city." And he added: "I respectfully ask the attention and co-operation as far as practicable of all publishers to whom he may come, believing that their compliance with his requests will greatly result in expediting the transmission of all mails to their destination, in much less time than has heretofore been practicable or possible."

This simple plan was the "Stating" of the mail; the plan inaugurated in the principal post offices the year before. It was accepted in

Hon. R. C. Jackson
Late Superintendent Second Division R. M. S.

due time and gave the relief so much needed, with advantage to the publishers and the Post Office Department. It was adopted a little later in all large publication houses throughout the country, and some of them very wisely took into their employ some of our expert distributers and placed them in charge of their mailing rooms.

A time came, however, some years later, when the increase of population, the rising tide of business, the intellectual and material development of the country demanded a wonderful increase of news and information of all kinds—spiritual, business, social and sensational. Information to be derived from books of essays, poetry, romance and history, and those works of positive scientific knowledge that are regarded as standard everywhere, on agriculture, mineralogy, mathematics, architecture, geometry, and astronomy. This demand was met by the enlargement of printing plants and publishing houses, and the establishment of new ones in different parts of the country, and when they were turning out their full capacity the volume of second-class matter pouring into their mailing rooms and into railway post offices and post offices was enormous; more than could be handled anywhere by the Post Office Department without unwarranted additional expenditure of money. Action was taken at once to have all these plants begin, or, if they were doing so, increase, the primary separation of their output, so as to keep a large per cent. of it out of their home post office, advancing its delivery and relieving the railway postal clerks from extra duty, many times, and the appropriation for clerk hire from demands that could not be met without detriment to the service at large.

In 1896, when we were very much embarrassed with this mail, the late Richard C. Jackson, who was one of our most intelligent and capable officers, with long and valuable experience in postal affairs in New York City, well acquainted with some of its people, and having the entree to its publishing houses, was placed in charge of the work of systematizing, improving, and enlarging the separations. He was a Christian gentleman, resourceful, diplomatic, and thoroughly reliable; was well-known personally to all the officers of our service and either personally or by reputation to thousands of our boys. He had the hearty support of our Division Superintendents, of the superintendents of mails in post offices, and the earnest approval of the General Superintendent. He made no mistakes and was eminently successful.

In 1896, Mr. Jackson made his first regular report, which showed that during the month of June of that year, publishers in sixteen of the principal cities, viz.: New York, Chicago, Philadelphia, Boston, St. Louis, Cincinnati, Baltimore, San Francisco, Minneapolis, Milwaukee,

Kansas City, Washington, St. Paul, Cleveland, Indianapolis and Brooklyn, sent into their respective post offices a total of 291,589 sacks of mail; of which 153,232 were so made up by the publishers that they were dispatched from the mailing offices without further separation, and 51,711 so made up that part of the distribution, which would have fallen upon the post office, was avoided. The remainder consisted of 86,580 sacks of miscellaneous or "mixed" matter, which was distributed wholly in the post office, and consequently was not dispatched as promptly as the other 205,009 sacks. These 86,580 sacks represented 29.7 per cent. of the whole, and as was said in my annual report for that year, this quantity we proposed to reduce, at the same time keeping pace with the growth of the mail. Remember, in this connection, that publishers separated very little to routes in those days

SEPARATION SCHEME FOR PUBLISHING HOUSES, 1896.

The schemes furnished to publishing houses provided for the separation of their newspapers and periodicals into two parts—states and directs. The first separation was the placing of the mail addressed to each state in a separate sack properly labeled, so that if it happened to be a distant state it could be dispatched from the post office of origin without being held for separation; and if it happened to be a nearby state it would go directly to the sorting table at the post office, at which it would be worked instead of passing through the preliminary separation to which all mixed mail must be subjected.

The second division—"directs"—consisted of placing all papers addressed to one post office in a separate sack properly labeled, so that it would not only avoid detention for separation at the office of origin, but would not need to be opened for separation until it arrived at the office of destination.

In the case of daily newspapers, and sometimes in the case of other periodicals, the publisher was called upon to make a separation for routes, this consisting of placing all papers for a certain R. P. O. line in a sack by themselves, properly labeled, so as to escape detention for separation at the office of origin, although the papers might have to be handled once or twice in the R. M. S. before reaching destination. The route separation was not availed of as often as the state or direct separations, because it required either expert knowledge on the part of the newspaper employees, or else consulting a technical list for the arrangement of the galley slips, figures being used alongside of each subscriber's name to indicate the particular R. P. O. line to which the paper should be assigned.

Any newspaper not made up in any of the three separations above described would be sent to the post office in a sack labeled "Mixed," and this meant that the individual papers would sometimes have to be handled twice in succession in the post office before they could be dispatched on the way to destination.

The country, east, west and south, received the benefit of Mr. Jackson's knowledge and experience, for after he had placed the separation system in progressive condition in the New York City publishing establishments, he visited other cities, and accompanied by Division Superintendents of Railway Mail Service, and sometimes by Superintendents of Mails in post offices, called upon the managers of these plants, held conferences with them on the subject that was so familiar to him, and labored to imbue them with his own enthusiasm and belief in the efficiency of this plan of expediting their mails, while saving the whole general mail from delay in dispatch by reason of the blockades superinduced by the enormous quantity of undistributed matter mailed by them daily. He was impressive, as a sincere man always is who understands his business thoroughly, and made excellent progress. But in most cases these visits were repeated several times, unless the Division Superintendent and the Superintendent of Mails were watchful, energetic and pleasantly aggressive. In that event he could turn his attention to some new and uncultivated field; sometimes a campaign would be entered upon which was prolonged because the concern was unwilling to assume additional charges, that it believed the Government should meet itself, but in the final "round up" they were all branded. Many times failure in some particular case would seem to be in sight, but a little more argument, accompanied by undeniable statements of facts, illustrations of the situation, showing what would inevitably be the results in the one case and in the other, etc., would cause them to yield. All that has been accomplished in this line of work, and it is very great, has been through the earnest efforts of the railway mail service, supported largely by "smothered" post offices. When we undertook to secure greater easement from want of room, distributers, and delay in dispatch of mails, brought about by the rapidly increasing volume of second-class matter, we did not expect to win "hands down." These pages show that the railway mail service has been compelled to fight persistently for every foot that it has advanced since its inauguration. Perhaps the fact that its pathway has not been cleared of obstructions by the law-makers, or strewn with flowers by those whom we struggled to benefit, may account for the bouquets thrown at it quite frequently in these days. Nevertheless it would not be safe to store its artillery and ammunition and rely upon a more liberal trend of disposition; it is best to be ready to step into the forum, the places of business, and to present reasons why what is urged is just, and in their interest; the wise business man is amenable to reason when he recognizes it.

Not being accustomed to have things go our way on first application, we were not disposed to be despondent because the large majority of the publication houses in the cities named declined to consider the matter; others had, and we were sure these would as soon as they realized that, notwithstanding all the Post Office Department could do for them, their competitors would enter states, cities, hamlets and crossroads quicker than they, so long as they continued to refuse to separate their mails.

In addition recommendation was made in 1895, "That section 3883, Revised Statutes, section 306, Postal Laws and Regulations, be so amended as to require publishers to make such primary separation of their periodicals for mailing as the Postmaster General may direct." It was also recommended that section 840 of the Postal Laws and Regulations—

Section 840. Canvas sacks may be taken by publishers.—Whenever, in any post office in large towns and cities, there is an extreme necessity of extending to publishers the privilege of taking canvas sacks to their printing offices to be there filled with printed matter for the mails, the postmaster must keep an exact account with each publisher of the number of sacks taken from and returned to his post office on every occasion. Besides the account kept in the post office for that purpose, pass books should be used between the several printing offices and the post office. No sacks should be delivered to any publisher, except on presentation of his pass book, in which he is to be debited with the number of sacks intrusted to him and credited with the number returned; and for the due return of all sacks so intrusted to him each publisher shall be held responsible—

be modified to read as follows:

(AMENDMENT.)

Postmasters may extend to publishers and others the privilege of taking canvas sacks to their printing or mailing offices, to be there filled with printed matter for the mails, upon the following conditions:

(1) That matter of the second and third classes sent to post offices must be made up, each state or route separate, where the quantity for any one state or territory is in excess of 50 pieces, except where the mail is made up at publication or mailing offices by routes under the direction of the postmaster or Superintendent of the Rail-

way Mail Service, or where the matter is all for one post office, for foreign countries, or for free county circulation.

(2) That each sack shall be labeled with a shipping tag, or other proper label, which shall show the route, office, state or territory to which the matter contained therein is to be dispatched, the name of the publication, if a regularly entered second-class publication, and the name and address of the printer or mailer, if mailed by other than the publisher. Where the quantity of mail matter for any state or territory is less than 50 pieces, such matter may be placed in one or more sacks labeled "Miscellaneous," the label or shipping tag to conform to above description in other respects.

(3) Postmasters must keep an exact account with each publisher, printer, or mailer, of the number of sacks taken from and returned to his post office on every occasion. Besides the account kept in the post office for that purpose, pass books should be used between the several printing and mailing offices and the post office. No sacks should be delivered for any publisher, printer, or mailer, except on presentation of his pass book, in which he is to be debited with the number of sacks intrusted to him and credited with the number returned, and for the due care and return of all sacks so intrusted to him each publisher, printer, or mailer, shall be held responsible.

A recommendation exactly like this one, or similar to it, appeared in my annual reports for eleven years, the last in 1906; but no action was taken. We accomplished much, but it has always seemed to me best that such important matters should have the sanction of law, because it takes them out of the domain of doubt and procrastination."

COMPARATIVE STATEMENT.

1896.

Number of sacks made up by publishers in the 16 cities named
so they were dispatched without re-separation 1,838,784

Number of sacks partly made up as above and advanced in
dispatch 621,324

Number of sacks of miscellaneous or "mixed" matter sent
to the post office for full distribution, and thereby delayed in dispatch 1,038,960
Or 29.7 per cent. of the whole.

1906.

Number of sacks received at same 16 post offices from publishers made up so as to insure first dispatch without additional separation 6,499,068

Number of sacks received at same 16 post offices from publishers so made up that a part of the distribution was saved therein and advance dispatch insured 1,918,260

Number of miscellaneous or "mixed" sacks, received by the same offices, from publication houses, and liable to considerable delay in dispatch for distribution 638,004

This was 7.1 per cent. of the whole; a reduction of 22.6 per cent. in ten years.

The whole number of sacks mailed, as above, by publishing houses in the 16 cities during the fiscal year 1896 was 3,499,068, and for the fiscal year 1906, 9,055,332; a gain in the ten years of 5,556,264.

The 1906 report shows that the list of 16 post offices embraced in the original statement had been extended to cover 150 post offices, at which publishing houses had mailed 14,703,408 sacks of second-class matter, made up as heretofore stated, of which only 9 per cent. was "mixed."

This is a reading age. Newspapers, magazines, journals, literary works of all kinds, travels, wars, heroes, philosophers, statesmen, history and general information abound. The papers and magazines are overflowing with information gathered from all parts of the world, and presented to the reader in beautiful descriptive language, which charms while it educates. Some of the magazines are wonderfully interesting and educational; the best matter of a literary character that can be obtained regardless of time, the number of trained men and women required to collect and develop it, and money, make them so.

It is one of the great glories of our country that this elevating material, some of it, can be found at most of our firesides; on the table in the living or sitting room around which the family gather after the evening meal to refresh their minds in conversation and reading; or on shelves in the library where the student and thinker is apt to seclude himself that his thoughts and impressions respecting the subject he is studying may be submitted quietly to the court of absolute knowledge. It is uplifting to know that our people are so eager for information, educational and physical development. This spirit will grow with the food it is fed upon, consequently the mail of this class will continue to increase with our intellectual capacity, and I hope that progressive, entertaining, educational, and elevating publications—all that are not distinctively immoral—will, but that which is should be religiously excluded from circulation in and out of the mail. We can depend upon our good friends of the field force of the Department to keep a watchful eye on this feature of the postal service, and the General Superintendent with the Division Superintendents, Superintendents of Mails in post offices, Assistant Superintendents, Chief Clerks; and the specialist, Assistant Superintendent C. H. McBride, the energetic and successful successor of Mr. Jackson, will see that publication houses do not forget that the splendid work they are performing in making up to states, offices and routes, is their salvation in the matter of quick delivery, and reasonable charges.

SPANISH AMERICAN WAR.

Thus far in its career the railway mail service has met and overcome every emergency that has confronted it.

Born about ten months before the close of the Civil War, and badly nourished in the beginning, it grew slowly for some years after its introduction, so slowly during the fiscal year ended June 30, 1865, an eventful period, that it did not become a factor in the disposition of the mails passing to and from the armies in the field. That became one of the missions of the old-established distributing post offices and other post offices in closer proximity to the columns maneuvering against the enemy. All these were strengthened as the mail increased sufficiently to separate it into armies, corps, divisions, brigades, regiments and sometimes companies, with the least delay possible, so that it might pass on at once to the soldiers addressed through the military postal system organized by the commanders of the army and their staffs, by authority of the Secretary of War, and with the advice and assistance of those who were regarded as experts in those days. This system became very effective as the war progressed, considering the difficulties encountered, such as the strategem employed by both armies to checkmate, disorganize, destroy or capture the foe; these movements often resulted in delaying the advance or hastening the retreat, through the burning of bridges; the capture, plundering and burning of wagon trains conveying supplies of all kinds and the mails to the boys at the front, and on the return trips those addressed to their homes in distant states. On such occasions the mails were plundered, and that not convertible to some purpose of the enemy cast into the flames to be burned with other non-convertible matter. Neither army had a monoply of this method of disposing of the correspondence of the enemy, but barring these unpleasant incidents the service was quite good.

I have said that the railway post office was not a factor in the disposal of the army mail during the Civil War; whatever relief it contributed to this was indirect and infinitesimal, consisting in such gain of time by the post offices mentioned as the partial assumption of the distribution of mail local to the lines, to star routes heading from offices on the lines, and to connecting intermediary lines, as the limited facilities and knowledge available permitted. But the service was very limited then; counting all its clerks, route and local agents, the force numbered but 612 two months after peace was declared, and it was two years later before the first full railway post office car was built and put in service. A cut of this car, the letter case of which I helped to label, may be seen on page 167. It was built in 1867. Previous to that time the whole service operated in apartments of cars, but by October, 1871, when the great fire which almost destroyed Chicago startled the business world, the number of employees in the whole service had increased to 1,582, and several additional lines of full railway post offices had been established. The second fire occurred in July, 1874, and swept through that section of the south side, which touched the southern-most line of the first fire, destroyed the post office and hundreds of other buildings; the force of the whole service then was 2,175, and full lines of railway post offices showed a fair growth. The third fire occurred in January, 1879, and deprived us once more of our official habitation; we had then accumulated 2,609 employees and many more full railway post office routes.

On each of these occasions the Chicago post office and ours also was left homeless and in most cases the fixtures and furniture disappeared very largely with the buildings. The first fire was the greatest by far, and had the railway post office cars and the clerks not been available the greatest blockade of mail ever known would have rendered that city almost helpless; but postal cars fully equipped with expert clerks were stationed on side tracks near where the depots stood and received, distributed, and dispatched to outgoing trains. All this has been described under the sub-heading "Fires." The same treatment was applied with excellent success in the other emergencies of like nature, and the people living in the city and those in the outside world were not deprived of the facilities necessary to communicate with each other. The system was pre-eminently successful, illustrating what a well-disciplined, determined, expert, energetic and faithful corps of railway postal employees can accomplish when emergencies inspire them to assume what the public recognizes as the most important work allotted to such an office as the one in Chicago, an office that never shirks work or responsibility, and that has always co-operated with the railway mail service in the fullest degree.

These experiences pointed out the best, most expeditious, and most economical way to handle large accumulations of mail in emergencies, and advantage was taken of it when war was declared against Spain by the United States on the 21st of April, 1898, and the President ordered the army mobilized, and issued a call for 125,000 additional troops on the 22nd of the same month and 75,000 later.

The army then in existence commenced to assemble in designated camps in southern and nearby eastern states. The Fifth Army Corps, which was composed more largely of regulars, trained soldiers, than any other, rendezvoused at Tampa, Lakeland, Jacksonville and Miami. It was camped on the threshold of Tampa and around it, so as to have at hand the most experienced soldiers when the hour struck for the invasion of Cuba; back of these were the camps of Chickamauga, Chattanooga, Camp Thomas, Falls Church (Va.), Hempstead (N. Y.), and later on at other places. In a brief time the mails began to pour into Tampa, Miami, Chickamauga, Camp Thomas, and were soon too large for those offices to handle, notwithstanding that the clerical force of each was increased largely and frequently, and then the Charlotte and Jacksonville, the Jacksonville and Tampa, the Waycross and Tampa and the Jacksonville and Miami railway post offices were reinforced and commenced to relieve the offices at or near the camps named. Soon full cars equipped with strong crews of railway postal clerks were placed on side tracks at Lytle, Ga., to handle the mails passing in and out of Camp Chickamauga. Later a line of 40-foot postal cars was placed on the Jacksonville and Miami route. On June 16, 1898, a 50-foot postal car of the Plant system, fully equipped with clerks, was placed on a side track at Tampa, and three days afterwards another, similarly equipped, was placed on the same track.

Thereafter the distribution and dispatch of the outgoing and incoming mail for and from the soldiers in camp near Tampa was accomplished in these cars, but this arrangement was not made until it had been demonstrated that the Tampa post office was not equal to the work. The mail was handled skillfully and promptly in the postal cars; it was separated to regiments and batteries, the same as in other camps where our cars were stationed, and was satisfactory in the main to the army. But when the Fifth Army Corps was embarked upon the thirty-five transports that were to convey it to Cuba, regimental organization was not observed closely in many instances, that is, sometimes parts of regiments were placed on two or three transports, and while it was the general opinion that the army would depart at once, it remained in the harbor several days, and during that time authorized representatives of the army called at the post office for the mail and returned with it to the transports and delivered it. The mail for a divided regiment was delivered to the detachment first discovered, who would open it, take out what was addressed to it and throw the residue with the outgoing new mail to the post office, instead of sending it to the transports carrying the other detachments. Thus each would be enabled to take out what belonged to it; that is, handle it as was customary on star routes—put the mail for all the offices on a route in a way pouch, which each postmaster opened in regular turn and relieved of the mail addressed to his office, replacing it with such as had accumulated therein, after the previous call of the stage, for other offices, then close and lock the pouch and hand it to the Jehu on the box, who cracked the whip over the backs of his mettlesome steeds and moved at a rattling pace to the next post office.

The treatment the mail received on the transports while they remained in the harbor caused considerable delay in its receipt by some of our brave soldiers, and put much additional labor on the clerks who rehandled the mail in the cars. This could have been avoided if the military postal service had been better systematized, or if the fact had been made known to the officer in charge of the workers in the cars, that some of the regiments were divided into two or more parts when the corps was embarked on the transports, and that each part, in such cases, was assigned to a different transport. If this had been done the mail for each detachment would have been pouched separately and the name of the transport to which it was assigned placed on the label. The easiest way to accomplish this was adopted by that old veteran, the senior superintendent of division, and himself a soldier of the Civil War, who is always ready for any emergency and has always had the confidence of his superior officers, Mr. Lynch M. Terrell, Superintendent of the Fourth Division, after he had made a thorough investigation of complaints entered by General Shafter and Inspector General Breckinridge; that is, he caused the mail to be made up by companies.

The destination of the transports being unknown to any one connected with the mail service when they steamed out of Florida Bay, and away from Key West for Cuba, it was necessary to forward the mail as fast as it was prepared for dispatch to Key West, that being the nearest point to deep water and Cuba, to be dispatched to the army and navy as soon as heard from, and the service secured of an army transport bound for the objective or real point of occupation; but before that time arrived a vast quantity of mail accumulated at Key West. This was dispatched on June 24, 1898, on the collier Lebanon to Santiago. The first mail received from General Shafter's command arrived at Key West, July 28, 1898. In the interim yellow

HON. LYNCH M. TERRELL
Superintendent Fourth Division R. M. S.
(See Appendix)

fever had made its appearance in Cuba with fatal results. Eben Brewer, the Postal Agent for Cuba, was stricken and died at Santiago, July 15th; he was succeeded by Mr. Kempner.

What was accomplished by the railway mail service at Tampa, Chickamauga, Camp Thomas, and Miami, was accomplished at other camps later, but at the three first named camps the capacity and resourcefulness of that service were severely tested and not found wanting. At the same time it must be admitted that, in comparison with the general distribution performed by the railway postal clerks on their regular runs, it is simple at the best, being in the nature of directs, consisting of regiments, companies, batteries, war vessels, and detachments; nor is it as difficult as that made in railway post offices stationed on side tracks near depots to handle the mails after the post office of a great city has been destroyed, and the hazard to life and limb is far less than that to which the railway postal clerk is subjected daily when on duty in times of peace.

The following letter shows that much anxiety was connected with the service however:

Atlanta, Ga., June 18, 1898.

Sir: On receipt of your telegram of the 13th instant, complaint of Inspector-General Breckinridge, regarding service at Port Tampa, Fla., I at once proceeded to that point, in the meantime instructing Chief Clerk Beaver to proceed immediately to Port Tampa and use his best efforts to relieve the situation.

On arrival at Port Tampa on the morning of the 15th instant, I found that Chief Clerk Beaver, with the aid of postal clerks off duty, had gotten the army mail in fairly good shape, and had arranged for a postal car to be placed on side track for the redistribution of the Fifth Army Corps mail.

Upon investigation I found that the mail for the army at Tampa and Port Tampa is made up by regiments and batteries, the same as we are doing at Chickamauga. The mails were being fairly delivered up to the time the troops went aboard the transports; then the trouble commenced. This was due to the fact that some of the regiments were assigned to as many as three or four transports. As they remained several days in the harbor, carriers from the steamers would call at the post office and take the mail for the several regiments to the steamers. This they would cut open, take out what they wished and throw the residue, together with outgoing letters, to the post office, instead of sending them to the other steamers carrying the regiment. The sack, not being labeled, would be thrown into the post office unnoticed by the postmaster or his two clerks, they having more than they could do to attend to the cancellation and delivery of outgoing mail. In many cases carriers from the steamers would come into the office, look through the sacks, and, finding a sack for the regiment to which they were assigned, would open it and take out such as they wanted, leaving the balance on the floor of the office. In this way the mail for the Fifth Army Corps was so thoroughly mixed that the force of the office was powerless to do anything with it. On Sunday, the 11th, a lieutenant and two experienced post office clerks were sent to the Port Tampa office to assist the postmaster in putting the mail in good shape, which they did. However, on Monday morning, representatives from the transports came to the office, and, as before, cut open the packages of letters and mixed them as they did on a previous occasion. Thus you will see that the railway mail service was not responsible for the handling of this mail in the Port Tampa office.

The Port Tampa office, also the Tampa office, has not the room and facilities for handling the large quantities of mails that they have been required to handle, which has resulted in more or less confusion.

Each of the regiments forming the Fifth Army Corps, now en route to Cuba, have left detachments in the vicinity of Port Tampa. We have great difficulty in securing names of companies forming these detachments. In order to facilitate the delivery of the Fifth Army Corps mail we are tying out letter mail by companies.

The redistribution of army mail at Port Tampa is under the personal supervision of Chief Clerk Beaver. With the help under his charge I feel assured that we will have no further trouble at that point as far as our branch of the service is concerned. The Fifth Army Corps mail we are holding at Tampa until further instructed.

Very respectfully,

L. M. TERRELL, Superintendent.

HON. JAMES E. WHITE,
  General Supt. Railway Mail Service,
Washington, D. C.

PHILIPPINES.

The mails for and from the troops assigned to the Philippines were not handled the same as those for the army and navy in Cuba, or in camps in Florida, Tennessee, and elsewhere, presumedly preparing for service on that island, except those that were afterwards withdrawn from these and assigned to the Philippines. These were made

HON. FRANK W. VAILLE
Superintendent Thirteenth Division R. M. S.
(See Appendix)

up in the railway post office cars at Tampa and Chickamauga as long as received.

Admiral Dewey moved into Manila Bay, May 1, 1898, and destroyed the Spanish fleet therein that day, and occupied Cavite on the 7th. On the 25th of the same month 16 bags of mail for Admiral Dewey's fleet were dispatched to Manila from San Francisco, Cal. On the 6th of June, Mr. Frank W. Vaille, Assistant Superintendent Railway Mail Service, Portland, Oregon, was ordered to proceed to San Francisco, to look after the mails to and from the Philippines, and to be ready to go to Manila at a moment's notice. As the order contemplated, Mr. Vaille on his arrival at San Francisco called on General Merritt, who had been ordered to take command of the land forces to be sent to the Philippines, and made arrangements for the transportation of himself and two clerks and such supplies and equipment as would enable him to establish a post office in the military camp at or near Manila.

On June 9th a station of the San Francisco post office was ordered in the Philippine Islands, and on the 15th Mr. Vaille sailed on the ship China for his destination. Before the China arrived at Honolulu, Hawaiian Islands, he gathered up the mail that had accumulated for the United States and Europe, also secured that which had been written on other vessels, lying in the harbor when he arrived and being tendered the use of the post office by the postmaster, made it up and arranged for its dispatch by the first vessel sailing from that port for San Francisco.

Mr. Vaille arrived in the harbor of Cavite July 16, 1898, and found Manila still in possession of the Spaniards. He came there with what was known as the Second Expedition under command of General Green, but, as was natural and right, was not landed until the troops were disembarked. In the meantime General Merritt, who was assigned as commander in chief of our troops on the islands, arrived, and three days later Mr. Vaille with his supplies and equipment went ashore, and on the 29th reported that he had a very fair office at Cavite. While waiting to be landed, he heard that the steamer Olympia would sail for Hongkong on the 18th, taking such letters as were ready for dispatch, with proper postage, to the United States Consul at Hongkong. This was in accordance with instructions from Admiral Dewey. Mr. Vaille called upon him and requested permission to dispatch a closed pouch for San Francisco direct, to contain all mail from the army and navy. This was denied, so he received mail on the China, made it up and dispatched it by the Olympia on the 19th. There were 1,535 letters, 4 packages and 4 papers. The postage amounted to

$121.15 and was placed in an envelope and sealed up in a sack addressed to the United States Consul at Hongkong. After he opened an office in Cavite he called on the Admiral and requested that a launch be provided him to collect the mails from the vessels and troops, distance about two miles from the office at Cavite. This was promised, but he was again advised that all mail must be sent via the United States Consul at Hongkong. The Admiral was simply giving such instructions as govern the navy under all similar conditions.

The Post Office Department was advised of the decision and communicated with the Navy Department at once; request being made that the Admiral be advised to allow Assistant Superintendent Vaille to handle the mail in accordance with instructions from the Postmaster General. This was agreed to and the representatives of both Departments advised of it by cable.

On July 31st Mr. Vaille informed the Department that Jackson and Evans, who were operating two steamers between Cavite and Hongkong, had agreed to carry a closed pouch, and said that the two vessels, with the United States transports that made occasional trips, would provide quite satisfactory service. On August 13th the army under General Merritt entered Manila. Mr. Vaille was with it and well to the front, as usual. He proceeded to the post office immediately and upon announcing himself was pleasantly received.

Mr. Vaille wrote under date of August, 1898:

"We entered Manila Saturday afternoon, August 13. I landed with the first party after General Merritt and at once announced myself at the post office, where I was very courteously received. I slept in the post office that night. Sunday morning I secured a letter from General Merritt to take possession of the post office and retain such employees of the office as I thought necessary for the proper conduct of the office in the maintenance of local service. Sunday afternoon I went to Cavite to arrange for the transfer of supplies from that point and returned Monday noon, having arranged to have all property there packed at once. I got across by private launch and could not transfer the supplies. Postmaster General Vallaenca, while very courteous, was very reluctant to turn over the government property, because the Captain General had not officially notified him that the city had surrendered, and, while the city of Manila might have surrendered, the records of his office pertained to the whole of the Philippines, and not to Manila alone. While I could have used force to clear the building, I thought it best to endeavor to have all the keys to desks and rooms in my possession, as everything was locked, and had I attempted to use force I would have found it necessary to force many doors. General Merritt gave me an order addressed to the Postmaster General to turn all property to me, to satisfy his wish to have something to show at Madrid for the abandonment of his trust. This evening, after hours of waiting, I received the keys to about everything here. I announced this morning the names of the clerks who would be retained, about 15 in all, and was surprised when I found in the course of the morning that the office was gradually deserted by all. Searching upstairs I found a labor union meeting in progress, composed of a majority of the 205 employees. An interpreter informed me that the Postmaster General had told them that they had not been released from their obligations to the Spanish Government, and that when Spain resumed control in a month or so their salaries would be paid them for all the time. If it is decided to retain possession here for any length of time a postmaster should be appointed for Manila. If I can arrange for a launch for the delivery and collection of mail to the fleet and to Cavite I will give our people a fine service. So far I know of no complaints. There has been no delay to outgoing or incoming mails for which this office was in any way responsible."

On the 20th of August twenty bags of mail arrived from Europe and Asia. This mail was worked under Mr. Vaille's directions and that addressed to the English, French, and German merchants was delivered that evening and the next morning. The Spanish mail could not be disposed of because the Spanish employees would not work. During the following week the matter was taken up with the Spanish merchants and with the editor of one of the papers, and it was explained to them that the Spanish employees in abandoning the office injured their people only, as their mail would not be touched until these men returned to work. The editor inserted a few words of wisdom in the columns of his paper, the merchants howled, and the unsorted mail on Sunday morning brought the Captain-General to terms and he sent a detail of officers to pick out the army mail, and ordered the old employees back to work. Soon after this occurrence Mr. Vaille cabled the Post Office Department, Washington, D. C., for authority to make such expenditures for the maintenance of the Manila post office as would insure first-class service; this to cover clerk hire, repairs, local transportation, etc. The Postmaster General granted this under date of August 29. The authorization relieved the army from furnishing feed for the horses in the post office stables, wagons for the transportation of the mails from the post office to the docks, and tugs for the transportation of it from the docks to the outgoing vessels. Thus the Manila post office was placed on a good footing, and, as it had been made a station of the San Francisco post office, the mails for the Philippine Islands, military and civilian, were dispatched to it from the latter; some of it made up to regiments was taken direct from the dock to regimental headquarters, thus avoiding considerable delay in delivery.

After the natives of the islands had been in insurrection against our government for some time, it became necessary to employ a larger number of transports to convey troops, munitions of war, and supplies of all kinds, and the mails from the states were dispatched on them, as well as mails from other countries. Some of these transports were faster than others; frequently one leaving San Francisco several days in advance of another would be overtaken at Honolulu by the latter, and as it was desirable to deliver the mails at Manila as quick as possible, transfers from the slow to the fast were made at that port. The number of vessels arriving and the frequency of transfers and departures resulted in some confusion; it was therefore deemed advisable to assign some experienced employee of the railway mail service at Honolulu, who, acting in unison with the postmaster, would superintend the transfers, keep record of them, report irregularities, etc., and the first selection for this assignment was Mr. J. M. Johnson, who had been Chief Clerk Railway Mail Service at Los Angeles, Cal.

The story of the character and conduct of the mail business of the Army of the Philippines from the day it steamed away from San Francisco, Cal., until it anchored in Manila Bay, near Cavite, and of the intelligent, earnest, but diplomatic efforts made by the officer in charge of it to supply the fleet and the few soldiers then there with mail from their homes; to collect, assort, and dispatch return messages to San Francisco; to establish a good working office at Cavite, pending the occupation of Manila and its post office; the wisdom shown in handling the recalcitrant clerks of the Spanish race who abandoned the office as soon as he took possession of it, and his management of the whole service there as Assistant Superintendent and Director of Posts, ought to have been expected from so able and experienced an officer of the railway mail service as Mr. Frank W. Vaille.

PORTO RICO.

The method of handling the mails for our forces in Porto Rico and for the residents of that island was similar to that pursued with respect to the Philippine Islands, but on a very much smaller scale. The area of the Philippines is 127,853 square miles and its population,

Hon. H. M. Robinson
Superintendent Twelfth Division R. M. S.
(See Appendix)

6,987,686; that of Porto Rico is 3,606 square miles and the population, 953,243, which did not make a spirited defense.

General Miles left Cuba with an expedition on the 21st of July and occupied the harbor of Guaneca, Porto Rico, on the 25th, and on the 28th received the formal surrender of Ponce, the second largest city on the island, without firing a gun. General Brooks sailed from Newport News, July 28th, for Porto Rico, and arrived just before hostilities ceased. There were a few more skirmishes, but nothing serious, and by virtue of the protocol, signed by both governments on the 12th day of August, hostilities ceased as soon as information of this fact was communicated to the commanders of the military and naval forces of each government, which was the following day.

Mr. Nathan Smith of the Post Office Department was appointed the first postal agent for Porto Rico, but did not have the pleasure of looking from its shores out over the beautiful waters of the Atlantic Ocean and the Caribbean Sea. On the 21st of July, Chief Clerk Robinson, with two clerks, reported to him at Newport News to take charge of the distribution and dispatch of the mails passing to and from Porto Rico. On July 23rd, Ponce was declared a station of the Washington, D. C., post office, and three days later Mr. Robinson was directed to assume the duties of the office vacated by the resignation of Mr. Smith, and on the 28th steamed away from Newport News en route to his new field of operation. He and his assistants arrived at Ponce, August 1, and were assigned quarters in the custom house by orders of General Miles. To fit these up for business, two distributing tables were taken from the old post office, which is located two miles inland, and others were built by carpenters detailed from the army. When these were placed, Mr. Robinson commenced receiving and delivering mails, and making them up for dispatch. This was on the 3rd, just nine days before the suspension of hostilities. On the 8th of August orders were issued to send all Porto Rico mail to the Washington, D. C., post office, to be prepared for dispatch, and on the 22nd arrangements were made whereby the War Department agreed to dispatch a steamer from New York every Wednesday for San Juan, Ponce, and Santiago. Preceding this the Postmaster General suspended the order of April 16th, discontinuing postal exchanges with Spain and her colonies, and on the 23rd of August, 1898, Guayama, Mayaguez, and San Juan were made stations of the Washington, D. C., post office. To these were added, on October 1st, Aguadila, Arecibo, Humacao, and Larez, and on the same day Mr. Robinson received authority to employ mail messenger between San Juan and Ponce, which covered very many of the important offices on the island. Later on railway post office service was established on a line of steamers between New York City and Porto Rico, and the service on the island was placed in much better condition than before. This was due to the peaceable spirit shown by the people, the compactness of the island, the close proximity to our shores, the shortness of the campaign, and the energy, capacity, and resourcefulness of Mr. Robinson, who remained in charge of the service in Porto Rico until relieved by the appointment of a Director of Posts, when he was reinstated as Chief Clerk, $1,600, and returned to the Fourth Division (July 19, 1899). He resigned to take effect July 31, 1900, and was appointed Special Agent and designated Assistant Superintendent Railway Mail Service, $1,600 per annum, August 1, 1900, and assigned to duty in charge of the mails of the army in China during the Boxer uprising of 1900, which lasted about eight months. In May, 1901, the Ninth Regiment, United States Infantry, sailed from China for the Philippine Islands and Mr. Robinson accompanied it and served there under the Director of Posts as his assistant until his resignation was tendered and accepted to take effect December 19, 1903; he was immediately reinstated as Chief Clerk of Railway Mail Service, Fourth Division; promoted to Assistant Superintendent, $1,600 per annum, May 18, 1904; promoted to be Superintendent of the Twelfth Division, $3,000 per annum, headquarters, New Orleans, La., to be effective November 11, 1908.

Mr. Robinson has served in many capacities and has always met the expectations of his superiors and friends.

The story of the upbuilding of the railway mail service since 1864, when the system now in operation in our own country had a limited introduction, reads almost like a fairy tale. There were then employed in the service, including railway post office clerks, route agents, mail route messengers, and local agents, 572 men; since then this number has been increased to 16,044, or more than 28 times, and all are designated railway post office clerks, and thoroughly educated, drilled, and disciplined in their occupation.

The track miles of routes has grown in the same period from 22,-616 to 217,116, or more than $9\frac{1}{3}$ times.

The annual miles has increased from 23,301,942 to 413,546,195, or more than $17\frac{1}{2}$ times.

The pieces of mail matter distributed from 864,700,000 in 1877, to 22,601,925,460, or more than 26 times.

The ratio of pieces distributed correct to each error known increased from 796 in 1873, to 3,264 in 1877, when the first report, including all classes of mail matter, was made, and to 12,396, in 1907; more than $15\frac{1}{2}$ times between 1873 and 1877, and more than $3\frac{3}{4}$ times between this later date and 1907; but during the former period only first-class matter was reported.

In case examinations the number of cards per examination averaged $65\frac{1}{2}$ greater in 1878, than in 1908—but the per cent. correct was $28\frac{1}{4}$ greater in 1908 than in 1878—the first year an annual report was made by the General Superintendent; this must be regarded as a striking record. If the data for the whole service back to 1873, were available it would be much more so, probably the showing would be 50 per cent., for it is known that at that date some divisions did not average 50 per cent. correct.

If, in considering the growth of the service, the amount of mail it handles and distributes, we also consider the material development of the country, we will realize that the one has progressed in about the same ratio as the other; that the process of settlement and development of any given territory always precedes the building of cities, towns, villages and hamlets, which increase in population and in trade importance as the country contiguous to them increases the yield of the products that are adapted to the soil.

These centers of population are stations or outposts where the output of the farms, mines, ranges, ranches, manufactories, and forests are bought and sold at remunerative prices, and that not needed for home consumption shipped by rail or water to the distributing centers to supply the deficiencies in other territories, in this and foreign countries. Correspondence of whatever character, commercial, professional, and social; the output of publication houses, including periodicals of all descriptions, pass into or through these communities on the way to their destinations. When we realize the magnitude of this we will understand why our postal establishment has grown so phenomenally in the past forty-five years, and its methods of transacting business been so largely modified in the interest of economy and simplicity; especially will we realize that the railway mail service has during that time surpassed all other branches of the postal service in the character and brilliancy of its work. Inquiry will reveal that this is due to the selections for appointment and for promotions as prescribed by the civil service laws and rules without any attempt at evasion; to thorough discipline, and to the retention of all employees who have proved accomplished in the occupation, gentlemanly in deportment and morals; to the humane and just treatment accorded them and to which they have responded with a devotion to their work that can not be excelled in interest, efficiency, industry, heroism, stability, fidelity and "esprit de corps." This spirit of comradeship and regard for the well-being of those with whom they are so closely associated, and for their families, is sublime and cannot be fostered too assiduously inside and outside of the service. The beneficial associations, whose membership is composed exclusively of those who are and have been employed as railway post office clerks, are auxiliaries of splendid worth to every member of the service whose name is upon their rolls, because they insure the widow and fatherless help in the moments of greatest distress, and come with cheer and comfort to those maimed and broken in accidents while on duty; they afford them social pleasures and intellectual feasts in their homes, and in national and division conventions and banquets. They should be endorsed and upheld by everyone in the service and by their friends outside.

The monthly journals and magazines are full of choice articles, and well written opinions upon almost all questions relating to the advancement of the interests of the men and the service. They are ably edited and conducted and deserve the widest circulation possible.

No one will doubt that it nearly broke my heart to separate myself from the chief office of such a thoroughly organized and efficient service, voluntarily, when I did, on account of ill health—as is shown in the following correspondence:

"On November 21, 1871, Captain White was advanced to Superintendent of the Sixth Division, which position he held with marked ability until honored with the appointment of General Superintendent on October 4, 1890.

"It was known recently that Captain White felt that his health made it dangerous for him to continue the constant strain upon his vitality, which added years had reduced. This feeling is expressed in his letter to the Postmaster General on January 4th, which included the offer of his resignation, as follows:

" 'DEAR SIR: My health having become so seriously impaired as to make it impossible for me to perform the duties of the office I hold in the railway mail service, with that force and activity essential to the best management of the service, and consequently to my own satisfaction, I deem it due to the service, the Department and myself that I tender you my resignation of the office of General Superintendent of the Railway Mail Service, which I do with great regret, and most respectfully request that it be accepted to take effect thirty days from this date.

" 'For the consideration shown me I am grateful and thank you sincerely—indeed, the pleasant greetings and the uniform kindness I have always received from the officers and employees of the Department with whom I have come in contact is and will be one of the most pleasant recollections of my life.'

"Postmaster General Cortelyou replied as follows:

" 'My Dear Capt. White: I have received your resignation as General Superintendent Railway Mail Service, under date of the 4th instant, with request that it be accepted for reasons stated, to take effect thirty days from date.

" 'In accepting your resignation, which I do with much regret, it is proper to say that the reasons you have assigned for this voluntary action reflect credit upon you.

" 'It gives me pleasure to speak in highest commendation of your exceptional career in connection with the one branch of the postal service, which is, perhaps, more largely indebted to your intelligence and organizing ability for its present efficiency than to the services of any other one person. Entering the postal service in 1866, after an honorable record of more than four years in the Civil War, in which you were severely wounded, you have passed through all the grades of the railway mail service from the lowest to the highest with an unblemished record and with the result of having mastered every detail of the organization you have presided over with great ability as General Superintendent for the past sixteen years. To have retained the confidence of both superior and subordinate officials through all changes of administration for so long a period is evidence of executive tact and wisdom of a high order, as well as of just and impartial administration.' "

CAPTAIN WHITE'S ADMINISTRATION.

No. of employees in 1890, when he assumed charge....	5,836
No. of employees in 1907, when he retired	14,357
Increase during the 17 years	8,521
Average annual increase	501
Miles of railroad carrying mail, 1890, when he assumed charge	154,779
Miles of railroad carrying mail, 1907, when he retired	207,237
Increase during the 17 years	52,458
Average annual increase	3,086
Annual miles carrying mail, 1890, when he assumed charge	214,715,680
Annual miles carrying mail, 1907, when he retired....	387,557,165
Increase during the 17 years	171,841,485
Average annual increase	10,108,323
Pieces of mail matter distributed, 1890, when he assumed charge	7,847,723,600
Errors in distribution	2,769,245

Pieces correct to each error 2,834
Pieces of mail distributed, 1907, when he retired......20,483,995,350
Errors in distribution 1,652,409
Pieces correct to each error 12,396
Increase in pieces distributed during the 17 years.....12,636,271,750
Average annual increase 743,310,103
Average annual decrease of errors 65,696
Average annual increase of pieces correct to each error   562
No. of case examinations, 1890, when he assumed charge   16,084
No. of cards handled 17,998,150
Correctly handled 16,059,814
Per cent. correct 90.24
No. of case examinations, 1907, when he retired...... 37,570
No. of cards handled 35,610,047
Correctly handled 35,162,574
Per cent. correct 98.74
Increased per cent. correct in 17 years 8.50
Annual increase correct .... .50
Pieces of mail separated for immediate city delivery, by
　　carriers, in railway post offices from July 1, 1890,
　　to June 30, 1907 9,581,426,222
Average annual separation for city delivery 563,613,307

The number of registered packages, cases, post office through registered pouches and inner registered sacks, railway post office through registered pouches and inner registered sacks and registered package jackets handled by the railway mail service during the seventeen years of Captain White's administration was 426,831,043; 17,714,501 for the fiscal year ending June 30, 1890, and 52,578,365 for the fiscal year ending June 30, 1907, an average annual increase of 2,050,815.

Note: Railway post office through registered pouches and inner registered sacks inaugurated April 1, 1902.

Registered package jackets inaugurated December 7, 1903.

ALEXANDER GRANT

succeeded Captain White March 1, 1907. He was appointed to the service originally January 31, 1872, at $650 per annum, and assigned to the line operating from Holly to Monroe, Michigan, which was later extended to Toledo, Ohio, the salary increased to $900 per annum, and the run was designated the Holly, Michigan, and Toledo, Ohio, route agency. March 26, 1874, he was transferred to the Chicago, Ill., and Toledo, Ohio, railway post office, with an increase of salary to $1,000 per annum, and September 28th,

HON. ALEXANDER GRANT
Tenth General Superintendent R. M. S.

of the same year, he was promoted to class 4, $1,200 per annum, which was reduced to $1,150 August 1, 1876, on account of reduced appropriations, which applied to all clerks of classes 4 and 5, $1,200 and $1,400 respectively.

This occurred about the time the first fast mail was withdrawn, though Mr. Grant served on it about six months as a clerk in charge before that happened.

May 11, 1878, he was promoted to class 5, at $1,300, and on August 30, 1882, this was increased to $1,400; in the meantime—January 1, 1880—he was relieved of service on the road by detail to the office of the Superintendent of the Ninth division, headquarters at Cleveland, Ohio, as examiner and remained so assigned until October, 1883, when he was detailed to the office of General Superintendent Thompson, headquarters Washington, D. C.; June 1, 1887, he resigned to take effect May 31, 1887, on which day he was appointed an Assistant Superintendent Railway Mail Service in the office of General Superintendent Nash, at $1,600 per annum.

On April 30, 1890, he resigned to accept appointment as Chief Clerk of the railway mail service (Bell, General Superintendent) that office having just been created by act of Congress and a salary of $2,000 per annum attached to it. July 31, 1897, he was promoted to be Assistant General Superintendent at $3,000 per annum, (White, General Superintendent) which was increased by act of Congress of March 3, 1903, to $3,500, effective July 1st, of that year.

Promoted to General Superintendent railway mail service March 1, 1907, $4,000 per annum.

It will be seen that Mr. Grant's experience in the service has been extensive and varied, and his training such as to qualify him well, with his natural and acquired ability, for the office that he holds.

His experience in the office of the General Superintendent was very valuable; he having served with six of those who were honored with the appointment. All of these, I believe, took him into their confidence and trusted him fully; under these conditions he could not fail to garner in his mind knowledge of the service, and methods of transacting business with those without, as well as within, the service. He is a student, an earnest, intelligent worker, has good judgment, and the best interests of the splendid corps of employees in his jurisdiction at heart, and will, I am sure, work with abundant good will to secure for all its members whatever benefits he believes them entitled to. My opportunities to know him well have been excellent, for he was one of "my boys" twenty-two of the thirty-five years of his service preceding my retirement. He was appointed in 1872 to a route in my division, then known as the Fourth, and remained there until the Ninth division was created in the latter part of 1877, when he was passed into that division. When I became General Superintendent, in October, 1890, he was the Chief Clerk of the service and he remained with me in that capacity and as Assistant General Superintendent until I retired in 1907. I had many occasions to commend him, none to reprimand. As Assistant General Superintendent he made many inspections of the service while investigating cases requiring the attention of my office, and often action by the Department; he was my eyes on such occasions; what he found he reported in clear and concise language.

When I retired I was satisfied that Mr. Grant would succeed to the office and that his administration would be successful I did not doubt, for no one realized as clearly as I did that he would be loyally supported by thoroughly trained Superintendents, and by a group of bright, active, and faithful Chief Clerks, working harmoniously and in full sympathy with the corps of educated workers from which we all graduated. The statement of what has been accomplished during the three years just past confirms that opinion.

Under Mr. Grant's administration the service has grown steadily; there have been no radical changes in methods of administration, as was to be expected where the head of the present was so closely associated with the chief of the last administration, but there have been many improvements, the benefits of which are noticeable and will increase with the growth of the service. Among these may be mentioned a revision of blanks with a view to securing uniformity throughout the service. This is the first general revision that has been made since 1894, and was indicated by the great growth of the service in the interim.

The facilities for the transaction of the business of the various offices of the service have been improved by the larger employment of labor saving appliances, such as typewriters, adding machines, addressographs, card index systems, etc. This larger use prevents a more rapid increase of clerk hire, and improves the character of the work.

Two additional divisions have been created. The Twelfth, with headquarters at New Orleans, Louisiana, comprises the states of Mississippi and Louisiana, with contiguous routes in Alabama, Arkansas, Tennessee and Texas. H. M. Robinson, Superintendent.

The Thirteenth, with headquarters at Seattle, Washington, comprises service in Alaska, Idaho, Montana, Oregon and Washington. Frank W. Vaille, Superintendent.

Many additional Chief Clerks have been created by promotion, and assigned where additional supervision was needed; this will have an excellent effect, for the service has not within my knowledge had as close supervision as was necessary for its greatest usefulness and efficiency.

The elimination of all old and unsatisfactory cars has been urged with vigor and the improvement in equipment is very noticeable. A great many steel cars have been built and a great many with wooden superstructure and steel under-frames. Arrangements have also been made whereby cars, whether full R. P. O. cars or apartment cars, that are reported to be in bad condition, will be inspected by the Inspectors of the Interstate Commerce Commission.

The benefits of Section 1,424, Postal Laws and Regulations, whereby a clerk injured while on duty will be allowed leave of absence with pay during the period of disability, not exceeding one year, and whereby the sum of $1,000 will be paid to the legal representatives of any clerk killed while on duty, have been during the past two years extended to substitutes. This was thought to be in the line of justice and is of material benefit to the seventeen or eighteen hundred men who are carried on substitute rolls.

A law has been passed imposing a penalty for mailing matter liable to injure the mails or the clerks or persons handling the mails. This is in the interest of the men and is a measure that has been urged by this office for a great many years.

The method of handling registered matter has been during the past year very much changed and simplified. The introduction of the package jackets and sack jackets has expedited very much the handling of this valuable class of matter and with the minimum amount of labor. The work of handling registered matter has been very much reduced as a whole, although it is not felt so much in the railway mail service as in the larger post offices where the bulk of the mail was formerly rehandled in transit, whereas now that work is almost entirely done by the railway mail service, either by making up jackets, sacks and pouches in the postal cars or by the establishment of registry terminals.

At the request of the First Assistant Postmaster General the railway mail service has, where practicable, assumed the duty of examining clerks in the mailing divisions of all first and second-class post-offices. While this imposes additional labor upon the railway mail service such work already has resulted in improvement of the service, and this will continue to grow.

To avoid the heavy transfer of mail at Chicago, arrangements have been made whereby storage cars will be passed from one depot to another, thereby avoiding the transfer of the same from depot to depot by wagon.

The increase in force has been about 2,296, or 16.25 per cent. Commencing July 1, 1907, the salaries of all clerks in the service who were receiving over $300 per annum were increased $100. The salaries of all Assistant Superintendents and Chief Clerks were increased $200. Those who had been receiving $1,800 were raised to $2,000, and those receiving $1,600 to $1,800. Commencing July 1, 1909, the clerks in charge of apartment runs on lines having no full R. P. O. service were increased $100, thereby putting those men on a parity with the men in charge of apartment car runs on full R. P. O. lines.

In the matter of expediting schedules there has been a very material improvement between St. Paul and Seattle. The Great Northern in October, 1900, placed in service a special mail train covering the distance from St. Paul to Seattle in forty-eight hours. This was a gain of about twelve hours. The Santa Fe and Rock Island-Southern Pacific Companies commencing February 20, 1910, shortened the time between Kansas City and Los Angeles of trains leaving Kansas City in the morning about three hours, so that they arrive at 2:30 and 3:30 p. m., instead of 6:00 and 6:55 p. m., as formerly. The Rock Island-Southern Pacific train leaving Kansas City at night was also expedited so as to arrive at Los Angeles at 7:35 in the morning instead of 1:30 p. m., as formerly. The time of Overland train 9, leaving Omaha at 9:30 a. m., is shortened so as to arrive at San Francisco at 10:08 a. m., instead of 1:08 p. m., as formerly. The fast Overland Mail on the Union Pacific has been divided into two sections—one for San Francisco and one for Portland, Oregon. The time between U. P. Transfer and Portland has been expedited about twelve hours, the connection leaving Omaha at 9:30 a. m. now arriving at Portland at 7:00 a. m., as against 6:30 p. m. New twenty-four hour trains between New York and St. Louis were placed in service by both the Pennsylvania and New York Central lines in November, 1909. These trains, like the eighteen hour trains for Chicago, are utilized for first-class matter only. The New York Central leaves New York at 2:45 p. m. and arrives at St. Louis at 1:45 p. m. the next day. This is a gain of about five hours. The Pennsylvania fast train leaves New York at 6:30 p. m. and arrives at St. Louis at 5:25 p. m. the next day. This is a gain of about four and a half hours and expedites all first-class matter for a very wide scope of country. There are corresponding fast trains with corresponding advantages in expedition east bound.

The agitation of the clerks for a travel allowance has continued and public sentiment and the sentiment in Congress in favor of the proposition has been steadily growing and is recognized as just and desirable by Mr. Grant, in fact, the bill making appropriation for next year now pending in Congress provides an appropriation of $250,000 for the traveling expenses of clerks, to be disbursed in the discretion of the Postmaster General. This of course will not enable the Post Office Department to pay the expense of all clerks who are away from home on their runs, but it is a recognition of their right to reimbursement and will undoubtedly lead to full payment of such expenses some time in the future.

The Civil Service Retirement idea is also growing very rapidly, and the endorsement of the idea by the President and several of the Cabinet officials has placed it in a much more favorable light. This is an idea that has been urged by this office for a great many years and Mr. Grant informs me in a recent letter that he is happy to state that the prospects for some legislative action in that line are much more favorable than they ever have been before, and I am very much pleased to hear it.

The statistical record made by the service up to the present date, June 30, 1909, of Mr. Grant's administration is:

Number of employees in 1907, when he assumed charge	14,357
Number of employees on June 30, 1909	16,044
Increase during the two years	1,687
Average annual increase	843
Miles of railroad carrying mail, 1907, when he assumed charge	207,237
Miles of railroad carrying mail on June 30, 1909	217,116
Increase during the two years	9,879
Average annual increase	4,939
Annual miles carrying mail, 1907, when he assumed charge	387,557,165
Annual miles carrying mail on June 30, 1909	413,546,195
Increase during the two years	25,989,030
Average annual increase	12,994,515
Pieces of mail matter distributed, 1907, when he assumed charge	20,483,995,350
Errors in distribution	1,652,409
Pieces correct to each error	12,396
Pieces of mail matter distributed during fiscal year 1909	22,601,925,430

Errors in distribution 2,156,227
Pieces correct to each error 10,482
Increase in pieces distributed during the two years.... 2,117,930,080
Average annual increase 1,058,965,040
Average annual increase of errors 251,909
Average annual decrease of pieces correct to each error 957
Number of case examinations, 1907, when he assumed
    charge 37,570
Number of cards handled 35,610,047
Correctly handled 35,162,574
Per cent. correct 98.74
Number of case examinations during fiscal year 1909.. 42,507
Number of cards handled 38,849,115
Correctly handled 38,415,308
Per cent. correct 98.88
Increased per cent. correct in two years .... .14
Annual increase correct .... .07
Pieces of mail separated for immediate city delivery in
    railway post offices from July 1, 1907, to June 30,
    1909 2,139,221,650
    (Being 1,006,882,940 for the fiscal year 1908 and
    1,132,338,710 for the fiscal year 1909).
Average annual separation for city delivery for the two
    years 1,069,610,825

The number of registered packages, cases, post office through registered pouches and inner registered sacks, railway post office through registered pouches and inner registered sacks, registered package jackets and lead seal sack jackets handled by the railway mail service for the fiscal year ending June 30, 1907, was 52,578,365, and from July 1, 1907, to June 30, 1909, during Mr. Grant's administration, 120,816,-491, being 57,416,566 for the fiscal year 1908 and 63,399,925 for the fiscal year 1909; an average annual increase of 5,410,780.

Note: Lead seal jackets inaugurated March 25, 1909.

CONCLUSION.

The uniform kindness and hearty support received from the faith-ful employees of the railway mail service during all the years I was connected with it, in supervisory capacities, made whatever success I achieved possible; without the earnest help of the whole corps, from the lowest to the highest, coupled with the loyal determination to build up the service, such results as were achieved could not have been obtained, and it is a source of satisfaction to me in these days to observe that my successor, and the old and new men back of him, are continuing the development, and harmonizing all parts of it in conformity with the laws of growth and the equities of justice.

If an officer knows that he has the loyal and affectionate regard of those whom he has been selected to command, and from among whom he rose by the blessings of Heaven, the faithfulness and in-tellectual ability of his comrades, and his own strenuous labor—physical and mental—he will continue the work with a cheerful spirit, and more determinedly than would be possible under less favorable conditions.

The belief that such an atmosphere surrounded me many times in the years that are gone, acted as a balm to a weary mind dwelling in an earthly tabernacle, battered and worn by nearly half a century's activity in the military and civil service of our very uncommon country.

Remembering this I pray you one and all to stand by your superior officers—and all have them—and the government, to the end that their work, and yours, may be thoroughly accomplished, and enjoyed as a symphony is by lovers of music.

APPENDIX.

Biographical Sketches of the Present Superintendents R. M. S.

Edward J. Ryan.

Born in Springfield, Mass., May 4, 1850. Educated in public schools of Chicago and Galesburg, Illinois; Worcester and Millbury, Massachusetts. Served in the Civil War from May to August, 1864, as drummer boy, 10th Regiment, Massachusetts Infantry, being then aged 14 years. Entered the railway mail service August 13, 1868, as a clerk in the Boston and Albany Railway Post Office at $1,200 per annum. June 2, 1869, promoted to head clerk same R. P. O., at $1,400 per annum. September 11, 1876, pay reduced to $1,300, account reduced appropriation, effective August 1, 1876. May 8, 1877, transferred to local agency, Boston, Mass. September 3, 1877, transferred back to the Boston and Albany R. P. O. May 17, 1878, promoted to $1,400, effective June 1, 1878. May 8, 1881, resigned, to take effect February 17, 1881. November 10, 1883, reappointed, Boston, Springfield and New York R. P. O., at $1,400 per annum (detailed). July 24, 1888, resigned, to take effect August 16, 1888. December 14, 1888, reappointed Boston and Albany R. P. O., $1,300. January 22, 1889, transferred to Boston, Springfield and New York Railway Post Office and promoted to $1,400 per annum (detailed). March 2, 1889, resigned, and appointed Assistant Superintendent at $1,600 per annum, same day. June 10, 1890, appointed Superintendent R. M. S., First division, $2,500 per annum, which was increased to $2,700 per annum, by Act of Congress, July 1, 1901, and to $3,000, by Act of Congress, July 1, 1903.

Victor J. Bradley.

Born in New York City, June 18, 1858. Educated in public schools, New York City, and afterwards in private academy, obtaining a general classical education. Entered the railway mail service in a temporary position in September, 1875, and became an assistant clerk of the Albany and New York R. P. O., effective November 1, 1875. During 1878 was appointed in charge of the divisional weighings, and on August 23, 1878, was appointed an assistant clerk of the New York and Washington R. P. O. Subsequently promoted as follows: To clerk, November 23, 1878; head clerk, June 30, 1880; chief clerk, December 30, 1884; Assistant Superintendent, January 17, 1889, in which position he served until February 2, 1895, when he was appointed Superintendent of Station H, New York City, which needed reorganization, especially in the distribution division. This work being finished he returned to the railway mail service, January 20, 1896, as Assistant Superintendent, and was promoted to Superintendent of the Second division, headquarters New York City, effective January 27, 1896, salary $2,500 per annum, which was increased by Act of Congress to $2,700, July 1, 1901, and to $3,000, July 1, 1903. In addition to the routine work of his position, Mr.. Bradley, like other superintendents, has served on many departmental commissions for the investigation of special postal problems, and was of special service to the commission appointed by the Senate of the United States and the House of Representatives in 1898-1899, to investigate and report upon the railway mail service of Canada, and the general postal service in England, France and Germany.

CHARLES W. VICKERY.

Born in Unity, Maine, March 22, 1840. Educated in the public schools of Boston, Mass., and in the high schools. Served in the Sturgis Rifles of Chicago, Illinois, from May, 1861, to November, 1863, during the Civil War. Entered the railway mail service March 13, 1867, in the Chicago and St. Louis R. P. O., at $1,000 per annum; promoted to head clerk, salary $1,400 per annum, July 1, 1870; transferred to the Chicago and Iowa City R. P. O., January 31, 1877, at same class and pay. Resigned August 10, 1880, to accept appointment as Assistant Superintendent R. M. S., at $1,500 per annum; promoted to Superintendent Third division, headquarters Washington, D. C., November 16, 1881, at $2,500 per annum, which has been increased twice by Act of Congress, viz: July 1, 1901, to $2,700, and July 1, 1903, to $3,000. He served part of the time during his original appointment as Superintendent, in charge of the Fourth division, headquarters Atlanta, Georgia. Resigned November 25, 1888; reappointed as Superintendent of the Third division March 26, 1889. Mr. Vickery's trend of mind is strongly mechanical, which has increased his usefulness to the service, especially in the matter of car building.

LYNCH M. TERRELL.

Immediately upon the first call to arms by President Lincoln, which occurred April 15, 1861, Mr. Terrell enlisted at Vincennes, Indiana, in a company called the "Old Post Guards," and with it reported at Camp Morton, near Indianapolis, Ind., April 20, 1861, and was mustered into service as First Lieutenant, Company B., 14th Indiana Volunteer Infantry; performed service during the West Virginia campaign under General McClellan, when he resigned on account of long continued poor health. He is a member of the Loyal Legion and of the Grand Army of the Republic. Entered the railway mail service December 8, 1869, as a clerk in the Louisville and Nashville R. P. O. In 1870 he was promoted to head clerk or clerk in charge; in 1871 he was detailed as chief clerk at Louisville, Ky. In June, 1871, was appointed a special agent of the Post Office Department and assigned to Texas, with headquarters at Marshall; afterwards changed to Dallas. This was before there were any railroads at Dallas, and Fort Worth was unknown. In 1873 he was transferred to Nashville, Tenn., and assigned as assistant to C. Jay French, who was then Superintendent of the Third division, which comprised the railway mail service south of the Ohio and west of the Potomac rivers, including Texas. When three new divisions were created in October, 1874, and the territory embraced in the original divisions was reapportioned, Mr. Terrell was appointed Superintendent of the new Fourth, which comprised the states of Alabama, Florida, Georgia, Louisiana, Mississippi, North Carolina and South Carolina, with headquarters at Chattanooga, Tenn., which were changed to Atlanta, Georgia, in 1876. In September, 1883, he was transferred to the Third division and in 1884 he was returned to the Fourth division at his own request. April 1, 1887, he resigned and on April 1, 1889, he was reappointed to his former position, which he still occupies. He is the senior Superintendent; always faithful, loyal and just to his superiors and subordinates; modest, tender-hearted, but a thorough disciplinarian.

CHARLES RAGER.

Born in New Brighton, Penna., February 2, 1861. Educated in the public schools of his native town. Entered the railway mail service March 17, 1881, in the Pittsburg and Chicago R. P. O., salary $900 per annum; promoted to class 4, at $1,150, November 21, 1881; promoted to class 5, clerk in charge, at $1,300 per annum, September 17, 1883. Removed December 9, 1887. Reappointed to the Pittsburg and Chicago R. P. O., April 29, 1889, salary $1,000 per annum; promoted to class 4, $1,150 per annum, June 24, 1889; promoted to class 5, clerk in charge, salary $1,300, April 12, 1890. Transferred to the Pittsburg and Cincinnati R. P. O., July 7, 1892, and salary increased to $1,400 per annum; detailed as chief clerk R. M. S., September 15, 1892. Appointed Assistant Superintendent R. M. S., $1,600, July 31, 1897; promoted to Assistant Division Superintendent, at $1,800 per annum, November 17, 1904. Promoted to Superintendent of the Fifth division November 25, 1905, at $3,000 per annum. In the number of employees and the amount of mail handled this is the largest division in the service, and it has made excellent records.

E. L. West.

Entered the railway mail service in the Chicago and Centralia R. P. O., March 24, 1880, at $900 per annum; transferred to the LaFayette and St. Louis R. P. O., same class and pay, December 6, 1880. Transferred to the Chicago and Effiingham R. P. O., February 7, 1881, and promoted to class 4, at $1,150 per annum. Transferred to the Chicago and St. Louis R. P. O., same class and pay, June 21, 1881; transferred to the Springfield and Gilman, Illinois, R. P. O., October 29, 1881, and salary reduced to $900 per annum; transferred to the Chicago and Centralia R. P. O., December 7, 1882, and promoted to class 4. $1,150 per annum. On April 27, 1885, was promoted to class 5, clerk in charge, and salary increased to $1,300 per annum; the line was afterward designated the Chicago and Cairo R. P. O. Resigned and appointed a Post Office Inspector, August 21, 1889, salary $1,200 per annum; reappointed March 8, 1890, and salary increased to $1,600 per annum. Resigned November 16, 1890, to accept transfer to the railway mail service as an assistant superintendent, without change of pay. Promoted to Superintendent of Sixth division November 18, 1899, salary $2,500 per annum, which has been increased twice by Acts of Congress—July 1, 1901, to $2,700 per annum, and July 1, 1903, to $3,000 per annum. This is the second largest division of the service; its record is first-class, and in it the "railway post office" was born.

Still. P. Taft.

Born in East Montpelier, Vermont, September 29, 1843. Educated in the public and normal schools of Oskaloosa, Iowa. Moved to Colorado in 1862. His first connection with the service was as a mail weigher on the Lake Shore and Michigan Southern Railway, November 15, 1876. When the weighing between Buffalo and Chicago ceased he was ordered to report to the superintendent at New York City, for assignment as "Supervisor of Weights" for the Second division; he remained in that assignment until about September 1, 1877. On the 30th of that month he reported to the Superintendent

R. M. S. at St. Louis, Mo., by direction of the General Superintendent, and was assigned as "Supervisor of the Weighing of Mails" for the Seventh division. He remained in this assignment until January 10, 1883, when he received a regular appointment in the railway mail service as a clerk of class 5, $1,300 per annum, in the St. Louis, Mo., and Atchison, Kansas, R. P. O. December 6, 1884, the salary was increased to $1,400. Resigned December 27, 1890, to assume the position of "Supervisor of Weighings" again, for the Seventh division. On July 1, 1891, he was reappointed to the R. M. S.; restored as a railway post office clerk, class 5, $1,400 per annum—the weighing having ceased. Resigned April 22, 1893, to accept appointment as Assistant Superintendent Seventh division, salary $1,600 per annum. Promoted to Superintendent Seventh division September 1, 1899, salary $2,500 per annum, which has been increased twice since by Act of Congress—July 1, 1901, to $2,700, and July 1, 1903, to $3,000 per annum.

A. H. Stephens.

Entered the railway mail service as a clerk of class 1, at $800 per annum, in the Ogden and San Francisco R. P. O. January 16, 1894; promoted to class 2, in the same R. P. O., at $900 per annum, February 12, 1894; promoted to class 3, at $1,000 per annum, March 10, 1898; promoted to class 4, same R. P. O., $1,200 per annum, May 24, 1899; promoted to class 5, same R. P. O., $1,300 per annum, April 2, 1900; increased to $1,400 June 19, 1900, and detailed as chief clerk; increased to $1,600 July 2, 1900. Promoted to Assistant Division Superintendent Eighth division, San Francisco, Cal., January 10, 1901, at $1,800 per annum. Promoted to Superintendent Eighth division, headquarters San Francisco, Cal., at $3,000 per annum, November 26, 1904.

George W. Pepper.

Born in Belfast, Ireland, October 22, 1852. Came to the United States with his parents two years later, and was educated in the public schools of Ohio. Entered the railway mail service in the Buffalo and Toledo R. P. O., at $1,000 per annum, June 12, 1872; promoted to class 4, at $1,200 per annum, April 5, 1873; promoted to class 5, at $1,400 per annum, January 25, 1875; reduced to $1,300 per annum, in the same R. P. O., August 2, 1876. Transferred and assigned to the middle division of the New York and Chicago R. P. O., August 1, 1882, account consolidation of the lines. Resigned April 2, 1889. Appointed Superintendent of the Ninth division, at $2,500 per annum, March 26, 1889, to take effect when he shall have executed the oath of office. Salary increased to $2,700 per annum July 1, 1901, in accordance with Act of Congress, and to $3,000 per annum July 1, 1903, in accordance with Act of Congress of March 3, 1903. Mr. Pepper is modest and active, a good and retiring officer. Had charge of one of the cars, equipped with a crew from the Ninth division, which composed the gold train, San Francisco to New York.

Norman Perkins.

Born in Lackawack, New York, and educated in the public schools of that place and in the seminary at Charlotteville, Schoharie County, N. Y. On the breaking out of the Civil War Mr. Perkins enlisted as a private in the 56th Regiment, New York Infantry. He was promoted during his service to corporal, color sergeant (carried the regimental colors from June, 1862, to June, 1863), first sergeant. Reënlisted in February, 1864. Promoted to second lieutenant, first lieutenant, and captain; was wounded and was honorably discharged in October, 1865. Participated in the Virginia, North and South Carolina campaigns, in the siege of Morris Island and Sumter, and was in many engagements. Is a member of the Grand Army of the Republic and of the Loyal Legion. Mr. Perkins entered the railway mail service in the La Crosse and Winnebago City, Minn., line, as a route agent, at $900 per annum, August 24, 1871. Salary increased to $940 per annum August, 1876. Transferred to the Chicago, Ill., and Sparta, Wis., R. P. O., at class 4, $1,150 per annum, February, 1877; promoted to class 5, clerk in charge, at $1,300 per annum, July, 1879; pay increased to $1,400, April, 1884, and detailed as chief clerk at St. Paul, Minn. Resigned to accept appointment as Superintendent Tenth division, April 1, 1889. Had charge of one of the cars, equipped with a crew from the Tenth division, which composed the gold train of 1892, San Francisco to New York. Removed June 19, 1893, and reappointed as Superintendent, June 26, 1897.

S. M. Gaines.

Born in Madisonville, Tennessee, June 22, 1859; was educated in the public schools of that place and in the Madisonville Academy. Entered the railway mail service at class 1, $880 per annum, in the Corpus Christi and Laredo R. P. O., March 20, 1882; transferred to the Palestine and Laredo R. P. O., at $900, June 26, 1882; permanently appointed at class 3, $1,000 per annum, September 11, 1882. Transferred to the St. Louis and Texarkana R. P. O., at class 5, $1,300 per annum, May 13, 1889, and served in the office of the Superintendent of the Eleventh division, by detail from the Palestine and Laredo, and from the St. Louis and Texarkana, until April 11, 1893, when he was promoted to Assistant Superintendent R. M. S., $1,600 per annum; November 26, 1897, he was appointed Superintendent of the Eleventh division, headquarters Fort Worth, Texas, at $2,500 per annum. Pay increased by Act of Congress, to $2,700, July 1, 1901, and to $3,000, by Act of Congress, July 1, 1903. Mr. Gaines has served on several committees appointed to consider and inspect mail equipment, such as lock pouches, cranes and catchers, tying devices, and interior arrangements of cars, and served well.

H. M. Robinson.

Born in Weard County, Georgia, August 25, 1858, and educated in the public schools. He entered the railway mail service as a clerk of class 2, at $900 per annum, in the Charlotte and Atlanta R. P. O., May 28, 1879; promoted to class 4, $1,150 per annum, July 7, 1880; reduced to class 3, at $1,000 per annum, May 18, 1881; promoted to class 4, $1,150 per annum, August 30, 1881; promoted to class 5, $1,300 per annum, August 27, 1882; reduced to class 4, $1,150 per annum, January 20, 1883; promoted to class 5, $1,300, August 1, 1883. Made chief clerk October 10, 1891, and pay increased to $1,400 per annum. November 23, 1898, promoted to Assistant Superintendent R. M. S., $1,600 per annum, and assigned to duty in Porto Rico. July 18, 1899, reinstated, at $1,600, as chief clerk R. M. S., Fourth division. August 3, 1900, resigned, to take effect July 31, 1900. August 1, 1900, appointed special agent and Assistant Superintendent R. M. S., $1,600, and assigned to China. December 21, 1903, resignation accepted, effective December 19, 1903, and restored to his old place in the Fourth division, R. M. S. May 18, 1904, appointed Assistant Division Superintendent, $1,600 per annum, Fourth division. November 11, 1908, appointed Superintendent Twelfth division, R. M. S., (new), $3,000 per annum, headquarters, New Orleans, La. See the Spanish-American War.

Frank W. Vaille.

Born in Springfield, Mass., on the 7th day of December, 1854. Educated in the public schools of that city and in Yale, from which he graduated in the class of 1876. Entered the railway mail service as local agent at St. Louis, Mo., September 4, 1877, class 1, $600 per annum. Appointment expired March 4, 1878. Reappointed February 28, 1878, salary $600. May 10, 1878, transferred to Pittsburg and St. Louis R. P. O., class 3, $1,000 per annum. July 8, 1879, promoted to class 5, $1,300 per annum. April 1, 1882, promoted to chief clerk R. M. S., at Indianapolis, Ind., and salary increased to $1,400 per annum. July 2, 1885, transferred to the Green River, Wyo., and Huntington, Oregon, R. P. O., at class 3, $1,000 per annum—this was made on his own request. July 29, 1886, transferred to the Omaha and Ogden R. P. O., at class 4, $1,150 per annum. December, 1886, promoted to class 5, at $1,300 per annum. May 25, 1889, transferred to the Chicago and Cincinnati R. P. O., class 5, $1,300 per annum. August 7, 1889, promoted to $1,400 per annum. December 17, 1890, resigned, and was appointed Assistant Superintendent R. M. S., and assigned later to the northwestern portion of the Eighth division, where he did excellent work until detailed June 6, 1898, to go to the Philippine Islands to assume charge of the mail passing to and from our army and to and from the citizens thereof. October 31, 1900, resigned as Assistant Superintendent R. M. S., and made Director of Posts of the Philippines. Reinstated as Assistant Superintendent R. M. S., after service in the Philippines, with headquarters at Portland, Oregon, March 7, 1901. July 1, 1904, pay increased by Act of Congress to $1,800 per annum. July 1, 1907, pay increased by Act of Congress to $2,000 per annum. July 1, 1909, appointed Superintendent Thirteenth division, R. M. S. (new), headquarters, Seattle, Washington, salary $3,000 per annum. Had charge of one of the cars of the gold train from San Francisco, Cal., to New York City, N. Y.

John W. Hollyday.

John W. Hollyday, Chief Clerk to the Second Assistant Postmaster General, was born and educated in Findlay, Ohio. In March, 1878, he was appointed in the railway mail service, serving on the New York Central and Lake Shore and Michigan Southern lines. He was detailed to duty in the office of the Superintendent, Ninth division, Cleveland, Ohio, for two years, 1881-1883, and then promoted to clerk in charge of one of the heaviest runs between Cleveland and Chicago, where he served until 1885, when he was transferred to the office of the General Superintendent Railway Mail Service in Washington, D. C. He filled various positions therein and was made chief clerk in August, 1897. March 1, 1907, he was promoted to his present position. Mr. Hollyday is married and has one child, a daughter. He served for ten years as vice president of the Mutual Benefit Association for the Third division, railway mail service, and has been an officer and director of the Post Office Department Immediate Benefit Association since its organization in 1891.